DIVIDED LOYALTIES

DISPLACEMENT, BELONGING AND CITIZENSHIP AMONG EAST TIMORESE IN WEST TIMOR

DIVIDED LOYALTIES

DISPLACEMENT, BELONGING AND CITIZENSHIP
AMONG EAST TIMORESE IN WEST TIMOR

ANDREY DAMALEDO

MONOGRAPHS IN
ANTHROPOLOGY SERIES

Australian
National
University

PRESS

For Pamela

ANU PRESS

Published by ANU Press
The Australian National University
Acton ACT 2601, Australia
Email: anupress@anu.edu.au

Available to download for free at press.anu.edu.au

ISBN (print): 9781760462369
ISBN (online): 9781760462376

WorldCat (print): 1054084539
WorldCat (online): 1054084643

DOI: 10.22459/DL.09.2018

Cover design and layout by ANU Press

Cover photograph: East Timorese procession at Raknamo resettlement site in Kupang district 2012, by Father Jefri Bonlay.

Contents

James J. Fox

Abbreviations

ADITLA	Associação Democrática para a Integração de Timor Leste na Austrália (Democratic Association for the Integration of East Timor into Australia)
AITI	Association for the Integration of Timor into Indonesia
ANP	Acção Nacional Popular (National Action Party)
ANU	The Australian National University
Apodeti	Associação Popular Democrática Timorense (Timorese Popular Democratic Association)
ASDT	Associação Social Democrática Timorense (Social Democratic Association of Timor)
ASEAN	Association of Southeast Asian Nations
Bakin	Badan Koordinasi Intelegen Negara (Indonesian Intelligence Coordinating Agency)
BMP	Besi Merah Putih
BRTT	Barisan Rakyat Timor Timur (East Timor People's Front)
CAVR	Comissão de Acolhimento, Verdade e Reconciliação de Timor Leste (Commission for Reception, Truth and Reconciliation in East Timor)
Celcom	Célular da Comunidade (community cell)
CIS Timor	Circle of Imagine Society in Timor
CRRN	Conselho Revolucionário de Resistência Nacional (Revolutionary Council of National Resistance)
CSEAS	Center for Southeast Asian Studies
CTF	Commission of Truth and Friendship
Depdagri	Indonesian Ministry of Home Affairs

DFAT   Department of Foreign Affairs and Trade

Falintil   Forças Armadas de Libertação Nacional de Timor-
                Leste (National Armed Forces for the Liberation of
                East Timor; military wing of Fretilin)

FECLETIL   Frente Clandestina Estudantil de Timor Leste (Front
                of East Timorese Students)

FITUN   Frente Iha Timor Unidos Nafatin (Always United
                Front of Timor)

FPBI   Front Pembela Bangsa Indonesia (Front of Indonesia
                Defenders)

FPDK   Forum Persatuan, Demokrasi dan Keadilan
                (Forum for Unity, Democracy and Justice)

FPK   Forum Pembela Keadilan (Forum for the Defenders
                of Justice)

Fretilin   Frente Revolucionária de Timor-Leste Independente
                (Revolutionary Front for an Independent East Timor)

Garda Paksi   Garda Muda Penegak Integrasi (Young Guards
                Upholding Integration)

Gerindra   Gerakan Indonesia Raya (Great Indonesia
                Movement Party)

GFFTL   Grupu Feto Foin Sa'e Timor Lorosa'e (Young Women's
                Group of East Timor)

Golkar   Golongan Karya (Party of the Functional Groups)

Hikbat   Himpunan Keluarga Atsabe (Atsabe Family Union)

HPPMAI   Himpunan Pemuda, Pelajar, dan Mahasiswa Anti-
                Integrasi (Association of Anti-Integration Youths and
                Students)

IDP   internally displaced person

IDR   Indonesian rupiah

Kesbangpolinmas Badan Kesatuan Bangsa, Politik, dan Perlindungan
                Masyarakat (Indonesian Agency for National Unity,
                Politics, and Community Protection)

KOKPIT   Komite Nasional Korban Politik Timor Timur
                (National Committee of East Timor Political Victims)

Komnas HAM	Komisi Nasional Hak Asasi Manusia (Indonesian National Commission on Human Rights)
KOTA	Klibur Owan Timor Ass'wain (Association of Timorese Heroes)
KTP	Kartu Tanda Penduduk (Indonesian identity cards)
LPMTI	Lembaga Perlindungan Masyarakat Timor Indonesia (the Association for the Protection of Indonesian Timorese Community)
Makasti	Masyarakat Komunitas Timor Timur (East Timorese Community Association)
Merah Putih	'Red and White', the colours of the Indonesian flag
MOBUDAN	Movimento Buka Dalan Foun
NGO	non-governmental organisation
NTB	Nusa Tenggara Barat (West Nusa Tenggara province)
NTT	Nusa Tenggara Timur (East Nusa Tenggara province)
Nurep	Núcleos de Resistência (nucleus of popular resistance)
OJECTIL	Organização da Juventude Catolica de Timor-Leste (East Timor Catholic Youth Organisation)
OJETIL	Organização de Jovens e Estudantes de Timor-Leste (Organisation for Youth and Students of Timor-Leste)
OPJLATIL	Organização Popular Juventude Lorico Ass'wain Timor-Leste (Popular Organisation of East Timorese Women)
PAN	Partai Amanat Nasional (National Mandate Party)
PD	Partai Demokrat (Democratic Party)
PDI	Partai Demokrasi Indonesia (Indonesian Democratic Party)
PKBI	Partai Kedaulatan Bangsa Indonesia (Indonesia Sovereign Party)
PNTL	Polícia Nacional de Timor-Leste
POT	Persehatian Orang Timor (United Timorese)
POTIBI	Persehatian Oan Timor Baucau Indonesia (the Baucau Indonesia Union)
PPA	Persatuan Pemuda Apodeti (Apodeti Youth Union)

PPI	Pasukan Pejuang Integrasi (Integration Fighters Force)
PPP	Partai Persatuan Pembangunan (United Development Party)
Renetil	National Resistance of East Timorese Students
RPKAD	Resimen Para Komando Angkatan Darat (Army Para-Commando Regiment), now Kopassus
SESPIM	Sekolah Staf dan Pimpinan (Staff and Leaders School of the Indonesian Police Force)
TTS	Timor Tengah Selatan (South Central Timor)
TTU	Timor Tengah Utara (North Central Timor)
UDT	União Democrática Timorense (Democratic Union of Timor)
UN	United Nations
UNHCR	United Nations High Commissioner for Refugees
UNIF	Front Persatuan Pendukung Otonomi (United Front for East Timor Autonomy)
UNOCHA	United Nations Office for the Coordination of Humanitarian Affairs
UNTAS	Uni Timor Aswain (Union East Timorese in Indonesia)

List of illustrations

List of tables

Acknowledgements

I write these acknowledgements in genuine recognition of the generosity, encouragement and support I received from many people and institutions without which this book would not have been possible. My greatest debt, however, rests with East Timorese in West Timor, without whom I would never have been able to learn such rich stories and experiences. I enjoyed every moment I spent with the Makasae people and this would not have been possible without the great friendship and hospitality of Agusto da Costa, Francisco Ximenes (Sico), Igidio Sarmento (Tuan Takur), Thomas Cardoso (Mau Rade), Bonifacio Ximenes, Cristiano Ximenes, Alfonso Fraga and Father Jefri Bonlay. I owe a great debt to the late Mauricio Freitas, who taught me a lot about the Waima'a people and their relationship with other Timorese groups.

I would like to thank my friend Mateus Guedes, whose company and support enabled me to trace different East Timorese groups in Belu. Among the Kemak people, I am indebted to the late Carlos Naibuti and the late Verissimo de Deus de Magelhaens, Djose Naibuti, the late Sico Pereira (Sico Naruk) and Januario Moreira, whose insights have taught me the complexity and diversity of their people. My work among the Idate people was made possible by the great support from Tio Sinuk (João Soares), Leopoldo Soares, Mateus Alves, Domingos Soares and Benyamin Emmy (Pak Guru). Armindo Mariano guided me into the pro-integration and cultural politics of the Naueti people. Katuas Lafaek, whom I met towards the end of my fieldwork, shared his knowledge of the Tetun Terik of Viqueque and their relationship with Wehali.

I owe great thanks to Ignasius Kali, the *Loro* of Lamaknen, for his personal archives and advice about cross-border migration, which helped me learn about Bunaq mobility. My good friend Stef Bere has helped with the translation of Bunaq poetic narratives. Maternus Bere and Hermino

Lopes also helped me understand the variations among Bunaq people and their cross-border relationships. I want to thank Mario Vieira for his support of my work among the Fataluku people.

I wish to thank Herman Seran and Joseph Seran, who helped me on my work among the Tetun Terik people. I enjoyed some long discussions with the late Blasius Manek, whose long experience and wide knowledge of Belu gave me insights into the political history of the region. I am also indebted to the Mambai people in Kereana village for their time and stories. My work in Dili has been made possible with great support from Charles Meluk, Sister Monica, Manuel Monteiro, Nug Katjasungkana, Armindo Maia and Dionisio Babo Soares. Basilio Araujo and Filomeno Hornay taught me the politics of pro-autonomy supporters, and Felisberto Amaral taught me Timorese border politics. It is my hope that this book will contribute to a better understanding of the rich and diverse cultural identities of East Timorese and recognition of their dignity as East Timorese in Indonesia.

I am indebted to the Circle of Imagine Society in Timor (CIS Timor) for their support during my fieldwork. In particular, I want to thank Winston Rondo for letting me be part of CIS Timor. I owe a great debt to my good friend Anato Moreira for sharing not only his knowledge of the East Timorese, but also his accommodation during my stay in Betun. Wendy Inta, Lius Leto, Mery Djami and Yanti Lina never ignored me when I interrupted their daily work with endless questions. Olkes Dadilado has been my great support since 2007 and I owe him a great deal. I would also like to thank my friends at the Regional Development Planning Agency of the East Nusa Tenggara provincial government for their generous support.

I have been inspired, encouraged and assisted by my guru, Professor Andrew McWilliam. *Mestre* Andrew supported my belief in the significance of this research and he patiently guided me beyond my PhD to bring this book to a nice conclusion. I enjoyed his wide knowledge of both West Timor and East Timor, but I always learned more from his critical comments and advice. I also owe a great debt to my *toulasik*, Professor James J. Fox, who taught me to think as an anthropologist and always directed me to consider my ethnography first. *Toulasik* Fox showed me the significance of history and guided me to interpret my ethnographic material in a meaningful way. He shaped my knowledge with his criticism. The way he challenged me to keep asking questions and broaden my understanding of regional and global ethnography has been profoundly influential. I want to express my gratitude to Professor Kirin Narayan, who provided great support in terms of writing style and the way I present and structure my argument.

I would like to thank Associate Professor Matt Tomlinson, Chair of the ANU Press Monographs in Anthropology Series Editorial Board, whose support was crucial for the publication of this book. I am deeply grateful to the following people, all of whom have read and commented on parts or all of the chapters in this book: Kathy Robinson, Phillip Taylor, Ken George, Andy Kipnis, Assa Doron, Jane Ferguson, Campbell Macknight, Pyone Myat Thu, Hans Hägerdal, Janet Hunt, Diana Glazebrook and Kathryn Dwan. My good friend Christine Mason helped me during my masters to stay focused on East Timorese issues. I owe great thanks to Karina Pelling for her cartography work. Thanks also go to Jan Borrie for her meticulous copyediting work. To the two anonymous reviewers, thank you for your helpful comments and constructive feedback.

Some parts of this book have been previously published elsewhere. Chapter 3 was published in the *Review of Indonesian and Malaysian Affairs* (vol. 48, no. 1, 2014: 159–81). Chapter 6 was published in *The Australian Journal of Anthropology* (vol. 29, no. 1, 2018: 19–34).

This book is a transformation of my PhD dissertation and I am most grateful to the Australian Department of Foreign Affairs and Trade (DFAT) and the Australia Awards Indonesia for funding my PhD journey, including 12 months of ethnographic fieldwork in Timor. I wish to thank the ANU Indonesia Project and SMERU Research Institute, whose financial support and generous grant enabled me to complete my manuscript. I also acknowledge the support of the Center for Southeast Asian Studies (CSEAS) of Kyoto University in providing me with an opportunity to revise and bring this book to completion.

Special thanks go to my parents for their constant prayers and to my brother, Aldy, for his great sense of humour. Finally, my love and warmest gratitude go to my wife, Pamela, my son, Quincy, and my daughter, Bindi, for their endless support and company, without which this book would not have been possible.

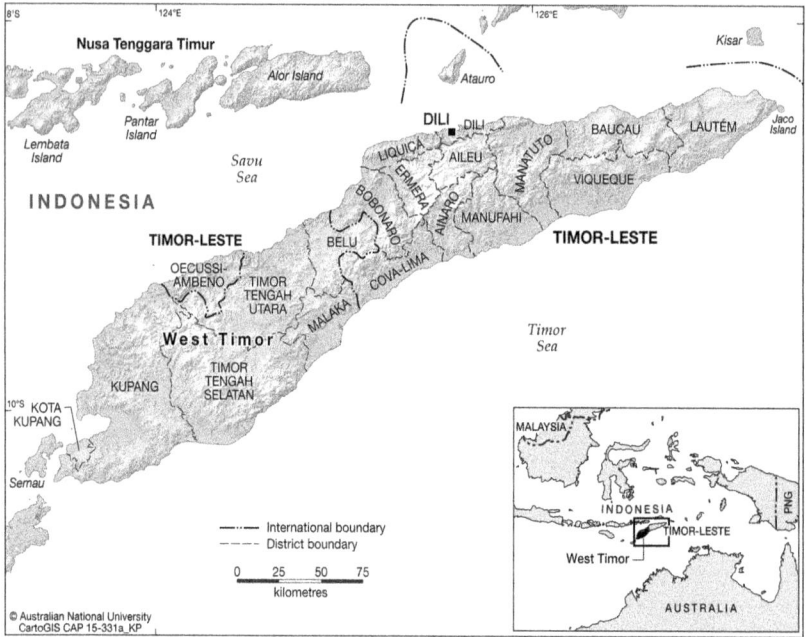

Map A.1 Timor Island

Source: CartoGIS, College of Asia and the Pacific, The Australian National University.

Preface

James J. Fox

Divided Loyalties is an ethnography of exceptional insight, analysis and theoretical significance. It is a work of engaged social inquiry based on intimate personal knowledge and local understanding of the island of Timor.

This book is a concerted attempt to examine the consequences of the disruptions that occurred after the United Nations–sponsored 1999 referendum on independence when hundreds of thousands of East Timorese fled or were moved en masse to West Timor. The majority of these East Timorese returned to their homeland, but large numbers chose to remain and to settle in different parts of West Timor.

Divided Loyalties examines the strategic settlement of these East Timorese, their diverse efforts at assimilation as distinct ethnic communities and the divided allegiances these efforts created. The critical feature of this study is its presentation of the mixed personal motivations involved in these efforts, the human dilemmas resulting from decisions taken and their effects on community relations.

Good ethnography depends on presenting a 'view from within'—one that provides analytical rigour but combines this with a sensitive presentation of the actions and motivations of the subjects of analysis. *Divided Loyalties* offers an ethnography that focuses on the central dilemma of the East Timorese: their demand for rights as 'displaced' Indonesian citizens coupled with their insistence on maintaining ancestral connections to their abandoned homeland. This book conveys the personal sense of struggle, sacrifice and the sadness of separation that pervade the efforts of these East Timorese to establish their new lives and livelihoods.

As an ethnography, this work is grounded on clear theoretical foundations that provide a glimpse of age-old processes of settlement and alliance common to Austronesian populations. Recourse to narratives of origin and the recognition of local precedence are highlighted in the contemporary discourse of the Timorese. The book describes the fashioning of a variety of these different modes of discourse to support successful resettlement.

Timor can be defined by its multiple migrations over centuries. The history of these migrations forms an underlying basis for the distribution of populations on the island and thus for both the island's social commonalities and its contemporary differences. There were previous migrations from east to west in the colonial period, particularly towards the end of the nineteenth and the beginning of the twentieth centuries, when the Portuguese began imposing a head tax on the populations they were attempting to control. *Divided Loyalties* draws on this earlier history to show how memories of these events continue to feed a discourse on relationships among the East and West Timorese and serve as the means of restoring relations from the past to the present. The nuances of this discourse are a paramount feature of this ethnography.

Andrey Damaledo's concern for the problems of the East Timorese began with their 1999 exodus to West Timor. As an Indonesian civil servant based in Kupang, he became involved in the initial reception and provisional settlement of these refugees. During this time, he conceived of the idea of doing a PhD, applied to The Australian National University and was accepted. He arrived in Canberra with tentative but determined plans for his doctoral research. His eventual thesis—based on further extended fieldwork—was awarded the Ann Bates Prize for the most outstanding thesis on an Indonesian topic. The Australian Department of Foreign Affairs and Trade (DFAT) also recognised Andrey's outstanding work and awarded him an Allison Sudradjat Prize.

For Andrey, however, the award of his doctorate was just the beginning. He immediately launched himself into other research on Timor. Fortunately, he was able to obtain a Fellowship from the Center for Southeast Asian Studies (CSEAS) at Kyoto University that has enabled him to revise his thesis for publication and undertake new research in both East and West Timor.

This book can therefore be considered as an initial ethnography with more to come in the future. It marks the beginning of a personal journey in advancing the ethnography of the island of Timor as a whole.

1

Lest we forget

Kupang, 8 May 2013. It was a bright Wednesday morning and I had just recovered from a two-hour motorbike ride from Betun to Atambua and a six-hour bus ride from Atambua to Kupang the day before. During the past few months, I had focused my work in Belu (and Malaka) district, near the border with East Timor, and planned to give myself a break in the provincial capital of Kupang. As I was transferring my field notes on Tetun people's displacement narratives into my laptop, a ring tone on my mobile phone announced a message. It was apparently not a short one:

> Good morning, my brother, my apology if this bothers you. On Saturday, the 4th of May, the 743 battalion force, led by the Deputy Battalion Commander cut down all of the banana trees which were planted by the East Timorese community on the side of Timor Raya road and along the drainage around the training field on the east of the Supporting Military Company [Kompi Bantuan] in Naibonat. The old banana fruits were taken home and the young ones were left scattered on the ground. Please pray for us as there has been an order for us to move out of this land we are living on because it belongs to the army. This is the order of the Provincial Army Commander of 161 Wira Sakti, Kupang. We are convinced that our brothers who were born on the west side of this Ancestral Land of Timor will pass along our suffering to the policy decision makers in this country. We are currently experiencing what the aphorism declares as 'after the sweet is taken, the remains are thrown away' [*habis manis sepah dibuang*]. Please do not ever forget the history. Thank you and God Bless You.

This message was sent by Francisco Ximenes, commonly known as Sico, the leader of the East Timorese community in Naibonat camp, Kupang district. Sico and his community fled to West Timor as a result of the destructive Indonesian withdrawal from East Timor in 1999. In that year, then Indonesian president B. J. Habibie announced there would be a popular referendum on autonomy offering East Timorese a tangible option to form their own state. Almost immediately, East Timorese militias, backed by the Indonesian military, began a campaign of violence to ensure that the province of East Timor remained a constituent part of the Republic of Indonesia (see van Klinken et al. 2002: 69; Bertrand 2004: 143). Throughout East Timor, intimidation and acts of violence took place. Initial attacks on residences soon escalated into a pseudo civil war. According to some accounts, soon after the United Nations (UN) announced that an overwhelming majority of East Timor's population (78 per cent) had rejected special autonomy within Indonesia—which was an effective rejection of continued Indonesian control over their territory—large numbers of people were killed in the East Timorese towns of Maliana, Oecussi, Suai and Liquiçá. The capital, Dili, and other towns were torched, about 1,000 people were killed and some 70 per cent of public infrastructure and private housing was destroyed (Dolan et al. 2004: 12; Robinson 2010: 161). As the intensity of violence increased, a stream of refugees left East Timor, many of them coerced into joining the militia exodus, and, by late 1999, an estimated 250,000 East Timorese (more than 30 per cent of the population) had fled to the neighbouring half of the island, West Timor, which was part of the Indonesian province of East Nusa Tenggara (Nusa Tenggara Timur, or NTT) (Amnesty International 1999; CAVR 2005).

Most of the displaced East Timorese were located in camps within Belu district, near the border with East Timor, and in Kupang district, near the NTT capital of Kupang. Naibonat camp is located near the Kupang district army reserve barracks and is one of the largest remaining camps for former East Timorese refugees. As a teacher during the Portuguese period who joined the Portuguese army in the years leading up to the decolonisation process, Sico certainly had a flair for emotional language. His melodramatic message, however, spoke to a sincere concern for his community. I immediately rang Sico for some clarification and agreed to catch up with him in Naibonat that afternoon. I asked Agusto da Costa, the former speaker of the Baucau district House of Representatives (in East Timor), who had initially introduced me to the Naibonat community, to accompany me.

We arrived in Naibonat at about 4 pm and headed straight to Sico's dwelling. 'As you can witness yourself', he said, pointing to where the remaining bananas had been left on the ground. Sico was not in his best form. Agusto, on the other hand, did not want to miss the opportunity to gain firsthand experience and immediately walked around the area with his camcorder capturing the scene while Sico continued to reconstruct events. 'Prior to the Saturday actions,' Sico began, 'there have been two important events taking place here.'

The first was on Thursday, 25 April 2013. About 8 am, two members of the 743 infantry battalion, dressed in their exercise uniforms, approached an East Timorese youth, Arlindo, and began to ask about his background and origins. They emphasised that the land belonged to the army and they were planning to build new barracks in the area, and implied that all the bananas should be cut down or the 743 infantrymen would do the job themselves. A similar encounter took place on the morning of Monday, 29 April 2013. This time it was a larger group of about 20 infantrymen, including the company provost, in their full formal uniforms. They approached Olivio,[1] who was standing in front of his dwelling, and explained to him their plan for the area. Like Arlindo four days earlier, Olivio politely advised them to see the neighbourhood leader (*ketua RT*) for a response.

Instead of following that advice, the next weekend, the army group cut down all the banana trees in front of the East Timorese who had planted them over the previous 12 years to support their livelihoods. Sico told me:

> We know that this land is owned by the army and that they can obviously do whatever they want with it. We also know that the bananas will grow again, but the problem is not the bananas; it is the way the army has acted. You know, those bananas were plants. It means someone has planted them and someone's labour has been invested in it. This requires respect and appreciation and this is the thing they have consciously ignored.

'But why didn't you try to stop them in the first place, then?' I asked.

---

1   Olivio and Arlindo are not their real names.

It seemed Sico had anticipated such questions: 'This was a bait [provocation], and they wanted us to bite. But we were also part of the Indonesian army and key players of this kind of game in the past.'

Sico arranged a community meeting for the next day to hear the views of his fellow Timorese. Apparently, the banana raid was one of their concerns, but the greater issue was an official letter from the commander of the battalion, who had given them a three-month deadline to move out and 'live in their own land'.

Thomas Cardoso, also known as Mau Rade, the former head of the intelligence unit in Baucau military district, loudly pointed out:

> The three-month deadline was an incredibly short period of time to pack all the things and move out, particularly when many of the community members did not have land and housing to move into. They knew we brought nothing from East Timor and now they are kicking us out of here. Are they trying to say that we should return to East Timor because that is our origin land? I suggest in the next three months we should remove our camps on to the main road, because that is the only place where we have access.

As others began to express their concerns, Sico stood up and reminded them about the army's provocation and they eventually agreed to address the issue in a peaceful and respectful way. In his concluding remarks, however, Sico looked at everyone and spoke gently:

> What we have to do is let people know that, for other Indonesians [and he suddenly turned his face to me and I realised I was the only person of non–East Timorese background present], the notion of Indonesia as the land where blood was spilled [*tanah tumpah darah*] is related to blood from the birthing process. But for us, the East Timorese, we spilled our own blood and that of our brothers and sisters to become Indonesian. This is the history they should always remember.

Citing the acronym made famous by Sukarno, Indonesia's first president, Sico declared: '*JAS MERAH*' (*jangan sekali-kali melupakan sejarah*, which translates as 'do not ever forget [your] history').

Sico and his community had calmly watched the army cut down their banana plants and received the letter to clear the camp they had inhabited since 1999. It looked as though they had passively accepted the provocation. In the ensuing days, however, Sico and his community made use of their own networks within the army to get their message across, even extending their reach across the provincial boundary to higher-ranking officers of the regional army command in Denpasar and army headquarters in Jakarta. In addition, the community initiated a series of engagements with their various representatives in the local parliament, human right activists, religious and political leaders as well as government officers at the national and local levels to find ways to resolve their grievances. What struck me during my involvement in these events was the absence of any suggestion of a return to East Timor. This commitment to remain in Indonesia suggests that, for many East Timorese, their existence in Indonesia—and West Timor, in particular—is no longer a transitory or liminal phase. They have moved on and are indeed East Timorese Indonesians.

The focus of this book is an ethnographic study of belonging and citizenship among former pro-autonomy East Timorese settlers such as Sico and his community who have elected to settle definitively in Indonesian West Timor. In particular, this book explores the way different East Timorese groups organise and represent their cultural and political interests in a new setting. In other words, this book seeks to highlight the diversity of East Timorese identities rather than to restrict them.

'Avoid two (potholes), hit four'

My interest in the East Timorese community struggling to make a new life in West Timor dates back a few years. In 2005, I became a public servant in the NTT provincial government. Having only heard stories of East Timorese issues from Malang in East Java, returning home and entering a government job where I could make use of my knowledge in the development of my region was an exciting prospect. My enthusiasm increased when the official appointment letter, signed by the provincial governor, clearly defined my role as regional resettlement planner in the Ministry of Labour and Transmigration, one of the key players in the East Timorese resettlement program. On the first day of my assignment, I was asked to join a team of transmigration officers to monitor the instalment of water pipelines from a recently built dam at Tulakaboak resettlement area, which housed many East Timorese.

Tulakaboak resettlement area is on the northern coast of Kupang Bay. It was constructed in 2001 as part of the emergency resettlement projects implemented for displaced East Timorese. Tulakaboak is in fact not that far from the provincial capital of Kupang, but poor roads mean it took five hours to reach the site by car. People living in the area commonly use the expression 'sili dua kena empat' (literally, 'avoid two [potholes], hit four') to describe the horrible road conditions. The resettlement area comprised 150, 6 m x 6 m houses for 75 West Timorese and 75 East Timorese households. It was located metres from the ocean, but, rather than an idyllic tropical coastal landscape, the area was covered mostly in bare rocks and thornbush. We could only find a sandy beach another 2 km to the north-east, in Panfolok, where fishing boats landed. In Tulakabaok, there was little evidence of crop cultivation. I walked around several blocks and found to my surprise that many houses had been disassembled and/ or left empty. It took another several blocks before I even encountered anyone who had remained in the area. The dam and pipeline project were not immediately my point of interest once I noticed that some people were reluctant to stay in the area. I managed to have a brief but effective informal conversation with some residents and received the clear message that the new houses had been abandoned because people had chosen to return to the camps to be closer to their families and livelihood networks.

The situation in Tulakabaok was apparently not a unique phenomenon. In Belu, many houses built for East Timorese are now housing animals (Kompas Online 2012). It is clear that even though the East Timorese have lived in West Timor for nearly two decades, the issues affecting them are far from resolved. My experience in Tulakabaok and what happened to Sico's community in Naibonat exemplify that dealing with East Timorese issues in West Timor is not simply a matter of physical housing needs. It requires an understanding of the way East Timorese perceive themselves as newly emplaced settlers and how they respond to the challenges they face. My concern in this book, therefore, is less with the pragmatic politics of humanitarian and development assistance than it is with examining the extent to which East Timorese adapt and attribute meaning to their emplacement, and how that meaning is negotiated, interpreted and contested by different East Timorese groups in West Timor.

Following the East Timorese in West Timor

The island of Timor lies in the Lesser Sunda archipelago in eastern Indonesia, north of Australia. The island covers some 34,000 sq km— approximately the size of the Netherlands. The terrain is rugged and mountainous, with plateaus covering most of the northern coastal range and a number of peaks in excess of 2,000 m high. The southern coastal area forms a wide plain with estuarine swamps and river deltas built up by progradation. The eastern half of the island, including the enclave of Oecussi and the islands of Atauro and Jaco, were under Portuguese administration for centuries before the 24 years of Indonesian occupation that ended in 1999. The western half of the island was under Dutch colonial administration, but formed part of the Indonesian state since its founding as an independent republic on 17 August 1945.

Thus, of all the Indonesian regions to which East Timorese migrated following the violent reaction to the independence referendum, West Timor presented the most immediately attractive. However, the very fact that it became the ultimate place of residence for the East Timorese who did not want to return to East Timor spoke volumes about the appeal of this half of the island. West Timor has never been a province of its own or an autonomous political entity, but is an integrated part of the composite NTT province that also includes the neighbouring islands of Flores and Sumba. In fact, the term 'West Timor' (Timor Barat) has always been alien to the people in the region, and has never been a point of reference or identification for people from neighbouring islands such as Sumba, Alor and Flores or even the proximate islands of Rote, Savu or Semau.[2] West Timor is simply a new directional term to distinguish the Indonesian part from the other half of the island, the independent state of Timor-Leste.

Administratively, West Timor comprises one municipality and five districts. Kupang municipality is the capital of the province as well as the centre for regional trade and services. Kupang district covers the hinterland of the capital. Further to the east are the districts of South Central Timor (Timor Tengah Selatan, or TTS) and North Central Timor (Timor Tengah Utara, or TTU), which border the East Timorese enclave of Oecussi. The final two districts are Belu, which borders the East

---

2   People simply refer to it as Timor rather than West Timor.

Timorese mountain district of Bobonaro, and Malaka,[3] which borders the southern Timor-Leste coastal district of Cova Lima. Ethnolinguistically, West Timor is dominated by the Meto-speaking people who occupy most areas in Kupang, TTS and TTU, as well as a few areas on the western side of Belu. Tetun-speaking people dominate the Belu and Malaka districts, which are also home to Bunaq and Kemak people. Kupang Malay is spoken in the capital, with a few remaining indigenous Helong-speaking people in centres such as Bolok and the island of Semau.

Although my engagement with the East Timorese began in 2005, almost all of the findings presented in this book are based on empirical research undertaken in Belu, Malaka and Kupang districts between October 2012 and October 2013, and during my return to Kupang, from January 2017 to February 2018. Because of the dispersion and diversity of the East Timorese people, I cannot confine my ethnographic inquiry to a specific territorial unit. Thus, during my first 12-month stay, I found myself frequently on the move. I conducted multi-sited ethnographic research by way of what Marcus (1995: 95) identifies as 'multiple sites of observation and participation that crosscut dichotomies such as the "local" and the "global", the "life-world" and the "system"'.

---

3   Malaka is a newly *pemekaran* district formed from Belu. *Pemekaran* (lit., 'blossoming') is the term used to describe the formation of new autonomous administrative and budgetary territories in Indonesia. While the formation of new administrative units within Indonesia has taken place since the early years of the republic, this process increased rapidly after the implementation of the Regional Autonomy Law no. 22/1999 and government regulation (PP) no. 129/2000. In 2004, the revised Decentralisation Law (no. 32) was enacted and, in ensuing years, the government reviewed the regulation and introduced PP 38/2007, which presently serves as the key regulation on the formation of new territorial administrations. In 1999, NTT comprised 13 districts and municipalities. In 2013, Malaka district was officially established and was added to the total of 22 districts and municipalities in the province.

Table 1.1 Statistics for NTT and West Timor, 2016

Description	NTT	West Timor					
		Kupang municipality	Kupang district	TTS district	TTU district	Belu district	Malaka district
Area (sq km)	47,931	180	5,526	3,947	2,670	1,249	1,161
Population	5,203,514	402,286	360,228	461,681	247,216	210,307	183,387
Male	2,577,953	206,129	184,314	227,877	122,209	105,187	88,709
Female	2,625,561	196,157	175,914	233,804	125,007	105,120	94,678
Population density (per sq km)	109	2,232	105	97	98	100	94
Number of districts	22						
Number of subdistricts	306	6	24	32	24	12	12
Number of villages and kelurahan (administrative villages)	3,314	51	177	278	193	81	127

Source: BPS (2017).

This idea of multi-sitedness is applied to research of the East Timorese in a series of activities across West Timor. The first principle is to follow the people. During my stay, I followed different East Timorese groups in their camps and resettlement sites. I visited three camps and seven resettlement sites in Kupang;[4] in Belu and Malaka, I visited one camp and 12 resettlement villages.[5] I participated in East Timorese community activities such as meetings, various celebrations and parties including two marriages, a birthday and a graduation, three mortuary ceremonies and funerals, a youth Christmas gathering and one cultural performance. By following people, I also tried to simultaneously follow their stories through numerous informal conversations and some semistructured interviews (see Agar 1980: 110). I conducted informal interviews with a diversity of women and men: young and old, politicians, government employees, farmers, labourers, traders, military personnel and members of the police force.

To explore their livelihood activities, I followed the money by joining some sharecropper farmers in their fields and following gamblers in their various pursuits. I also tried to follow different conflicts and reconciliation processes, including undertaking two week-long visits to Timor-Leste in July 2013 and March 2017. My initial intention was to visit people in the districts, but time constraints restricted my engagement to selected human rights activists and non-governmental organisation (NGO) personnel working on repatriation issues.

Archives provided another source of information for my research, including Portuguese and Dutch colonial records focusing on displacement and cross-border migration. This archival research allowed me to reconstruct the political history of Timorese population mobility. Other sources included a wide range of government and NGO documents and reports, as well as local newspapers.

The final point after following different East Timorese groups over a decade is the significance of time and space. Time and space inform and transform East Timorese identity. In other words, to understand East

---

4   The three camps are Naibonat, Tuapukan and Noelbaki. The seven resettlement sites are Boneana, Manusak, Raknamo, Naibonat Sosial, Naibonat 100, Oebelo Atas and Oebelo Bawah.
5   The camp is Tenu Bot. The resettlement sites are Dirun, Kabuna, Manumutin, We Liurai, Kinbana, Haliwen, Harekakae, Weoe, Betun, Kobalima Timur, Raimea and Sulit. While I focused most of my observations in those three districts, along the way from Kupang to Belu (and Malaka), I stayed overnight in TTU and TTS districts to collect stories of East Timorese there.

Timorese identity is to be able to distinguish the ways in which stories are shared in different settings. Without such understanding, or at least an awareness of it, it is likely we will miss the underlying message that East Timorese try to convey.

Let me illustrate the different verbal expressions in different times and places through a story of my engagement with Verissimo de Deus de Magelhaens. The leader of the Aitarak militia known as Group Nine, Verissimo was in charge of the Vila Verde area in 1999. He was one of the main participants in the local roulette-type gambling game called *bola guling* in Atambua. Introducing myself as a researcher writing about Timorese identity politics, I first met Verissimo in November 2012 in his shelter in Tenu Bot camp. Our first conversation lasted for two hours and was full of expressions about the way he had defended Indonesia and the 'Red and White' (the colours of the Indonesian flag).[6] The next day, I visited him again, and he explained that he had been struggling for Indonesia since 1975. He was one of 300 Atsabe youths who crossed the border in 1975 to be trained by Indonesian special forces (RPKAD (Resimen Para Komando Angkatan Darat, Army Para-Commando Regiment), now Kopassus) in Belu to become a partisan force.

When I returned to talk to him a week later, he vented his criticisms of Timor-Leste:

> What kind of independence do you have if you don't have your own currency? Timor-Leste are now following the Americans and they let the Australians control their oil. Is this what you call independent?

In our next conversation, he began to express his detachment from East Timor: 'I have bought my own land and I don't care about East Timor. My focus is to make money and build my house here.'

In this formal setting, we can see how Verissimo expressed his strong allegiance to Indonesia and announced his sense of personal deterritorialisation. In so doing, he silences his longing for his homeland in his attempt to impress on me his pure commitment to Indonesia. As time went by, I began to deal with him on a daily basis and, after a while, he asked me to visit the construction site of his new house. Walking together while observing the builders mixing concrete, our conversation in this setting started to change.

---

6   A typical topic for most, if not all, former East Timorese militiamen with whom I spoke.

Verissimo told me that although he had decided to build his house in West Timor, his obligation towards East Timor would never be forgotten. When we returned to his shelter and ate together, he recalled several attempts on his life since his arrival in West Timor. These were made in response to Verissimo's efforts to protect pro-independence supporters who joined his evacuation group. He was almost killed when he tried to send these pro-independence supporters back to Dili in 2000. 'But I knew what I did and the ancestors knew it, too,' he said, describing his successful efforts and how the ancestors' blessings had kept him safe. In this different setting, I did not hear much about Indonesia. What I heard instead were stories of Verissimo's longing for Atsabe and East Timor.

In late August 2013, I visited Verissimo one evening, at about 8 pm. His shelter was rather quiet so I asked where everyone was. He said he had just sent his wife to Timor-Leste because his mother-in-law was gravely ill. He had given his wife almost all of his savings (about IDR20 million, or A$1,900) to make sure everything was taken care of. Two days later, his mother-in-law passed away and Verrisimo sent one of his sons with more money—the money he had saved to complete his new house in Kabuna village (Belu district). He now redirected these savings to the mortuary rituals and funeral arrangements in Atsabe.

Verissimo's actions represented the opposite of the views he had expressed not so long ago—that he no longer cared about East Timor. After more than 16 years in temporary shelter, in May 2016, Verissimo moved out of Tenu Bot camp to settle permanently in Kabuna village. His oldest son has been working in Dili and his other children cross the border frequently to visit their home village in Atsabe. Sadly, Verissimo passed away in December 2016, only eight months after moving into his own house on his own land. He was buried in his backyard, but only temporarily, because, in his final words, Verissimo wished that one day his children would return his remains to Atsabe for a reunion with his ancestors.

Verissimo's story exemplifies two striking features of researching East Timorese in West Timor. First, space forms part of the identity that East Timorese attempt to maintain and negotiate. In the public domain, East Timorese will expose their prescriptive narrative of 'defending the Red and White' as a form of allegiance to Indonesia. In their private domain or in informal settings such as gardens and rice fields, kitchens and dining rooms, stories of their relationship with ancestral land resonate louder. This suggests that East Timorese stories are situational and expressed verbally for specific purposes. This also brings the issue of time into consideration. On average, my shortest conversation with these people lasted about four hours. In most instances, we talked for the whole day and there were numerous times when we finished our conversation beyond 2 am. During this seemingly endless talk, the information I was seeking was often expressed only at the very end of our conversation—when I was too tired to memorise even a short statement.

The second feature is related to action. The actions of East Timorese often speak louder than their words and sometimes help to explain what is not expressed verbally. It is also interesting, in this case, that while some East Timorese announce their political allegiance to Indonesia, they never really escape their cultural obligations towards East Timor. Performing cultural obligations does not require announcement; action speaks for itself and is what an East Timorese does as an East Timorese. Seen in this light, I would like to emphasise that investigating East Timorese requires a significant investment of time combined with continued observation and reflection on data from different settings.

Navigating East Timorese complexity

The most notable challenge of a multi-sited ethnographic approach is the fact that one simply cannot follow everything, especially when the journey time between districts is up to six hours by road. While it is difficult to provide a comprehensive picture of any one Timorese group, such an approach did enable me to develop a broad network of relationships with various East Timorese groups and to observe similarities and differences among them. Following different East Timorese groups in West Timor led me to recognise their complex identities and dispersion. Because of their number and spread, there have been various attempts to simplify the situation of the East Timorese living in West Timor.

Labelling them as refugees, or militias—and therefore brutal, violent and intolerant—is one of the more potent of these simplifications. This, however, provides little understanding of the complexity of East Timorese identity. These East Timorese might have had Indonesia as their destination when they left East Timor after the referendum, but it would be a mistake to perceive them as a uniform community economically, politically, socially, geographically or ideologically or, crucially, as ethnically homogeneous. In other words, examining the life of the East Timorese means recognising that they are not one, but many.

Plate 1.1 An East Timorese procession in Raknamo resettlement site, Kupang, October 2012

Source: Father Jefri Bonlay.

It has been estimated that more than 14,000 government employees and about 6,000 members of the military and police force with their core and extended families left East Timor. About 4,500 government employees were part of the Indonesian Ministry of Home Affairs (Depdagri) and decided to resettle and continue their career in various government agencies in NTT.[7] Army personnel and police officers have also continued their service in various squads throughout NTT and continue to draw salary and other employment benefits within the Indonesian security forces. Over time, they have also become eligible for pensions and retirement benefits under the Indonesian civil service system. Apart from this formal sector, many East Timorese are subsistence farmers. Some still live in camps, surviving by working as sharecroppers on land owned by local West Timorese.

From a political point of view, these people were formerly associated with four political factions of the pro-autonomy campaign in 1999: the East Timor People's Front (Barisan Rakyat Timor Timur, or BRTT), the Forum for Unity, Democracy and Justice (Forum Persatuan, Demokrasi dan

---

7   Their decision to transfer to the Indonesian civil service in Kupang protected their service benefits and salary.

Keadilan, or FPDK), Integration Fighters Force (Pasukan Pejuang Integrasi, or PPI) and the more recently formed Alliance of Sociopolitical Organisations Supporters of Autonomy (Aliansi Orsospol Pendukung Otonomi). Many have transformed themselves and continue to pursue their political ambitions through mainstream Indonesian political parties.

The East Timorese who have decided to remain in West Timor come from all 13 districts in Timor-Leste. They came in different waves by different modes of transportation. People from the eastern parts of East Timor, such as Baucau, Lautem and Viqueque, now reside in Kupang district, in the far west—the area to which they were conveyed by the Indonesian air and sea evacuation efforts. East Timorese from the central and border regions joined the land evacuation and currently reside in the border districts of Belu and Malaka.

Religiously, most East Timorese are Catholic, but there are about 500 Protestant East Timorese who built their own church in Silawan village along the international border; most are former members of the Balibo congregation. There are also about 150 East Timorese Muslims who have settled in Boneana on the western tip of Timor.

From a gender perspective, women have always been integral to East Timorese society in West Timor and I have noticed they are always keen to meet new people in their community. Whenever I approached an East Timorese household, I was always introduced to the mother and/or wife of that family; however, that was all. Following introductions, the women would disappear into the house and any further interaction with that family was limited mainly to the father and/or husband. There is an East Timorese expression '*feto rona deit, mane poder barak liu*', which means a 'woman should only listen because it is the man who has more power' (see Pakereng 2009: 8). This expression does not mean that women are powerless compared with men. Rather, it refers to the different gender roles and authority in dealing with outsiders or guests. And, indeed, women were only occasionally present during my visits, and only then to serve me food and drink. Rarely was I able to engage them in conversation, and I tended to rely on the views and reflections of fathers and husbands, who readily voiced their opinions. As I dealt mostly with men, my research has a distinctively masculine cast and offers little in the way of women's perspectives. But I note that in spite of these cultural barriers, a few East Timorese women do have leadership roles in resettlement politics or negotiate access with their village counterparts.

East Timorese are diverse in their political, geographical and religious backgrounds and, crucially, not all East Timorese belong to the same ethnic group. The *Language Atlas of the Pacific Area* (Wurm and Hattori 1981–83, cited in Fox 2003: 6), for instance, recognises 17 different languages in East Timor and at least double that number of dialects. These different ethnolinguistic groups are currently dispersed throughout West Timor. From their mode of evacuation, the current location of these different groups can be viewed as a reversal of the map of East Timor. Ironically, among the major ethnolinguistic groups from the eastern part of Timor-Leste, those from the far east choose to reside in Kupang district, while people from the west of Timor-Leste are concentrated in the border areas, in Belu and Malaka districts (see Chapter 2 for location details).

The final point to add to the complexity of East Timorese residing in West Timor is their numbers. Upon the arrival of the East Timorese in 1999, the UN High Commissioner for Refugees (UNHCR) estimated that 250,000 people had crossed into West Timor. As of 31 December 2002, the UNHCR officially declared the end of refugee status for those East Timorese and, by May 2003, it claimed 225,000 people had returned to Timor-Leste, with only 25,000 East Timorese remaining in West Timor. Later that year, for the purposes of the 2004 Indonesian general election, the Indonesian Ministry of Home Affairs conducted a registration census and found that 125,455 East Timorese remained in Indonesia, with 117,616 living in NTT. In 2005, the Indonesian Government announced the end of humanitarian and development assistance for East Timorese and the NTT conducted another census, which estimated that 104,436 East Timorese were resident in the province, 90 per cent of whom were located in West Timor. Drawing on additional data, I estimate there to be more than 88,000 East Timorese in West Timor: 18,000 in Kupang and about 60,000 in Belu and Malaka, with 10,000 in TTU and TTS (see Table 2.6).[8]

---

[8] I was fortunate that my fieldwork coincided with another registration census on East Timorese conducted by the most reliable census agency, Statistics Indonesia. This was funded by the Indonesian Ministry of Public Housing as part of its housing project for East Timorese. On completion of the census, I flew to Jakarta and visited the ministry to view the results. To my surprise, the project manager advised me that his office could not release the official results because they had no idea 'who are these East Timorese in West Timor'. He told me that everyone in West Timor seemed enthusiastic to be recognised as East Timorese because they knew registration often resulted in development assistance. On the other hand, there were some East Timorese groups who refused to be registered. The result of the census had still not been released by the conclusion of the housing project in 2014.

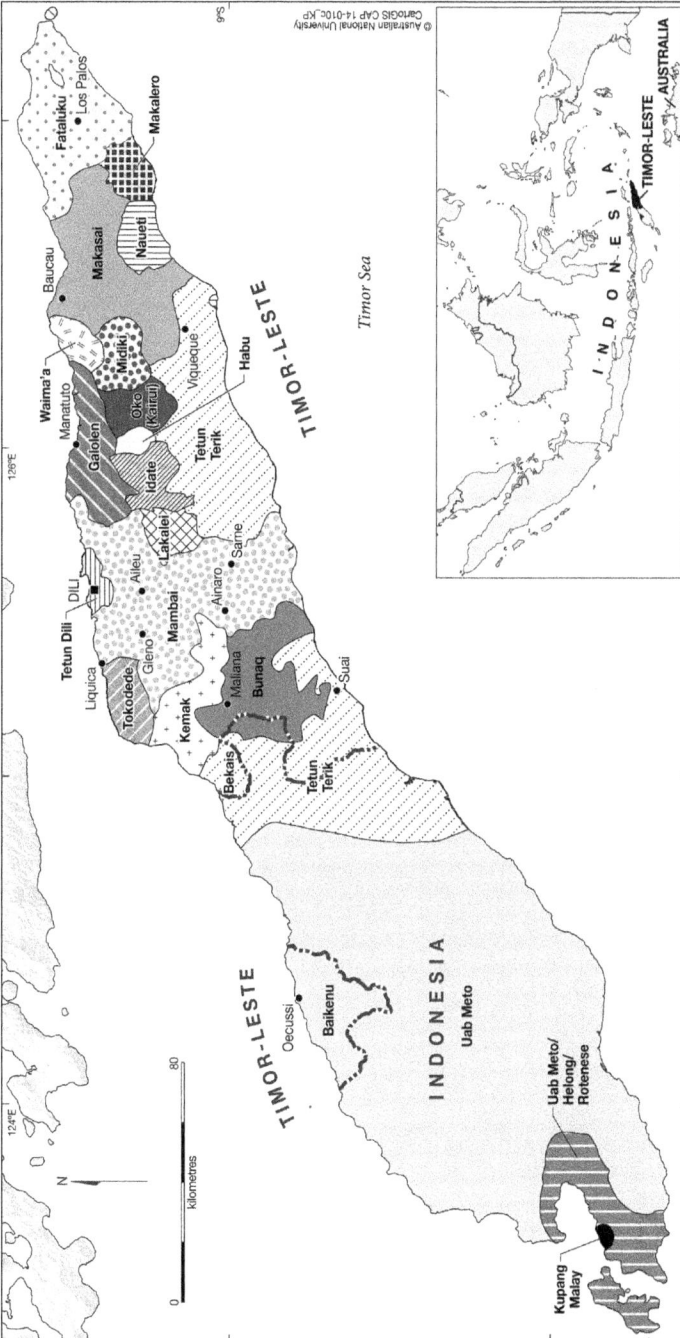

Map 1.1 Timorese ethnolinguistic groups

Source: CartoGIS, College of Asia and the Pacific, The Australian National University.

On displacement, belonging and citizenship

This book sets out to understand the way in which different East Timorese groups in West Timor have rebuilt their lives after the violent and destructive separation from their homeland. A handful of studies have looked at this issue, but the East Timorese—like many refugees and communities displaced by conflict—are often labelled as passive victims of the external macropolitical situation that forces them to flee their homeland in search of security and protection as well as humanitarian services (see, for example, IDMC 2010, 2015; ICG 2011; UN-Habitat 2014). This understanding of displacement illustrates the relations of power that operate within refugee movements and the politics surrounding humanitarian aid (Kunz 1973: 131; Shacknove 1985: 276; Zetter 1991: 51). What it lacks, however, are perspectives on the lived experiences of those refugees or displaced people.

Anthropological analysis can shed light on this issue, particularly if we follow Harrell-Bond and Voutira's (1992: 7) definition of refugees as:

> people who have undergone a violent 'rite' of separation and unless or until they are 'incorporated' as citizens into their host state (or returned to their state of origin) find themselves in 'transition', or in a state of 'liminality'.

A significant contribution of liminality to the understanding of displacement is the idea that transition is inherently a transformative process rather than a fixed event. Liminality 'occurs in the middle phase of the rites of passage which mark changes in an individual's or a group's social status and/or cultural or psychological state' (Turner 1974: 273).

This transformative process reminded me of Manuel Conceciao, a Kemak elder whom I met during my visit to Manumutin village in Belu district in 2013. As a former head of a village in Atsabe, in East Timor, Manuel had mobilised hundreds of his villagers to West Timor after violence broke out in Ermera following the referendum. While they were camped in the football stadium on the outskirts of Atambua, Manuel organised the return of most of his followers to their home village. At the same time, he approached Carlos Naibuti, an influential Kemak elder from the house of Bei Leto, an established Kemak group in Belu district whose members originally came from the village of Deribate, in Ermera subdistrict of Hatolia and who had migrated to West Timor in 1912. Recognising their shared ancestral land in East Timor, Manuel performed a ritual exchange and gifted woven cloths (*tais*), goats and some 'money for betel-nut' (*uang sirih-pinang*) to Carlos. In return, Carlos offered his land in Manumutin village for Manuel and his followers to settle down. There are currently more than 70 Kemak households of Atsabe origin living on the site.

Despite the involuntary nature of his people's flight, Manuel's effort exemplifies the case that displaced people are not passive victims of violent conflict. Rather, they remain active social agents who continually try to create and recreate meaning about their displacement. Displacement, in other words, is not necessarily about loss of place, but is a transformative process of 'place-making, of regaining control and establishing oneself in the new life circumstances' (Korac 2009: 7). The transformative process of displacement and cross-border migration has also changed the way we understand citizenship. In this context, we must explore another form of transnational and multiple belonging in which newcomers are not only trying to maintain a relationship with their place of origin, but also actively working 'to protect themselves against discrimination, gain rights, or make contributions to the development of that state and the life of the people within it' (Glick Schiller and Fouron 2001: 25). What is clear from these studies is that individuals or a group of people can belong to more than one nation-state and they can also move back and forth within and between nation-states.[9]

The way Manuel secured his land through cultural exchange highlights the significance of the notions of origin, ancestry and alliance in our understanding of East Timorese placemaking and citizenship practice in West Timor. East Timorese, like other Austronesian societies, use their ancestral land of origin to mark their identity and to claim belonging to a particular locality (Fox 2006c; McWilliam and Traube 2011). Here, locality is not about physical setting. Rather, I read it as a 'phenomenological quality' (Appadurai 1996: 178) that entails a series of interconnected places forming ancestral pathways. In this sense, when the East Timorese consider their land of exile as forming part of their ancestral pathways, their displacement is one that entails not only loss and separation, but also alliance and connection.

---

9   Discussion of transnational citizenship among immigrant communities generally revolves around ideas of multicultural citizenship (Kymlicka 1995), cultural citizenship (Rosaldo and Flores 1997; Rosaldo 2003), diasporic citizenship (Laguerre 1998) and flexible citizenship (Ong 1999). For a discussion on the dynamics of citizenship in the modern nation-state, see Bloemraad (2006) and Reed-Danahay and Brettell (2008).

'Moving back and forth'

This book follows people like Manuel to depict alternative versions of human experience that are vital for our understanding of placemaking, national identity and citizenship practice among formerly displaced people. This book is divided into three general sections to demonstrate different aspects of East Timorese displacement and citizenship practices.

Chapters 2 and 3 locate East Timorese displacement in their historical and macropolitical contexts. Here, I am concerned to illustrate the different ethnohistorical waves of East Timorese displacement to West Timor that occurred from early 1900 until 1999. These chapters also highlight the way external institutions such as the UNHCR and the Indonesian Government deal with the East Timorese and construct their identity as outsiders and/or an inferior type of citizen. The long history of East Timorese displacement and their position in the contemporary refugee/ internally displaced person (IDP) geopolitical arena present a distinct perspective on the challenges of placemaking practices.

From the historical and external encounters, I shift the focus of my discussion to the internal dynamics of East Timorese placemaking practices. Chapters 4 and 5 represent the significant ideas of origin, ancestry and alliance among different East Timorese groups. These chapters compare and contrast the experience of East Timorese who share ancestral alliances with others in West Timor with those who do not. This exercise provides an argument that, while the identity of many refugees and displaced communities has undergone deterritorialisation, the discourse and actions of East Timorese in West Timor reveal locality to be a significant feature of belonging to a place.

Following cultural ideology, the next two chapters turn my focus to East Timorese political ideology. Here, I seek to highlight the significance of East Timorese narratives of suffering and sacrifice to maintain a relationship with their homeland as well as to foster their new identity in Indonesia. This includes the way they have transformed the political landscape of the region. I end with a reflection on East Timorese vernacular citizenship to describe the complex ways they perceive themselves in the Indonesian part of Timor.

When I embarked on this study, an East Timorese elder said of their continuing border crossings that 'we are like ants, moving back and forth but we always remain as one' (*ita ema nu'u dei nehe tau malu//nu'u nehek tau malu dalan lakotu*). The structure of this book, as a study of people on the move, is also one that moves from the past to the present, from the external to the internal, from outsiders to insiders and from the cultural to the political. I hope through these movements I have not only chronicled the journeys of East Timorese whose lives have been overturned by extraordinary events, but also recovered stories of their dignity and struggle to maintain connections with their homeland and move on with their lives in Indonesia.

2

Spirit of the crocodile

I heard it said that there was once a crocodile who had lived for many
hundred[s] of years in a swamp and whose great dream was to grow and
reach a phenomenal size.

So begins poet Fernando Sylvan's (1988: 29) narrative of the island
of Timor. It continues:

However, not only was he a small crocodile, he also lived in a very confined
place. Only his dream was large.

A swamp, of course, is the worst possible place to live. Shallow, stagnant
water hemmed in by strange ill-defined banks, and above all lacking in
food to tempt a crocodile … 'I must get out of here and look for food
further afield' …

At that moment, a lively young lad happened to pass by, humming
to himself.

'What is the matter, Crocodile? You are in a bad way! Have you broken
your legs? Did something fall on you?'

'No, I have not broken anything. I am all in one piece. It is just that
although I am small, I cannot carry my body any more. I'm too weak even
to find a way out of this sweltering heat.'

The lad replied, 'If that is all it is, I can help you.'

And with that he went up to the crocodile, picked him up and carried him to the edge of the swamp. What the lad failed to notice as he carried him, however, was that the crocodile had perked up considerably: his eyes brightened and he opened his mouth and ran his tongue round his saw-like teeth.

'This lad must be tastier than anything I have ever eaten', thought the crocodile, and imagined stunning the lad with a lash from his tail and then gobbling him up.

'Do not be so ungrateful', replied the other voice inside him.

'But the need justifies the end.'

'That may be, but remember it is also shameful to betray a friend. And this is the first friend you have ever had.'

'So you expect me to do nothing, and starve to death?'

'The lad rescued you when you needed him. Now, if you want to survive, it is up to you to look for food.'

'That is true …'

Therefore, when the lad placed him on the wet ground, the crocodile smiled, rolled his eyes, shook his tail and said: 'Thank you. You are the first friend I have ever had. I cannot give you anything in return, but if you [have] never been further than this swamp we see all around us, and would like one day to travel abroad, to cross the sea, come and see me.' (Sylvan 1988: 29–32)

In many origin narratives, Timor Island is mythically perceived as the embodiment of a crocodile—wary and wanting. These narratives also represent the Timorese people as friendly to outsiders but at the same time resisting unfriendly treatment—exemplified by the various rebellions by different ethnic groups in East Timor against Portuguese colonial rule. These rebellions led to various waves of population movement across the border to West Timor. In its discussion of East Timorese displacement, the Commission for Reception, Truth and Reconciliation in East Timor (Comissão de Acolhimento, Verdade e Reconciliação de Timor Leste, or CAVR) points out that 'most individual East Timorese alive today have experienced at least one period of displacement. Many have experienced several' (CAVR 2005: 72).

This chapter takes this idea further by examining East Timorese displacement across the border to West Timor from Portuguese colonial times until 1999.[1] In this attempt, I do not intend to limit myself to ethnohistorical accounts. Rather, I move on to explore what happened in the early years after the East Timorese decided to stay in West Timor. In short, this chapter is about dispersion and encounters. The dispersion part attempts to trace and reconstruct the political history of East Timorese displacements. It covers the rebellion-induced displacement in the early Portuguese colonial period until the early twentieth century (1912–14). I then outline another population movement across the border during the Japanese invasion of Timor in the early 1940s, before describing the displacement that occurred in the mid-1970s when a decolonisation process was under way and the Indonesian military invaded East Timor. The second part of the chapter deals with the displacement that occurred in 1999 and early interactions between displaced East Timorese and West Timorese. An underlying objective is to demonstrate that displacement in Timor is not a new phenomenon and therefore an understanding of its complex patterns and variations is crucial to our understanding of contemporary resettlement and emplacement in West Timor.

Early colonial encounters

The Portuguese presence in Timor began with successful expeditions to support the Queen of Lifau/Ambeno in 1641 and to establish a settlement in the 1650s (Hägerdal 2012: 150–1). After nearly a century of relative peace and mutual trade, at the beginning of the eighteenth century, Portugal dispatched its first governor to Timor and imposed a head tax on the Timorese. The Timorese did not wait long to respond to this policy. In what was known as the 'battle of Cailaco', 15 kingdoms from Oecussi to Ermera united against the Portuguese in violent resistance in late October 1726 (Durand 2011: 3–4). In their attempt to lay siege to the Timorese stronghold, Joaquim de Matos, the Portuguese commander, reported:

> [O]ur people could not do more, for it was necessary to climb up one by one and without a shotgun, giving the hand to the other person so they could also step up from the low to the high place. And the enemy threw rocks, which was like an inferno, smashing everyone who was in front of

---

1   The first Timorese refugees were the Oirata people who fled to Kisar Island in 1714. 'They came from Loikera, that is, Loiquero close to the eastern cape of Timor' (Hägerdal 2012: 336–7).

them. The sight of that stopped our people who were in the trenches and posts from gaining on the enemy below, because of the risks involved. (Sá 1949: 49–50, cited in Hägerdal 2012: 340)

The Cailaco stronghold finally fell after six weeks of fighting. Describing the aftermath of the bloody battle, de Matos wrote to the governor of Timor:

[T]here was neither a settlement nor a sign of one that was not burnt down. Seventy-two of their trenches were destroyed, among which were some of considerable strength. They had stone parapets apart from the large poles and thick beams on which they were built, with ditches of a good size all around, very sharp bamboo sticks full of poison, which were dug into the roads … And all people were brought away from them. Many provisions were burnt, without them being able to impede it, or preserving them to feed these people, although I gave orders to spare much of it. Of buffaloes, our men took more than 2,000 as booty. Of severed heads, 152 were shown to me, apart from the other dead that they buried. Concerning the 168 prisoners and the principal leaders, they confessed that in the besieged fortress, more than 300 people died from wounds and suffocation [heat exposure], including men, women and children, and some leaders; so that one can assume that the enemy had more than 700 dead. On this occasion I lost 39 soldiers. I do not speak of the wounded, of which there was a large number. (Sá 1949: 51–2, cited in Hägerdal 2012: 341)

Despite this devastating defeat and the destruction of their villages, events at Cailaco inspired further resistance, which continued until 1728. The continuing Timorese resistance and attacks on the Portuguese culminated in the killing of the Portuguese governor Dionísio Gonçalves Rebelo Galvão in 1766, and relocation of the colony to Dili in 1769. With the establishment of their new settlement in Dili, the Portuguese increased the head tax and introduced forced labour. Again, the Timorese responded, with the *reinos* (domains) of Laclo and Ulmera on the coast east of Dili rising against the oppressive policies of the Portuguese. In 1861, warriors from these *reinos* marched on Dili, set up an advance post and managed to cut off food supplies to the Portuguese centre of administration. The Portuguese Government then secretly approached and made a deal with the Timorese rulers of Liquiçá, Ermera, Cailaco, Deribate, Leimean, Atsabe, Caimauc and Maubara to fight on their side against the rebels who were allied with the rulers of Hera and Manatuto. At the end of the fight, the Portuguese and their Timorese allies were victorious and had 'captured over one thousand buffalos, four hundred horses … as well as large quantities of maize, rice and domestic livestock', although it was reported that the Laclo chiefs had managed to escape (Davidson 1994: 143).[2]

The Kemak rebels

After a series of battles more than two decades after the first Laclo uprising, in 1888, the Portuguese finally received an official declaration of loyalty and vassalage from 13 *reinos* in the eastern part of East Timor— namely, Ulmera, Vemasse, Baucau, Bercoly, Venilale, Barique, Manatuto, Laleia, Laicore, Cairuhy, Laclo, Lacluta and Caimau. The central, western and south-western parts of East Timor, on the other hand, remained self-governing and proved constant irritants to the Portuguese. 'All *reinos* of the west were in revolt … and so were the twelve *reinos* of the central west and seven of the southern *reinos*', wrote the newly appointed governor, José Celestino da Silva, on his arrival in Dili in May 1894 (Davidson 1994: 181). With their colonial territories in Africa restricted and having been diplomatically humiliated by the British ultimatum in 1890, the Portuguese empire in Lisbon saw an ongoing rebellious Timor as another devastating blow. As a military officer, da Silva therefore came to Timor with a clear mission: restore pride and honour to Lisbon through glorious battle against the Timorese rebels (Davidson 1994: 174).

Without wasting any time, da Silva began a campaign into the western part of East Timor in the early months of 1895. Under the leadership of the regional military commander Alferes Francisco Duarte, da Silva made the border people of Obulo and Marobo his first target. They had 'decided to revolt against Portuguese authority to the point of threatening to fly the Dutch flag' (Davidson 1994: 184) and needed to be punished for their disloyalty. Duarte's initial attack was unsuccessful and he was forced to call on Dili for reinforcements. In April 1895, da Silva sent an additional 6,000 *morradores*[3] and artillery pieces under the command of Captain Eduardo da Câmara, an experienced soldier who had served in India and Mozambique, to defeat the Obulo and Marobo, who had assistance from

---

2   For detailed discussion of the anti-Portuguese movement, see Hägerdal (2012: 335–409) and Kammen (2016: 61).
3   *Moradores* are citizen militias who fought alongside the Portuguese forces. They were initially recruited in Dili (Durand 2011: 5). Another group of citizen militia during the Portuguese colonial period was called *arraias*. These 'two groups were clad and armed in the same manner but they differed in their relations to the colonial government' (Davidson 1994: 165).

their allies in Cailaco, Atabai, Baboi, Balibo and Fatumean. Even with these additional troops and weapons, it took another month to defeat the Obulo, at the end of May. In his depiction of the battle, da Câmara admitted:

> the inhabitants [of Obulo] have a notable aptitude for war and can hurl a *zagaia*[4] fifty meters to bring down a man; with swords they are no less fearful and we can only be sure of dispersing them with gunfire. (Davidson 1994: 185)

After this successful campaign, Captain da Câmara—without orders from Dili and without waiting for additional troops from Oecussi—brazenly marched into the *reinos* of Cova, Fatumean and Forem (Fohorem). The Timorese warriors, however, wiped out da Câmara's forces and all of his officers. The captain himself was decapitated and Lisbon was under pressure to act forcefully in response. In the bigger picture, this incident provoked the largest military occupation of Timor. As the *Revisa Militar* journal in Lisbon noted in October 1895, 'without stringent punishment, without an effective and responsible occupation which subdues and disempowers the treacherous *regulos* … our dominion will remain as it is now, fictitious' (cited in Davidson 1994: 193).

In the ensuing months, an additional 300 troops from Africa arrived in Dili to support Governor da Silva's large-scale military operation. The intention was not just to capture those responsible for da Câmara's death, but also to make the Portuguese colonisation of Timor a reality. Therefore, rather than aim initially for Cova, Fatumean and Fohorem, the governor began his campaign from Cotubaba. In a bloody, aggressive and rampaging attack, the Portuguese forces—with the support of Timorese allies from Maubara, Atsabe, Cailaco, Ermera, Deribate and Leimean—'pillaged, burned and killed all they encountered' and, eventually, after 10 days, 'Cotubaba was completely destroyed [and] not even the smallest tree remained standing', according to Captain Francisco Elvaim, the leader of one of the Portuguese forces (Davidson 1994: 195).

> Such was the terror they created that the government forces arrived at the village of Sui-Laran [a hamlet in the present day village of Aidabaleten in Atabae] to find the *Liurai* [ruler] and all his people had fled, 'abandoning everything, even food and household utensils'. (Davidson 1994: 195)

---

4   *Zagaia* is similar to *assegai*, which means 'spear'. On other Timorese weaponry, see Forbes (1884: 409) and Jolliffe (1978: 35).

From Cotubaba, they marched on to Balibo and Sanir. The *liurai* from Balibo approached Captain Elvaim and surrendered. This was not the case in Sanir (Sanirin). At the village of Dato-Lato, the captain asked the villagers to hand over Cotubaba fugitive leaders he believed had found refuge there. A village representative admitted:

> they had some refugees but the *principais* and their livestock had fled to Cova. Refusing to believe this, the Portuguese commander ordered his men to attack the village and after a tenacious resistance lasting four days, Dato-Lalo finally fell when the shells from the field gun dislodged them from their fortified mountain peak. (Davidson 1994: 196)

Recalling the horror of the battle, the captain recorded: '[I]n the morning, the central square was strewn with more than one hundred bodies, stripped, decapitated and horribly mutilated' (cited in Davidson 1994: 196). The victory over Sanir was not all good news for the local allies of the Portuguese. Dom Thomas, the *liurai* of Atsabe, considered that 'to attack Sanir was to attack Atsabe' and therefore he did not wish to continue his support for the next campaign, into Cova (Davidson 1994: 197). Another ally who deserted and pulled out their troops was the Kemak-speaking group from the *reino* of Deribate (Davidson 1994: 198).

In spite of the broken alliances, the Portuguese forces continued their campaign and marched into Cova. To their surprise, there was no resistance whatsoever from the Cova warriors. When they entered the ritual centre of the village, all they found were the severed heads of Captain da Câmara and some others hanging from a lulic tree. The people of Cova had already fled into Dutch territory to the west (Davidson 1994: 197). With Cova now under Portuguese control, in October 1896, Governor da Silva ordered his forces, under the leadership of Alferes Duarte, to march to Deribate and punish the people there for their desertion (Davidson 1994: 198). The initial resistance around the sacred woods of Talo was vanquished and the rebel warriors joined their *liurai*, chiefs and remaining villagers in a subterranean cave surrounded by rock walls some 2 m thick in an area called Dede-Pum. Duarte decided not to launch an attack on such a well-defended position, and simply surrounded the cave. In time and facing dehydration inside the cave, small groups crept out every night to fetch water, but never returned as they were shot dead by Duarte's forces. The remaining rebels cried out for negotiations on the eighth day, but the *liurai* refused to surrender and Duarte's army 'brought out twenty-one prisoners, only two of whom were men'. As there was no sound from the cave on the twelfth day, Duarte went in and found the remains of men and women, 'most in a state of complete putrification'. In his report, Duarte estimated there to have been about 400 bodies. The *liurai*, however, were not there; they had managed to escape (Davidson 1994: 199).

At the end of these military campaigns in the west, the *reino* of these Kemak-speaking people from Deribate, 'along with those of Cotubaba, Sanir and Cova, were declared extinct in 1897' (Davidson 1994: 199). Teófilo Duarte, a Portuguese traveller who visited Cova in the 1940s, observed:

> there were large parts of Cova once noted for their comparative prosperity that remained empty and uncultivated thirty years later despite the Governor's plan for a military colony to be established there. (Cited in Davidson 1994: 202)

A record of the early settlement of Kemak people in West Timor can be found in the daily journal of a Jesuit priest, Father J. Erftemeijer. He found Kemak people from Cotubaba settled in the hamlet of Fatukmetan, approximately 4 km east of the port of Atapupu (Seran et al. 2010: 183). According to the local people, the name of the king who brought them to Fatukmetan was Alexander Mau Mali. The king came from the house of Parlara and arrived along with people from nine named houses: Dudu Basa, Railelo, Hatu Male, Mane Morin, Lapasin, Umbirun, Koturan, Dair and Taimali.

In his visit to Wehor, 5 km east of Atambua, in November 1913, Father Erftemeijer noted about 2,000 Kemak people from Sanirin were settled there. Kemak of Sanirin origin can also be found in and around the border villages of Tohe, Maunmutin and Lamaksanulu. From Wehor, Father Erftemeijer continued his journey to Sadi and found another 900 Kemak-speaking people there. He also observed people's livelihoods and wrote about different kinds of domesticated livestock, including horses and water buffalo. He was informed that the name of their leader was Kes and they had settled there in 1901 (Seran et al. 2010: 183).

The largest movement of Kemak people was of those from Deribate. It was recorded that in May 1912 about 2,000 people from Deribate crossed the border and entered West Timor. Meanwhile, an additional 7,000 people were hiding in caves along the border, waiting to leave the Portuguese colony (Davidson 1994: 258–9). Carlos Naibuti who was the oldest descendant of the Kemak of Deribate origin, told me in his house in Tenu Bot that, after the crossing, his ancestors temporarily stayed along the border. After two years, and through peaceful negotiations and agreement with the ruler of the Lidak domain, who controlled most of what is now Atambua, they moved further west and settled in Tenu Bot, on the outskirts of the Atambua civic centre.

Table 2.1 Displacement of Kemak people between 1900 and 1912

Ethnolinguistic group	Current location			Approximate number of people
	Kabupaten/ kota (district)	Kecamatan (subdistrict)	Desa (village)	
Kemak from Cotubaba	Belu	Kakuluk Mesak	Kenebibi	n.a.
Kemak from Sanir	Belu	Kakuluk Mesak	Kabuna	2,000
		Raihat	Maunmutin	
			Tohe	
		Lamaknen	Lamaksanulu	
Kemak from Leolima, Leohitu and Atabae	Belu	Tasifeto Timur	Sadi	900
Kemak from Deribate (Hatolia), Leimea and Atabae	Belu	Atambua	Manumutin	9,000

Sources: Davidson (1994); Seran et al. (2010); and author's interview with Carlos Naibuti.

The Tetun 'returnees'

After more than 30 years of extensive military campaigns, only in the late nineteenth century were the Portuguese 'able to exert their influence on the interior of Timor' (Fox 2003: 11). As they had all of the *reinos* under control, the next step in the colonisation effort was to exploit them. Under the leadership of Filomena de Camara, who arrived in Dili in 1910, a head tax—increased from 1 to 2.5 patacas (equivalent to 2 shillings, 4 pence)—was immediately implemented. This policy produced different reactions from the *reinos* in the southern part of the country. A Dutch colonial report noted:

[T]he *regulos* of Manufahi and Raimean conferred with the *regulo* of Camenasse ... and decided they could not pay the tax ... A decision was made to go to the Military Commander at Suai and ask for a reduction in the tax ... The gathering mass of people, preparing to come to Command site was reported to the Commander by Chinese traders ... He misunderstood [and presumed] it was an attacking force and with his garrison, and several Englishmen from the Petroleum Company based in Suai, made their way to a ship based offshore before the people of Raimean were sighted. (La Lau 1912: 657–8)

The *liurai* of Camenaça approached the Dutch border authority seeking permission to cross over and stay. He came with his three chiefs and 750 people and their livestock. The request was granted and they were permitted to settle in South Belu. Many other chiefs and their people from the western and south-western regions of East Timor soon followed (La Lau 1912: 657–8). According to Francillon (1967: 53), these Tetun people from Suai were commonly called '*ema malaik*' or 'people who fled'; however, these newly arrived Tetun people did not perceive themselves as refugees or people who had fled from war. The term *ema malaik*, as Francillon further explained:

[was] resented since they insisted on the fact that they did not really run away but merely returned to the lap of Wehali, the mother, as would a child do with his mother when in difficulty. (Francillon 1967: 53–4)

In their own terms, displaced Tetun from Suai and the Camenaça area of East Timor perceived their journey to refuge not as a flight from their homeland, but as a return to their ancestral land of origin.[5] More than 2,200 Tetun 'returnees' arrived in southern Belu in the early twentieth century, settling in Betun, Kletek and Besikama. Some maintained the names of their origin places such as Suai and Kamanasa (Francillon 1967: 54).

The maintenance of the origin placename is exemplified by the Tetun people in Lakulo village in Besikama. These people are most likely the descendants of the three chiefs who came with the ruler of Camenaça to the Dutch border. According to these people's oral history, the present-day Lakulo village is derived from their home village of Lakulo/Laclo in the Suai area of East Timor. Their ancestors migrated to West Timor during the war of Boa Ventura (Dom Bona Ventura), comprising three named

---

5   A return to 'Wehali the mother and the father' (*ina no ama Wehali*) (Therik 2004: 49).

houses: Tolu Bei, which is recognised as *ina no ama* ('the mother and the father'); Kara Saen, which is recognised as *mane ulun* ('the eldest child'); and Suri, recognised as the *mane ikun* ('the youngest child').

They established their initial settlement in Besikama and named it Lakulo Tasi, because it was near the sea. According to Domi Yos Seran, the elder of Kara Saen house and the first head of Lakulo Webriamata village, several years after the arrival of their ancestors on the Besikama coast, one of the rulers in Lakulo, Na'i Lulik Lia Kobe, made a visit to Besikama. He travelled south through Suai and arrived on the coast of Besikama to see the situation of his people and to ask whether they were willing to return. As most of the people opted to stay, the king went to the house of the ruler of Besikama to 'give away' (*fo baa*) his people to the local ruler.

The Lakulo people stayed on the coast of Besikama until the late 1930s. In 1939, Besikama was swept away in a great flood of the Bena Nain River and Lakulo Tasi settlement was entirely buried under sediment. As a result, the people moved a little further into the interior, to the place where they grew food. The Tolu Bei clan occupied the area of Kubaklaran and named it Lakulo Kubaklaran. Kara Saen occupied the area of Webriamata and named it Lakulo Webriamata, while the Suri clan moved into the Weain area and named it Lakulo Weain. The Tolu Bei clan later expanded and cultivated the land around Wekmidar village, naming it Lakulo Sunan, and around Badarai village, a location they identify as Lakulo Laensukabi.

By the mid-1960s, it was estimated 500 people of Lakulo origin were living in the area. In 2016, they numbered about 4,000 people. Despite their conviction that their ancestors came from East Timor, nowadays they always refer to themselves as '*oan fehan*' ('people from the plain/ coast'). *Oan fehan* is the same term by which southern Tetun-speaking people identify themselves.

Table 2.2 Displacement of Tetun people between 1911 and 1912

Ethnolinguistic group	Current location			Approximate number of people
	Kabupaten/ kota (district)	*Kecamatan* (subdistrict)	*Desa* (village)	
Tetun from Suai and Camenaça	Malaka	Wewiku	Lorotolus	750
			Webriamata	n.a.
			Badarai	n.a.
		Malaka Tengah	Kletek (Suai)	1,020
			Kamanasa	635
			Fahiluka	450
			Umakatahan (Matai)	160
		Weliman	Lakulo	n.a.
		Rinhat	Weain	n.a.
			Wekmidar	n.a.

n.a. = not available

Sources: La Lau (1912: 658–9); Francillon (1967: 52); and author's interview with Domi Yos Seran, former head of Lakulo Webriamata village.

The Bunaq refugees from the east

The early twentieth century also marked the arrival of Bunaq-speaking people from the East Timorese Maucatar enclave in West Timor. Maucatar was in the north of Suai, but was controlled by the Dutch in accordance with the 1859 treaty. This treaty, however, also acknowledged the Noimuti enclave to the south of Oecussi as part of Portuguese territory. Another convention was negotiated in 1904 and an agreement was reached to cede Maucatar to the Portuguese and Noimuti to the Dutch (see Fox 2003: 14–16). This agreement nevertheless left residual issues over territorial boundaries and culminated in the Lakmaras incident in 1911. Violent conflict in Lakmaras and the subsequent retreat of the Dutch from Maucatar caused about 5,000 predominantly Bunaq people to move to West Timor (Francillon 1967: 52; Schapper 2011: 175–6). Initially, they moved eastward to Lamaknen, but with little land available there, they went further south until they reached Wehali land. According to

Francillon (1967: 54), more than 400 Bunaq arrived in Wehali land during this period and they eventually settled in Labarai (75 people), Nataraen-Uma Fatik (200 people) and Manumuti Benai (150 people).[6]

Table 2.3 Displacement of Bunaq people between 1911 and 1912

Ethnolinguistic group	Current location			Approximate number of people
	Kabupaten/ kota (district)	Kecamatan (subdistrict)	Desa (village)	
Bunaq from Maucatar	Malaka	Kobalima	Lakekun Lakekun Utara Litamali Kamanasa (Labarai)	5,000
		Kobalima Timur	Alas	
		Malaka Tengah	Umanen Lawalu (Manumuti Umafatik)	

Sources: Francillon (1967); Schapper (2011).

World War II refugees

After 1912, the Portuguese colonisation of East Timor continued unchallenged until an intervention by Allied forces in late 1941 led to occupation by Japan. The Japanese invaded Timor on 20 February 1942 and stayed until they surrendered in August 1945. Their three-year occupation caused large displacement of Bunaq people. The Japanese attack in August 1942 caused the Bunaq from Fohorem who supported the Allied forces to flee across the border into West Timor and settle in the village of Namfalus, in southern Belu. For those who supported the Japanese, such as the Bunaq from Lebos village in Bobonaro, movement to West Timor helped them avoid reprisals after the defeat of the Japanese. They were accepted by the Bunaq in Lamaknen and established their village of Lakus in northern Belu (Schapper 2011: 173–5).

---

6   I note there was also a migration of Meto-speaking people from Oecussi enclave during this period, most of whom merely crossed the border to North Central Timor (TTU), but others moved further west to South Central Timor (TTS) and Kupang. See Ormelling (1957) and Ataupah (1992).

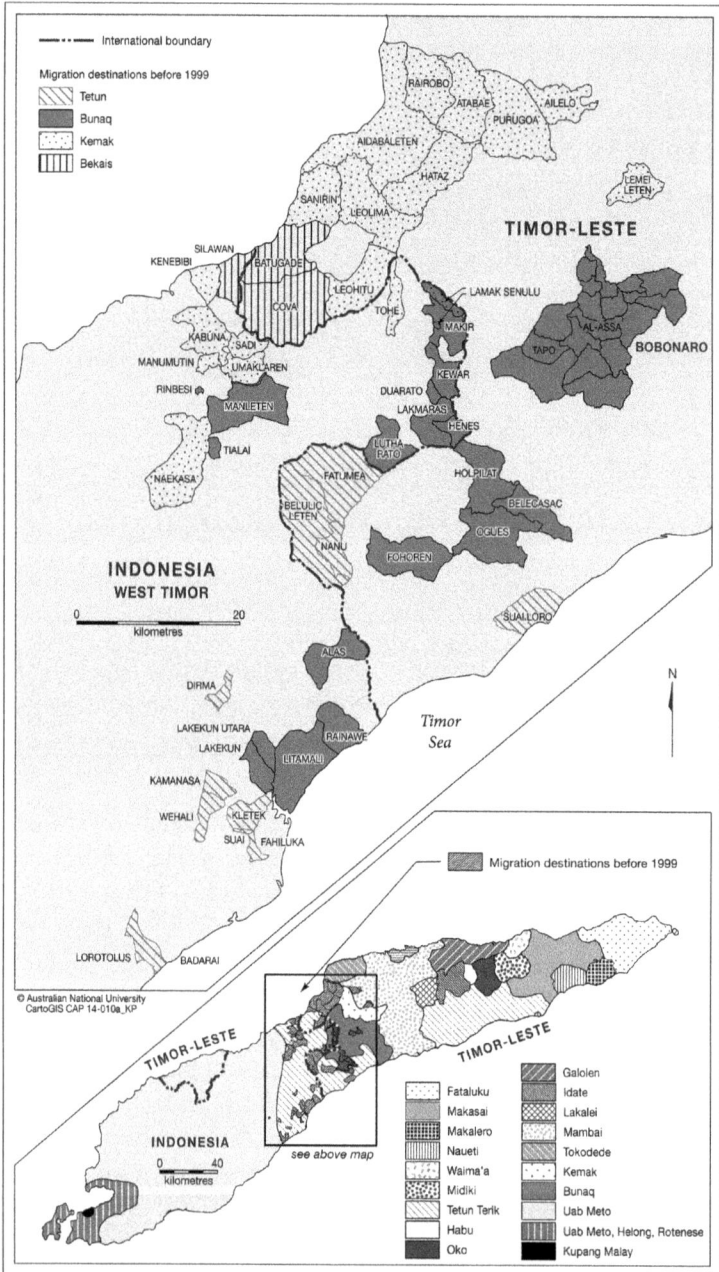

Map 2.1 East Timorese migration to West Timor during Portuguese colonisation

Source: CartoGIS, College of Asia and the Pacific, The Australian National University, with author's analysis.

Table 2.4 Displacement during World War II, 1942–45

Ethnolinguistic group	Current location		
	Kabupaten/kota (district)	Kecamatan (subdistrict)	Desa (village)
Bunaq from Ololo	Belu	Lamaknen	Kewar
Bunaq from Lakus	Belu	Lamaknen	Kewar
Bunaq from Fohorem	Malaka	Kobalima	Rainawe

Source: Schapper (2011).

Political upheaval and Indonesian invasion

After the end of World War II, the Portuguese resumed their colonial rule over East Timor, until the political situation changed in Portugal in the 1970s. In April 1974, the regime of Marcelo Caetano was overthrown by the Portuguese Movement of Armed Forces in the so-called Carnation Revolution (Kammen 2016: 121). In addition to the restoration of democracy in Portugal, the new administration extended to the colonial territories, including East Timor, the right to determine their own future and become independent if they so wished. News of the revolution and decolonisation agenda quickly reached Timor. Timorese did not want to miss the opportunity to become independent, so they started to mobilise their political activities towards liberation.

On 11 May 1974, some former representatives of the National Action Party (Acção Nacional Popular, or ANP), the only political party that functioned in East Timor during the Caetano regime, joined with plantation owners to form the Democratic Union of Timorese (União Democrática Timorense, or UDT). Over a week later, the Timorese trade union teamed up with members of an anticolonial clandestine group and formed the Social Democratic Association of Timor (Associação Social Democrática Timorense, or ASDT). The ASDT was later renamed the Revolutionary Front for an Independent East Timor (Frente Revolucionária de Timor-Leste Independente, or Fretilin). In late May, another association formed, initially called the Association for the Integration of Timor into Indonesia (AITI), later changed to the Timorese Popular Democratic Association (Associação Popular Democrática Timorense, or Apodeti). Other smaller groups established during this period included the Popular Associations of Monarchs of Timor (Associação Popular Monarquia Timorense), which was later renamed the Association of Timorese Heroes (Klibur Owan Timor Ass'wain, or KOTA), the Democratic Association for the Integration of East Timor into Australia (Associação Democrática para a Integração de Timor Leste na Austrália, or ADITLA) and the Timor Labour Party (Partido Trabalhista).

In August 1974, the UDT launched a coup, but was effectively countered by Fretilin, which sparked further political upheaval in East Timor. This resulted in approximately 40,000 refugees fleeing to the Indonesian territory of West Timor (Babo-Soares 2003: 55). The remaining Portuguese in the territory withdrew and Fretilin declared the independence of East Timor on 28 November 1975. A few days after the declaration of independence in Dili, the UDT and Apodeti, directed by the Indonesian Intelligence Coordinating Agency (Badan Koordinasi Intelegen Negara, or Bakin), signed a declaration of integration (Aditjondro 1994: 8). On 7 December 1975, a few hours after the conclusion of an official visit to Jakarta by then US president Gerald Ford and secretary of state Henry Kissinger, the Indonesian army launched a military invasion of East Timor.

The East Timorese who took refuge in Indonesia were encamped in Belu district on the border. In late January 1976, the Belu district government conducted a registration census and estimated that more than 37,000 East Timorese had moved into the region. These refugees were dispersed across eight subdistricts: Lamaknen, East Tasifeto, Representation of East Tasifeto, West Tasifeto, Representation of West Tasifeto, Central Malaka, East Malaka and Atambua. Following their ancestors, the refugees utilised their social kinship relations to validate their connection to their chosen camp. The Tetun-speaking people, for instance, choose to stay in central and eastern Malaka. The Kemak from Marobo were encamped around the Kemak area in Haekesak, along the border. The Kemak from Atsabe chose to stay in Tenu Bot, a large area occupied by Kemak of Dirubati origin since their arrival in 1912. The Bunaq, on the other hand, chose to stay in the Lamaknen area. Many Bunaq refugees also went further into the Sukabiren area of Atambua.

Table 2.5 Displacement during the civil war and Indonesian invasion, 1975–79

No.	Ethnolinguistic group	Location			Approximate number of people
		Kabupaten (district)	Kecamatan (subdistrict)	Desa (village)	
1	Bunaq from Bobonaro	Belu	Lamaknen	Lamaksenulu	7,307
				Makir	372
				Kewar	1,750
				Duarato	10
			Lamaknen Selatan	Lakmaras	287
				Henes	271
				Lutha Rato	160
			Tasifeto Timur	Manleten	3,542
				Tialai	63
			Atambua Selatan	Rinbesi	4,435
Total for Bunaq					18,197
2	Kemak from Marobo (Bobonaro)	Belu	Tasifeto Timur	Sadi	556
			Raihat	Haekesak	6,355
3	Kemak from Atsabe	Belu	Atambua	Manumutin	1,649
			Tasifeto Barat	Naekasa	3,432
Total for Kemak					11,992
4	Tetun from Balibo	Belu	Tasifeto Timur	Silawan	5,726
Total from Tetun Balibo					5,726
5	Tetun from Suai	Belu	Malaka Tengah	Wehali	109
			Malaka Timur	Dirma	1,048
Total for Tetun Suai					1,157
Total for all ethnic groups					37,072

Source: Archive of Belu District Government, with author's interpretation.

Plate 2.1 East Timorese from Bobonaro in Atambua, 1974
Source: Ignasius Kali.

In July 1976, Indonesian president Suharto declared East Timor the 27th province of the Republic of Indonesia. Following improved security and stability in East Timor, East Timorese refugees began the return journey to their homeland. The Indonesian Government facilitated this return, which concluded in 1979, when the last group of East Timorese refugees was transported back to Atsabe and Bobonaro.

Indonesian military occupation and the 1999 displacement

The military occupation of East Timor led to more than two decades of violent conflict and resistance by East Timorese pro-independence supporters. After the fall of president Suharto and his 'New Order' regime in May 1998, the incoming Indonesian president, B. J. Habibie, made the issue of East Timor central to his agenda. In January 1999, he announced there would be a popular referendum offering wideranging autonomy or independence for East Timor. During the political reform in the lead-up to the referendum, the Indonesian military developed a plan to 'protect the integration' by forming militia groups in all districts of East Timor—with violence used on occasions against those who supported independence (Robinson 2008: 102). As the intensity of violent conflict between pro-autonomy and pro-independence supporters increased in the lead-up to the referendum, people began to flee.

Those who fled East Timor in this early stage were mostly of NTT origin or those who had come from other parts of Indonesia. Most had migrated to East Timor after the Indonesian occupation seeking employment or for business purposes. One month before the referendum took place, the NTT government reported that nearly 3,000 households (approximately 12,000 people) from East Timor had been dispersed across six districts in NTT. Of this number, however, only about 900 households claimed East Timor as their origin. Others claimed NTT, East Java, South Sulawesi, Bali and West Nusa Tenggara province (NTB) as their origin (Pos Kupang 1999).

The departure and evacuation of predominantly East Timorese took place almost immediately after the result of the referendum was announced. Januar Achmad, a medical doctor who set up a team of volunteers for relief services in West Timor between late 1999 and early 2000, observed:

> [O]n 4 September 1999 the first shipment of 1000 refugees arrived in Kupang harbour and was received by the governor of the NTT ... Initially, only a few tents were available, so most of the [East Timorese] refugees were settled in the football stadium, government buildings and schools. [Others] just slept in the open air with no shelter at all for a few weeks. Wealthier East Timorese first stayed in hotels. Later they rented houses in the city and villages around the camp. Some of the refugees also moved out from the camps and rented rooms or houses in the villages where they could. [The refugees who had no money] stayed in churches, empty offices, or public camps. (Achmad 2003: 196)

In early 2000, it was estimated that about 250,000 displaced East Timorese were dispersed across more than 200 camps in West Timor (Campbell-Nelson et al. 2000: vi). These camps varied significantly in terms of their construction, the number of residents and location. Some were built in designated sites with organised barracks and public sanitation; but others comprised temporary tarpaulin tents with no public facilities. For those who had prior relationships based on shared ethnicity, the local people accommodated them in their houses or built extra rooms for them in their gardens. Regardless of variations, the camps were located within existing villages and most sat alongside existing local residential arrangements. This situation was often referred to as 'the poor assisting the needy', because poor West Timorese farmers had to share their limited land and water resources with the incoming refugees.

Plate 2.2 East Timorese children in Tuapukan camp, one of the few camps established in 1999 remaining in Kupang district
Source: Andrey Damaledo.

Most residents of the camps in West Timor have returned to East Timor, mainly with the support of the UNHCR's repatriation program, which commenced in 2000. The official determination or classification by the UNHCR of East Timorese—displaced in 1999—as 'refugees' concluded in 2002; however, the Indonesian Government continued its repatriation program until 2005. For those East Timorese who decided to stay in West Timor, the Indonesian Government and international development agencies have provided support for housing, resettlement and livelihoods. These programs have facilitated the dispersion of different East Timorese groups into various locations across West Timor.

In Kupang district, the Makasae-speaking people are clearly dominant numerically and territorially, with approximately 4,500 living in hill towns, such as Raknamo and (Upper) Oebelo, and on the plains, such as in Naibonat, Manusak, Tuapukan and Noelbaki. An estimated 3,800 Fataluku-speaking people dominate the central plain area of Kupang, particularly in Oebelo and Manusak. In the central and eastern regions of Kupang district, there is also a large group of Tetun Terik people from Viqueque in Tanah Merah, Oefafi, Tuapukan and Merdeka, while others have moved further north to the Sulamu area. There are about 2,500 Tetun Terik from Viqueque in total.

Plate 2.3 East Timorese resettlement site in Oebelo, Kupang district, housing Fataluku-speaking people from Lautem district
Source: Andrey Damaledo.

In addition to these dominant groups, about 1,500 Naueti-speaking people (from Baucau district, East Timor) reside in Manusak and Naibonat. A similar number of Idate-speaking people (Manatuto district) are found in the hilly areas of Raknamo and Naunu. In areas such as Naibonat, Manusak and Raknamo, there are smaller groups of Galoli-speaking people (Manatuto), with about 500 residing in Empat Air and Dua Air resettlement site, which is part of Naibonat, and about

750 Waima'a-speaking people (Baucau) near the Naibonat graveyard. About 200 Midiki and Kairui people (Manatuto/Baucau) have settled in Raknamo; about 300 Mambai-speaking people (Ailieu/Manufahi) have also settled in Raknamo and Manusak; and about 100 Makalero people (Lautem) and 50 Sa'ani people[7] (Lautem) live in Manusak.

In contrast to those in Kupang, different East Timorese groups in the border region of Belu and Malaka districts are found in higher numbers and are more dispersed. The Bunaq-speaking people, with a total population of more than 11,000, are the largest group, with the majority currently residing in the predominantly Bunaq villages of Raihat, Lamaknen and South Lamaknen in Belu, and along the southern border of Kobalima and Eastern Kobalima in Malaka district. About 7,000 Kemak-speaking people are also following their predecessors by residing on the outskirts of Atambua, in places such as Tenu Bot, Sadi, Haliwen, Hali Ulun, We Liurai and Kabuna. Along the northern border, about 1,200 Bekais-speaking people (Bobonaro district) are accommodated in the land of their forebears, in Silawan and Tulakadi. Along the southern border, an estimated 6,000 Tetun Terik people from Suai chose to stay in Malaka district, particularly in Betun, Kletek and Kamanasa areas. Belu and Malaka host other East Timorese groups who did not have a previous ethnic relationship. For example, about 4,500 Tokodede-speaking people from Liquiçá are currently staying on the north coast of Belu, around the port of Atapupu. In the highlands of Belu, roughly 500 Idate-speaking and 50 Habu-speaking people have resettled in the Kinbana region. The Mambai people from the central highlands of East Timor are found in the western side of Belu district and the highlands of Malaka district; there are approximately 2,500 currently resettled in areas such as Labur, Rafae, Leun Tolu and Kereana.

---

7   The Sa'ani language is spoken by people from the villages of Barikafa and Kotamutu in Lautem subdistrict of Luro.

Plate 2.4 A Fataluku woman in her house in Oebelo Atas resettlement area in Kupang district
Source: Andrey Damaledo.

Plate 2.5 Resettlement site for East Timorese in Kabuna village, Belu district, housing Kemak people from Atsabe
Source: Andrey Damaledo.

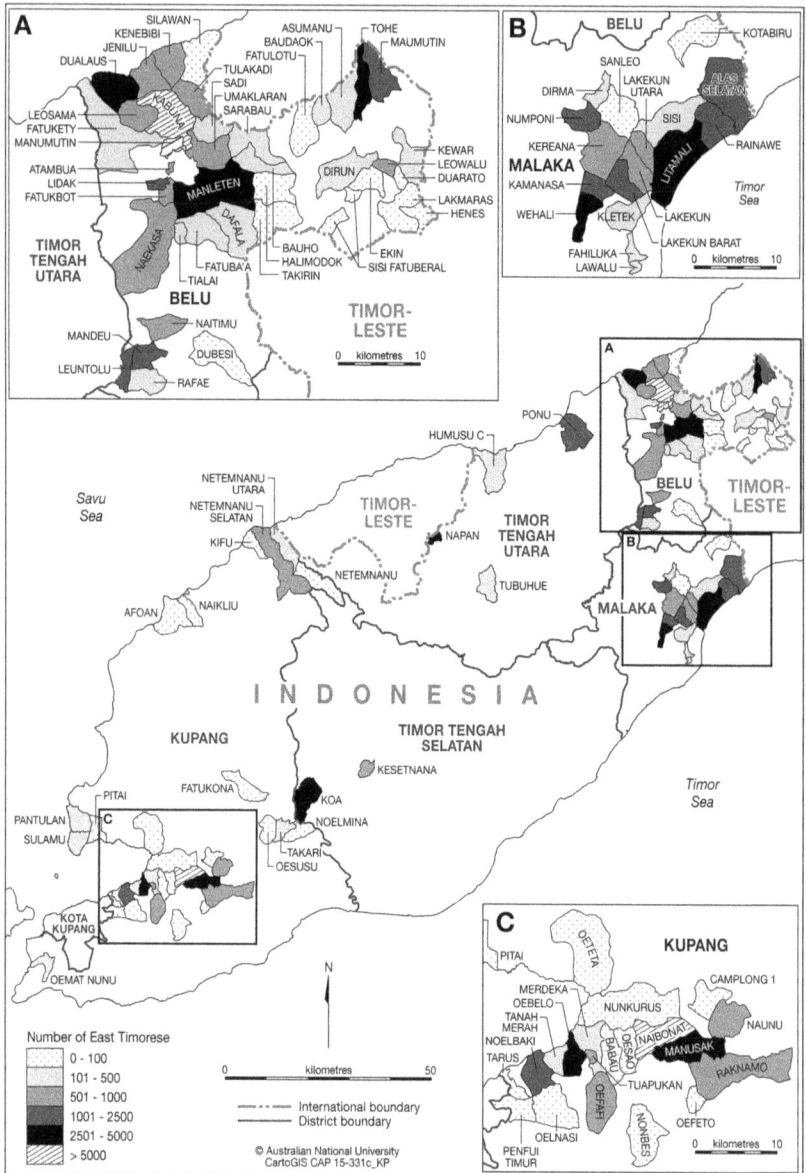

Map 2.2 Number and location of East Timorese in West Timor, 2016

Source: CartoGIS, College of Asia and the Pacific, The Australian National University, with author's estimation.

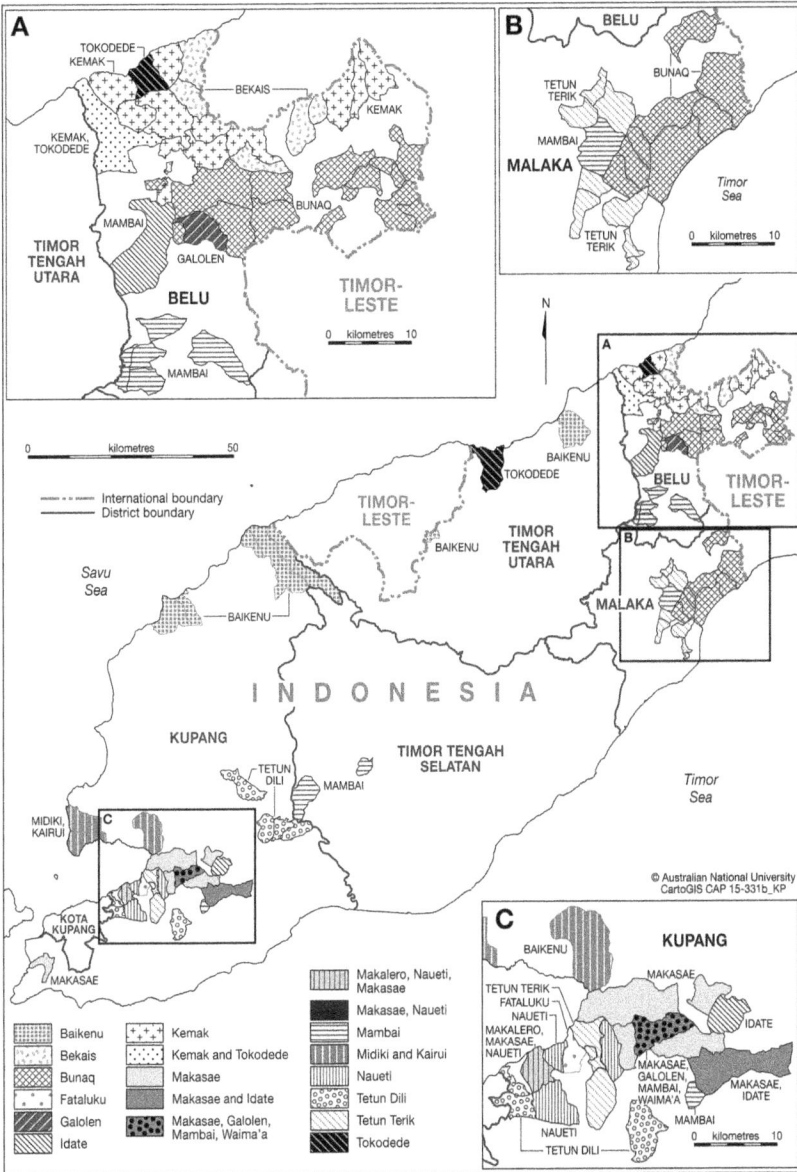

Map 2.3 East Timorese ethnolinguistic groups in West Timor, 2016

Source: CartoGIS, College of Asia and the Pacific, The Australian National University, with author's analysis.

Table 2.6 The number and location of East Timorese ethnolinguistic groups in West Timor, 2016

District	Subdistrict	Village	Dominant ethnolinguistic group	Estimated number of people
Kupang	Kupang Timur	Naibonat	Makasae, Galolen, Mambai, Waima'a	5,100
		Manusak	Makasae, Fataluku	2,510
		Tuapukan	Tetun Terik, Makasae	930
		Merdeka	Tetun Terik	470
		Babau	Naueti	80
		Oefafi	Tetun Terik, Naueti	650
		Nunkurus	Makasae, Waima'a	15
		Oesao	Makasae	64
	Kupang Tengah	Noelbaki	Naueti, Makalero, Makasae	1,800
		Tanah Merah	Naueti	200
		Oebelo	Fataluku	3,100
		Oelnasi	Naueti	36
		Penfui Timur	Tetun Dili	3
		Tarus	Tetun Dili	20
	Kupang Barat	Oematnunu	Makasae	422
	Fatuleu	Naunu	Idate	770
		Camplong I	Makasae	50
	Amabi Oefeto	Raknamo	Makasae and Idate	940
		Oefeto	Mambai	79
	Takari	Takari	Tetun Dili	150
		Noelmina	Tetun Dili	49
		Oesusu	Tetun Dili	31
		Fatukona	Tetun Dili	7
	Sulamu	Sulamu	Midiki, Kairui	196
		Pantulan	Midiki, Kairui	156
		Oeteta	Midiki, Kairui	13
		Pitay	Midiki, Kairui	3
	Amfoang Timur	Netemnanu Utara	Baikenu	274
		Netemnanu Selatan	Baikenu	507
		Kifu	Baikenu	33
		Netemnanu	Baikenu	38
	Amfoang Utara	Naikliu	Baikenu	35
		Afoan	Baikenu	12
	Amarasi	Nonbes	Tetun Dili	39

District	Subdistrict	Village	Dominant ethnolinguistic group	Estimated number of people
Timor Tengah Selatan	Mollo Barat	Koa	Mambai	2,400
	Mollo Selatan	Kesetnana	Mambai	100
Timor Tengah Utara	Bikomi Utara	Napan	Baikenu	2,600
	Kota Kefamenanu	Tubuhue	Baikenu	250
	Biboki Anleu	Ponu	Baikenu	1,200
	Insana Utara	Hamusu C	Tokodede	250
Belu	Lamaknen	Leowalu	Bunaq	790
		Dirun	Bunaq	380
		Duarat	Bunaq	60
		Ekin	Bunaq	43
		Kewar	Bunaq	134
	Lamaknen Selatan	Henes	Bunaq	20
		Lakmaras	Bunaq	70
		Sisi Fatuberal	Bunaq	80
	Raihat	Maumutin	Kemak	1,650
		Tohe	Kemak	4,840
		Asumanu	Kemak	400
	Lasiolat	Baudaok	Bekais	250
		Fatulotu	Bekais	100
	Tasifeto Timur	Silawan	Bekais	100
		Tulakadi	Bekais	860
		Umaklaran	Kemak	600
		Fatuba'a	Galolen	500
		Bauho	Bekais	150
		Dafala	Bunaq	150
		Halimodok	Bunaq	50
		Manleten	Bunaq	4,000
		Sarabau	Kemak	120
		Takirin	Bunaq	34
		Tialai	Bunaq	150
		Sadi	Kemak	250
	Kota Atambua	Atambua	Kemak	800
		Manumutin	Kemak	9,000
	Atambua Selatan	Lidak	Bunaq	1,900
		Fatukbot (Asu Ulun)	Kemak	700

District	Subdistrict	Village	Dominant ethnolinguistic group	Estimated number of people
	Kakuluk Mesak	Fatuketi	Kemak and Tokodede	430
		Jenilu	Tokodede	660
		Kenebibi	Kemak	855
		Dualaus	Kemak	2,550
		Kabuna	Kemak	5,000
		Leosama	Kemak	715
	Tasifeto Barat	Naekasa	Idate	900
		Naitimu	Mambai	750
	Nanaet Dubesi	Dubesi	Mambai	80
	Raimanuk	Mandeu	Mambai	1,450
		Leun Tolu	Mambai	1,100
		Rafae	Mambai	280
	Sasita Mean	Kereana	Mambai	400
Malaka	Kobalima	Rainawe	Bunaq	2,000
		Sisi	Bunaq	500
		Litamali	Bunaq	3,600
		Lakekun Utara	Bunaq	700
		Lakekun	Bunaq	850
		Lakekun Barat	Bunaq	1,800
	Kobalima Timur	Kotabiru	Bunaq	2,210
		Alas Selatan	Bunaq	60
	Malaka Tengah	Kletek	Tetun Terik	400
		Kamanasa	Tetun Terik	2,500
		Fahiluka	Tetun Terik	125
		Lawalu	Tetun Terik	350
		Wehali	Tetun Terik	3,000
	Malaka Timur	Dirma	Tetun Terik	160
		Sanleo	Tetun Terik	25
		Numponi	Tetun Terik	1,150
Total				88,363

Note: Because of the unavailability of secondary information, these estimations do not take into account East Timorese residing in Kupang municipality.

Source: Author's estimation from various sources.

Conclusion

This chapter has traced another path in Timorese history by reconstructing patterns of population displacement and mobility from East to West Timor. There are two main points to draw from the exercise. First and foremost, there have been large number of migrations among different East Timorese groups since at least the seventeenth century.[8] During the colonial period, violent conflict and political disputes played the major roles in these migrations. This pattern changed during the period of Indonesian occupation. In his examination of the displacement of East Timorese in 1975 and 1999, Robinson (2008: 115) argues:

> forced displacement was not the incidental or inevitable consequence of armed conflict in East Timor, but an intrinsic element of the political strategies adopted by the Indonesian military and by East Timor's pro-independence movement.

Reflecting on these arguments and learning from the 1999 displacement, I would like to add that displacement also demonstrates East Timorese resilience and ability to adapt and maintain their cultural identity in a situation of disadvantage. While many who were displaced within East Timorese territory have returned to their land of origin (Thu 2012), what is evident is that East Timorese displacement has also been the beginning of people's subsequent resettlement and emplacement. In fact, it was only after the 1975 displacement that most East Timorese returned to East Timor. Most of those involved in other displacements have remained living in West Timor and made the best of it.

The tendency for permanent resettlement leads to the second point about cultural patterns of migration. The politics of colonisation and military occupation might have caused people to flee, but the ways they have resettled indicate it was not a random migration. Instead, it was a process of following paths of alliances and/or creating new ones. Migration and resettlement before 1999 tended to follow the path whereby specific ethnolinguistic groups, particularly in the border areas, retraced their previously established ethnic relationships, which eventually led them to resettle among their kin groups in West Timor. Since 1999, however, different East Timorese groups have been displaced and have resettled

8   For the migration of Loiquero people to Oirata village in Kisar Island, eastern Indonesia, see Hägerdal (2012: 336–7).

widely across West Timor, as far as the western point of the island. For these groups, displacement provides an opportunity to develop a new alliance with West Timorese with whom they previously had no relationship. The encounter between different East Timorese groups and West Timorese has not always been easy. Schapper (2011: 175–6) encountered a similar phenomenon when she traced the historical resettlement of displaced Bunaq who fled to West Timor as a result of violent conflict between the Dutch and the Portuguese in 1911. Although these people now proudly proclaim themselves as 'the first refugees from East to West Timor', Schapper notes that it took them nearly two decades of moving from place to place as a result of land disputes with the local Tetun people before they were able to settle in several villages in Lamaknen and the Raihat subdistrict of Belu, in the 1930s. The complex dispersion of the 1999 displacement made the encounter between East and West Timorese even more difficult, with various conflicts and disputes between the two communities. In spite of these conflicts, many East Timorese have remained and have been able to reconstitute viable settlements and livelihoods from a position of political and economic marginality. In Sylvan's (1988) narrative of the formation of Timor Island, the crocodile finally went to the open sea. Along with his stranger friend, the crocodile stayed on the move, until finally settling down and turning itself into what is now the island of Timor.

> Time passed, and one day the lad returned …
>
> The lad settled himself on the crocodile's back, as if in a canoe, and they set out to sea. It was all so big and so beautiful! What astonished them most was the open space, the size of the vista that stretched away before and above them, endlessly. Day and night, night and day, they never rested. They saw islands big and small, with trees, mountains, and clouds. They could not say which was more beautiful, the days or the nights, the islands or the stars. They went on and on; always following the sun, until the crocodile finally grew tired.
>
> 'Listen, Lad. I cannot go on. My dream is over.'
>
> 'Mine will never be over …'
>
> The lad was still speaking when the crocodile suddenly grew and grew in size until, still keeping his original shape, he turned into an island covered with hills, woods, and rivers.
>
> And that is why Timor is the shape of a crocodile. (Sylvan 1988: 33–4)

3

'Refugees', 'ex-refugees' and 'new citizens'

Sitting in an office of the Indonesian Agency for National Unity, Politics, and Community Protection (Badan Kesatuan Bangsa, Politik, dan Perlindungan Masyarakat, or Kesbangpolinmas) of the Belu district government, near the border with Timor-Leste, I was asked to outline the topic of my research while seeking permission to conduct fieldwork. Kesbangpolinmas is the local government department with the authority to issue official consent for research activities in the region. 'My research examines the experience of different East Timorese groups who are currently living here in Belu', I explained, in an effort to summarise the aims and scope of my project. 'If you are looking for the East Timorese,' the officer in charge responded, '[they] are dispersed across the district, so you have to travel around.' While reviewing my proposal, he moved on, 'and as you are doing so, I would like to advise you that, in Belu, the East Timorese are called "new citizens" [*warga baru*]'. As I was about to leave the office with the fieldwork approval letter in hand, the officer reminded me: 'The East Timorese are to be no longer considered "refugees" [*pengungsi*] or "ex-refugees" [*eks pengungsi*], but as "new citizens" of Belu District.'

This chapter examines the way labelling is used to accommodate the entitlements of displaced East Timorese and how they have sought to respond. Analysis of the definition and application of labelling is longstanding and ongoing. Labelling in sociological terms is often associated with deviance. Theorists argue that labelling creates a sense of being 'outsiders' for those so labelled and therefore restrains their social interaction (Becker 1963; Matza 1969). Anthropologists using comparative analysis argue that the size and complexity of a society present conditions under which official labelling works (Raybeck 1988: 392–3). From the perspective of public policy, labelling is often perceived as imposed political action that involves 'conflict as well as authority' (Wood 1985: 347). While differing in their analytical approaches, each perspective shares a common view that identity labels are ascribed to groups of people for the purpose of control in a situation of often disputed power relations.

In the context of displacement, Harrell-Bond's (1986) examination of the politics of humanitarian aid offers a clear picture of the bureaucratic and administrative exercise of power and control through labelling people as 'refugees' and the implications that carries. Harrell-Bond (1986: 3) argues that governments both create and sustain conditions of dependency when they label someone a 'refugee'. The notion of labelling is further elaborated in the work of Zetter (1991: 51), whose analysis of the impact of a housing resettlement scheme in Cyprus shows that being labelled a refugee can come to mean a number of things over time and this imposition shapes the behaviour of refugee communities. Labelling, in Zetter's (1991: 59) view, essentially illustrates 'conditionality and differentiation, inclusion and exclusion, and stereotyping and control'.

Among East Timorese in West Timor, forms of labelling have varied over time. On their arrival in West Timor in late 1999, displaced East Timorese were identified as 'refugees' by the UNHCR in contrast to the category of IDP applied by the United Nations to people internally displaced within East Timor. In 2001, when East Timorese decided to stay in Indonesia, they were considered 'ex-refugees' by the Indonesian Government. As they moved on and sought to integrate themselves into local communities, they were called 'new citizens', even though before East Timorese independence they were already Indonesian citizens. I argue that these externally constructed categories have denied the agency of the displaced East Timorese and brought unintended consequences that have shaped their new lives in West Timor. In response, displaced East Timorese engage in various socioeconomic and political activities to show they have not submitted to the labels they deem to be derogatory. By actively exercising their citizenship rights and responsibilities, the East Timorese in West Timor show that those who have objectified, marginalised and denied their autonomy might have stalled their access to potential resources.

I begin by looking at the displacement process during the last turbulent months of 1999. In so doing, I trace how the category 'refugee' had a significant impact on the way humanitarian assistance was promoted and delivered. I then examine the way in which the Indonesian Government has sought to manage the East Timorese who decided to stay in West Timor. I argue that the categories of 'ex-refugee' and 'new citizen' are problematic conceptually and hinder efforts at integration by the East Timorese themselves. Finally, I outline various activities that are articulated by different East Timorese groups as a considered response to their labels.

Labelling 'refugees'

> The militia and elements of the military invited all the villagers in Los Palos to come for a meeting at the village hall. The message was clear that everybody must immediately register and then leave East Timor. Those who stayed on would be consider pro-independence followers and would be killed. (Achmad 2003: 192)

This is the story of Fernando da Costa, a farmer from the village of Luro in the East Timor district of Lautem, and the way he and his family were forced to flee East Timor in September 1999. Fernando and his family of nine arrived in Kupang on 15 September 1999 after a night sailing on an Indonesian navy ship. They were then transported by military truck to Tuapukan camp.

Tuapukan is one of the largest East Timorese camps remaining in West Timor. It is located some 24 km outside the NTT capital of Kupang. In early 2000, Tuapukan camp hosted about 30,000 East Timorese from the districts of Lautem, Viqueque, Baucau, Aileu and Manatuto. Most have since returned to Timor-Leste under the repatriation program. Some others have joined the resettlement program and moved to surrounding villages such as Oebelo, Raknamo, Manusak, Oefafi and Merdeka. When I visited the area in February 2009, there were more than 300 households remaining in Tuapukan camp, mostly from Viqueque, with a few from Baucau and Manatuto. I was introduced to Mama Olandina Ximenes from Ossu village in Viqueque district, East Timor. As we sat and watched the children running around the shelters, Mama Olandina vividly recalled the events that changed her life forever:

On 8 September 1999, we were transported by the Indonesian army from Ossu to Viqueque, and later spent about four nights on the seashore before we boarded the ship. We heard the sounds of gunshots everywhere and all of us were crying as we thought about our families who were left behind. The local army commander [Danramil] said that all of us should be on board, and yet we never knew where they were going to take us. On the morning of September 17, we were moored in Kupang Bay. On the shore, several military and police trucks were waiting. We disembarked and were taken to this place [Tuapukan refugee camp]. I had no idea where I was at that time. This area [Tuapukan] used to be nothing but an empty land. No-one was living in this area but us and also a few houses near the main road. I kept crying as I remembered my relatives who were not here with me. But the soldiers and some other women said that we should not be worried because they would be joining us soon. And indeed, within about the next four months, people kept coming and coming, on a daily basis.

Mama Olandina is a widow with three children. Her husband was recruited by the Indonesian army and served as a combat soldier. He was killed by Falintil guerillas during one of their insurgencies in Viqueque in September 1996. A striking similarity between Mama Olandina's and Fernando's stories is the involvement of the militias and the military in their displacement process. The Indonesian term used to describe a displaced person is 'pengungsi', which refers to both refugees and IDPs. But Mama Olandina's and Fernando's accounts illustrate the notion of 'refugee' that is generally used in the global political sense to describe a displaced person. As clearly exemplified in the 1951 UN Convention Relating to the Status of Refugees:

> [a refugee is] any person who owing to a well-founded fear of being persecuted for reasons of race, religion, nationality, membership of a particular social group or political opinion, is outside the country of his nationality and is unable, or owing to such fear, unwilling to avail himself of the protection of that country. (UNHCR 2010: 14–15)

This definition upholds certain entitlements for people granted refugee status; they should be offered not only legal protection, which they would not receive in their own country, but also social and humanitarian services (Shacknove 1985).

In anticipation of this humanitarian emergency, on 12 August 1999, then Indonesian minister for social welfare Justika Baharsjah made a visit to Kupang and met the governor of NTT. They discussed various responses to the expected influx of some 100,000 refugees from East Timor, including evacuation, transportation and preparation of temporary accommodation sites across the region. The governor also decided to allocate five staff from each department in the provincial government to support these humanitarian services. The number of refugees apparently nearly tripled the initial estimation and the Indonesian Government welcomed the UNHCR and other international agencies to address the East Timorese refugee problem in West Timor.

On 15 September 1999, the UN Security Council passed Resolution 1264 to authorise the establishment of a multinational force to restore peace and security in East Timor. This resolution also stressed—no less than three times—that the refugees must be allowed to return safely to East Timor (UNSC 1999). This resolution indicates that East Timorese who fled to West Timor were categorised as refugees as defined by the 1951 Refugee Convention. Four days after the resolution was passed, UNHCR high commissioner Sadako Ogata arrived in Kupang, accompanied by her staff from Geneva and the Indonesian Coordinating Minister of Welfare and Poverty Alleviation. The team flew by helicopter to visit the East Timorese refugees who were camped in Haliwen football stadium in Belu district. They then flew back to Kupang to observe the refugees encamped in and around the sports complex in Oepoi, near the office of the NTT governor. The next day, Mrs Ogata continued her mission to Jakarta and held a meeting with president Habibie to discuss UNHCR support. On 22 September 1999, president Habibie announced the position of the Indonesian Government to support the East Timorese refugees who decided to return to East Timor. This led to the establishment of UNHCR field offices in Atambua and Kupang (Achmad 2003: 204). In the government statement, displaced East Timorese were identified as *pengungsi* or refugees, and not IDPs.

During the first three months of the operation (October to December), the UNHCR facilitated the return of 82,527 East Timorese refugees. At the same time, about 43,000 people made their own way back to East Timor (Dolan et al. 2004: 17). Fernando and his family were among those first East Timorese returnees. Most refugees returned to their former settlements, while others resettled in Dili, contributing to a dramatic swelling of the capital's population in that period. In January 2000, however, half of the East Timorese refugees were still in West Timor. Amnesty International (1999) observed that the 'crisis is not yet over'. In the Tuapukan refugee camp, for instance:

there were 174 people [who] died [between] September 1999 [and] the beginning of December 1999. In one two week period alone—from 22 November to 1 December 1999—32 children and three adults died in the camp from infectious diseases such as chronic diarrhoea, malaria and tuberculosis. (Amnesty International 1999: 3)

Despite this ongoing humanitarian crisis in West Timor, it was the post-conflict situation in East Timor that became the main focus of the international intervention. This is exemplified by the funding distribution of the UN Office for the Coordination of Humanitarian Affairs (UNOCHA). The first comprehensive UN appeal for donor support in October 1999 managed to garner about US$199 million. Unfortunately, less than 10 per cent of those funds were allocated for West Timor (UNOCHA 1999, cited in Bradt and Drummond 2008: 75). The World Health Organization (WHO) 'had no dedicated funding for refugee-associated activities in West Timor for five months' and the UNHCR did not place its first health coordinator in West Timor until five months after the health crisis began in the refugee camps in West Timor (Bradt and Drummond 2008: 75). The situation became more complicated when rioting East Timorese militias killed three UNHCR staff in Atambua (the capital of Belu district) on 6 September 2000.

While there was an ongoing need for humanitarian assistance, the issue of East Timorese refugees in West Timor was not the main focus of international intervention. I would argue that there was a prevailing assumption that those East Timorese who had fled to West Timor and were subsequently categorised as refugees were perpetrators of the destruction and killing in East Timor, therefore they did not deserve the attention of the international community. From 1 January 2003, the UNHCR no longer recognised as refugees those East Timorese who stayed in West Timor (UNHCR 2002). With the end of their refugee status, the East Timorese in West Timor were considered by the UNHCR to be Indonesian citizens and its support was gradually withdrawn from West Timor. UNOCHA followed suit and ceased its activities in West Timor soon after (Sunarto et al. 2005: 29)—a decision that reinforced Shacknove's (1985: 276) comment that an 'overly narrow conception of "refugee" will contribute to the denial of international protection to countless people in dire circumstances whose claim to assistance is impeccable'.

Labelling 'ex-refugees'

On 6 June 2001, with improving sociopolitical conditions in East Timor, two options were officially offered to the East Timorese then living in Indonesia: return to East Timor or remain in Indonesia. East Timorese were asked to vote on these options in a process facilitated by the Indonesian Government. Although the process was criticised as a 'sham' due to suspected militia propaganda during the voting, 98 per cent of the 113,794 East Timorese in Indonesia decided to remain there (Smith 2002: 73). In response, in a cabinet meeting in Jakarta three months later, the Indonesian Government outlined the 'National Policy to Accelerate the Handling of Refugees' (*Kebijakan Nasional Percepatan Penanganan Pengungsi*).[1] At this point, the Indonesian Government continued to use the term *pengungsi*, albeit with a change in reference to that of IDPs rather than refugees. The policy consisted of three components: repatriation (*repatriasi*), relocation (*permukiman kembali* and *transmigrasi*) and empowerment (*pemberdayaan*).

The national policy did not specify East Timorese as its sole target because in the wake of the fall of Suharto's New Order government, Indonesia was hosting the single largest population of IDPs in the world by 2001 (Hedman 2008: 4).[2] In addition to the East Timorese, the term *pengungsi* in the national policy covered displaced people in the Indonesian regions of Aceh, Papua, Kalimantan, Sulawesi and Maluku.[3] The concurrent displacement of such a large number of people throughout the archipelago made the job of improving the lives of displaced people a daunting task. The Indonesian Government also recognised that East Timorese displacement was different from other internal displacement in Indonesia because of its complex geopolitical situation. Following the referendum, East Timor was no longer part of the Indonesian unitary state, which is why, politically, the East Timorese who came to West Timor were initially identified as refugees and managed by the UNHCR. In response to a satisfactory post-conflict normalisation process in Timor-Leste, the UNHCR declared the refugee status accorded to East Timorese would cease on 31 December 2002. At this time, the UNHCR also claimed that

---

1   For further discussion of the use of *pengungsi* with reference to refugees and IDPs, see Hugo (2002).
2   According to the Indonesian National Coordination Agency for Disaster Management and the Handling of Refugees, there were about 1.3 million IDPs in Indonesia in late 2001 (Hugo 2002).
3   For comparison, see Duncan (2008: 213).

some 230,000 of 250,000 East Timorese refugees had returned to Timor-Leste. Following this announcement, the Indonesian Government, in its attempt to define a clear target for the national displacement intervention policy and to differentiate the East Timorese from other Indonesian IDPs, transformed the UNHCR refugee label and identified the East Timorese as 'ex-refugees' (*eks pengungsi*).

Labels such as 'ex-refugee' legitimated displaced East Timorese claims for assistance from the government. Ex-refugee also meant that the repatriation program to Timor-Leste would be continued with the support of the Indonesian Government. During this intervention, the government facilitated the repatriation of an additional 1,300 East Timorese. In addition, nearly 7,500 houses for East Timorese have been constructed in West Timor and some 500 East Timorese families have migrated to other regions, including Sumatra, Kalimantan and Maluku. After these interventions, in 2005, the Indonesian Government considered the issue of East Timorese in West Timor had been resolved and declared that there were no longer any ex-refugees from East Timor. Later that year, however, the NTT government conducted a registration of all resident East Timorese and found that 104,436 East Timorese had stayed in NTT, 90 per cent of whom were residing in West Timor (Satkorlak PBP NTT 2006).

The fact that many East Timorese opted to remain in West Timor rather than be repatriated challenged this externally constructed ex-refugee label. In explaining the situation, Wise (2006: 188), in her work on East Timorese refugees in Sydney, argued that a return to East Timor has never really been an option for those who had their life connected to and successfully engaged in Australia. East Timorese who chose to stay in West Timor, however, had different reasons, related to their different political and sociocultural circumstances. At the end of my conversation with Mama Olandina, I asked whether she had any plans to return[4] to East Timor, as repatriation was still being supported by an NGO tasked with this responsibility. She replied:

---

4   Wise (2006: 183) has also pointed out that many East Timorese in Australia were happy to return to Timor-Leste after independence, although they have to 'engage in various strategies to renegotiate a sense of home, post-exile'. The International Crisis Group (ICG 2011) has also outlined different factors that influence East Timorese in West Timor to return, however, its report focuses more on return as repatriation. Taking the diversity of East Timorese groupings in West Timor into account, I note different ideas of return, including the notion of being in West Timor as a return, a return to visit Timor-Leste and an eventual return (after life).

For those who supported independence, it was safe for them to return to East Timor, but for us who have stood for the *Merah Putih* [the 'Red and White', the flag of Indonesia], we are considered enemies. We would put our life in danger if we went back there. Furthermore, although we suffer here, personally, I chose to stay because I want to continue the fight for that which my husband paid for with his own blood [for Indonesia].

The week after my meeting with Mama Olandina, I visited Oebelo, a neighbouring village. Here, there are two main sites of East Timorese settlement, Oebelo Atas (Upper Oebelo) and Oebelo Bawah (Lower Oebelo). Most of the East Timorese living in Oebelo come from the Los Palos district in far eastern Timor, but there are also people from Dili, Viqueque and Baucau. After Sunday mass, I was introduced to one of the East Timorese elders who lived next to the chapel, Bapa Matheos from Dili, who invited me to sit in front of his house, where he shared his experience:

I never wanted to leave East Timor in 1999. I don't know how many battles I have been involved in, as I have fought for Indonesia since 1975. I ran with bullets in my body [he showed me the wounds in both his legs] and am still alive, so I preferred to die rather than abandon East Timor without a fight. It was shameful. Most of the Indonesian supporters fled Dili as we were told that we must retreat to Indonesia on 4–6 September. My wife and children had gone ahead. I cried desperately, but said to myself, 'Over my dead body will anyone send me out of East Timor'.

I insisted on staying [to fight] but on 17 September 1999, the army held a meeting at the office of the provincial military command in Dili, and the commander instructed us to leave East Timor or we would face him and the Indonesian army, our own friends. I was ready to face my foes, not my friends. It was frustrating as we were forced to surrender and leave East Timor without having any chance to defend it. Afterwards, I went to Alor [Island] for a couple of months, and then spent Christmas in Soe [the capital of South Central Timor district], and eventually ended up here [in Oebelo] in April 2000. I was the only one in the family who was in favour of heading to Indonesia and I decided to stay here because it is my political ideology. My parents, my brothers and sisters—they are all in Dili.

Bapa Matheos shares almost identical views about Indonesia with Mama Olandina. They suggest that, for many East Timorese in West Timor, Indonesia is regarded not as the place from which they came, but the nation to which they chose to belong. Aspinall (2003: 128), in his discussion of Acehnese in contemporary Indonesia, argues that integral to an understanding of emerging postcolonial nationalism in Indonesia are three distinct elements: 'a nationalist future of modernity and liberation, the construction of a nationalist history stretching back to antiquity, and an official emphasis on ethnic diversity'. Many Indonesians, according to Anderson (1999: 8), are 'still inclined to think of Indonesia as an "inheritance"'.

For many East Timorese, however, Indonesia is not something they have inherited but something for which they have struggled and sacrificed. This is why living as a displaced person in West Timor is something an East Timorese must bear at all costs as the consequence of their attempt to preserve Indonesia and their (political) belonging to that nation. It is a sacrifice they must make for their struggle (*perjuangan*) to defend the 'Red and White'.

Labelling 'new citizens'

In early March 2004, almost all the relevant parties involved in East Timorese displacement intervention were invited to Kefamenanu, the capital of North Central Timor (TTU) district to share their experiences and seek ways to improve their support for the East Timorese. During three days of meetings, the Bishop of Atambua, Monsignor Anton Pian Ratu, SVD, put forward his idea of 'new citizenship' (*warga baru*). According to the priest, who also chaired the Forum for Communication among Religious Leaders (Forum Komunikasi antar Pimpinan Agama): 'Our brothers and sisters from East Timor who have decided to stay in Indonesia and maintain their Indonesian citizenship were uncomfortable to be identified as ex-refugee.' As a solution, he went on to propose that perhaps they should be called 'new citizens'[5] of Belu or TTU district.

In 2005, the Indonesian Government declared the end of official humanitarian assistance for the East Timorese across the country. This also signalled the transformation of labelling activities into a domestic frame. At this stage, the 'new citizen' label was recognised as a way to accommodate

---

5   'New citizens' was coined to facilitate the process of integration. Although the label has been widely ascribed to the East Timorese, its official recognition was actually limited. The East Timorese were issued the same Indonesian identity card as other Indonesians. The label was not adopted in the 2010 national population census. The recent census by Statistics Indonesia as part of the resettlement project funded by the Ministry of Public Housing did not issue additional identity cards, but merely put a sticker on the door of a house or a shelter as a sign of completed registration.

the East Timorese into Indonesian society. As a label, however, it was not appealing to funding bodies, either the international agencies or the Indonesian Government. Oxfam Great Britain, for instance, chose the term 'uprooted people' in their transitional shelter and livelihood projects between 2005 and 2008. Around the same period, CARE International employed the term 'IDPs' for their community integration and local economy project. UN-Habitat went further and came up with the notion of 'ex-IDPs' in their capacity-building project (2011–13). The Indonesian Government also deployed various terms. The Ministry of Social Affairs used the nomenclature 'victims of social disaster' (*korban bencana sosial*) to support the East Timorese in 2007. Most recently, the Ministry of Public Works and Public Housing identified the East Timorese as 'people with low incomes' (*masyarakat berpenghasilan rendah*), using a term deployed across Indonesia. As part of this project, they assigned Statistics Indonesia to conduct a registration census of the East Timorese and made use of the 'new citizen' label by identifying the East Timorese as 'new citizens of East Timor origin' (*warga baru asal Timor Timur*).[6]

While the registration census was proceeding, I made a visit to the East Timorese camp in Naibonat village, 32 km from Kupang. During a discussion with a handful of Baucau elders, one of them, Cristiano Ximenes, who is often jokingly called 'the professor', made a comment about his status as a new citizen:

> I don't know why they called us 'new citizens'. You know, I was born a Portuguese citizen because East Timor at that time was an overseas province of Portugal. When Indonesia came in, I joined Indonesia and became an Indonesian citizen and I am still an Indonesian citizen up to now. If for this reason I became a new citizen then who are the local [existing] citizens [*warga lokal*]?

Cristiano draws our attention to established citizenship as a category contrasting with 'new citizens'. This dual categorisation is further exemplified in comments made by the former speaker of East Timor's provincial parliament, Armindo Soares Mariano. When I met him in his house, he posed the following questions:

> Why weren't the people [migrants] from Java, Sulawesi or any other places in Indonesia who come and stay in this area identified as new citizens? Why is it only us from East Timor?

---

6   For further discussion of various refugee labels, see Zetter (2007).

Without waiting for my response, Armindo continued:

> We [the East Timorese] are moving to West Timor because East Timor is no longer part of Indonesia. We were Indonesian citizens and we are still Indonesian citizens and not new citizens.

Here, Armindo takes the ideas of sameness and difference to problematise the 'new citizen' label.

Plate 3.1 Registration sticker identifying a house occupied by East Timorese, Belu district
Source: Andrey Damaledo.

The deployment of oppositional categories by both Chris and Armindo suggests that the 'new citizen' label is another category for asserting priority and superiority within Indonesian society. This understanding is implicit in Chris's intent: why should we become new citizens if we were Indonesian in the first place? It is clear that instead of integrating people, as was initially intended, the 'new citizen' label has been divisive and has created a perception of East Timorese as an inferior class of citizen. This situation relegates many East Timorese who have decided to maintain their citizenship and integrate with their fellow Indonesians to the margins of the Indonesian national imagination.

The impact of labelling

Labelling activities have diverse impacts on the lives of displaced people. Waldron (1988) argues that bureaucratic labels fail to articulate the salient factors that make up the refugee identity. In fact, government procedures have led to gross misinterpretation or even nonrecognition of existing problems and have resulted in ill-conceived policies and programs. Labels such as 'refugee', 'ex-refugee' and 'new citizen' have impacted on East Timorese experiences of displacement and involvement in the pre-referendum and post-referendum conflicts in terms of their eligibility for humanitarian and development assistance.

This situation has often been politicised by the local government during its annual planning and budgeting process.[7] With its limited financial capacity, local government tends to exclude the 'problem' of the East Timorese despite the fact these people have been living in their administrative areas for almost 15 years. When I discussed this issue with government officers across West Timor, their response was similar: 'Displacement is not our responsibility, but that of the central government.' Therefore, 'we will pass along your concern to the central government' is the typical answer of the NTT governor and the heads of district (*bupati*) whenever a demand for clarity and transparency is raised by the East Timorese community.

The impact of this exclusion is clearly exemplified in Oebelo Bawah resettlement site, which houses many East Timorese from Los Palos. Every year during the monsoon, the resettlement site floods. At the peak of the rainy season in February 2009, more than 30 families were evacuated from their houses to the chapel by the side of the main road. They remained there for four days because deep floodwaters had swamped their houses and surrounding areas. I visited Oebelo in the aftermath and observed how people struggled to get rid of the mud and make their houses liveable again. The surrounding landscape is lower than the road and makes the resettlement site a perfect spot to catch all of the run-off water during the rainy season. Yet I found no floodway or drainage system

---

7 I note that the Kupang district government allocated IRD519 million (approximately A$49,000) in its 2012 budget to support the central government's relocation project for the East Timorese. However, as emphasised by the district secretary (*sekretaris daerah*), the fund was allocated to facilitate the removal of East Timorese shelters that had created slum areas around new government buildings. Essentially, the fund served the interest of the government rather than that of the East Timorese community.

installed. The initial permanent resettlement site was completed in 2004 and a larger one was built by the Indonesian military in 2007–08, but no additional investment was made by the local government to protect the East Timorese settlement from flooding.[8]

References to 'refugees', 'ex-refugees' and 'new citizens' may call into doubt the trustworthiness of the East Timorese. An East Timorese camp coordinator, regarded as a camp representative based on his management role during the 1999 evacuation process, explained that his people encountered difficulties obtaining bank loans because of concerns they might return to Timor-Leste without repaying them (Sunarto et al. 2005: 33). In another case, some East Timorese learned of their exclusion from the social protection program providing direct cash assistance (*bantuan langsung tunai*) to the poor. This program was funded by the central government as compensation for increasing oil prices, but was managed by local authorities (The Jakarta Post 2009).

Proactive response to labelling

Many displaced East Timorese acknowledge that the humanitarian and development program has the objective of trying to improve their socioeconomic conditions in contemporary Indonesia. But they also know that the various labels that accompanied those interventions have brought unintended consequences and hindered their integration into local communities. This is why displaced East Timorese chose to resist being labelled by asserting their rights and responsibilities as Indonesian citizens. I want to suggest that this represents a proactive response whereby the East Timorese are able to identify opportunity and mobilise resources to distance themselves from these labels and at the same time confirm and realise their imagined ideal of maintaining Indonesian citizenship.

Different East Timorese groups respond in their own way. Many are actively trying to work through the formal political system and join Indonesian political parties to represent their communities. During each of the past three local parliamentary elections (in 2004, 2009 and 2014), politicians

8   The flood occurred just one month after 'extraordinary event' (*kejadian luar biasa*) status was removed from the surrounding area. It was imposed after a diarrhoea outbreak in January claimed the lives of four children and two elders in the resettlement site. While the latter deaths could have been caused by other illnesses, the former were the result of a lack of potable water and poor sanitation. I noted no change—apart from a neighbourhood pathway—when visiting the area in 2013.

of East Timorese origin have been elected to office from Indonesian mainstream political parties. Currently, there is one East Timorese-born representative in the NTT parliament. At the district level, better progress is evident, with one representative in the Kupang district parliament and three in Belu district. Some East Timorese have attempted to run for national parliament, but so far without success. In the government sector, some have managed to attain high-level managerial positions in government departments in West Timor.

East Timorese have also engaged in informal strategies to further their interests. In their attempts to secure land on which to settle, for example, East Timorese in Naibonat village in Kupang district handed the responsibility for locating and negotiating for land on their behalf—either land in the camp or land nearby—to the camp coordinator. Other groups, such as those camped in Belu district, prefer to work collectively by using existing ethnic and kinship networks. But the basic aim is the same everywhere. Through cash payments or credit instalments, by late 2006, more than 2,000 displaced East Timorese families had been able to legally obtain land either in or near their former camps (many are currently in the process of certification).

These proactive responses are revealed not only through the way landownership has been secured, but also in the way both men and women engage in a range of income-generating activities. Some are labouring on local farmers' land or renting and making use of such land; others are working as middlemen, taking agricultural products from the subdistricts to trade in the city. Some women weave cloth (*tais*). Some also make money by tapping palm trees to sell the juice or ferment it into a popular alcoholic drink (*sopi*). Duarte Dos Santos, from Fatuboro village in Liquiçá district, who is now settled on his own land in Belu district, recalled:

> When we were here in 1999, this was a camp, but now as you see this land is ours and we have managed to buy it from the local landowner after 2001–2002. We are farmers. We are not civil servants who have a regular income but it does not mean we can't do anything. I saw palm trees when I was looking for some fire wood, I climbed and tapped the juice, and I took it to the market and it was sold out. Every day I climb up to eight palms and I have made money to purchase the land. In fact, we can save some for the children's education. (Djami 2006: 12)

Once land and housing have been secured, the main focus for East Timorese is their children's education. Francisco Ximenes, a leader of the East Timorese community from Baucau, once told me after celebrating the achievement of national senior high school accreditation for the school in Naibonat:

> When we were about to leave East Timor, our families who decided to stay reminded us, if you remain in West Timor, the children's education has to be your top priority. We are not living in that memory, but living for that memory.

It was the only school in the entire Kupang district that qualified for accreditation, and the majority of its students were displaced East Timorese. 'The East Timorese can also make the Kupang district proud, you know,' he added with a big smile.

Conclusion

This chapter has discussed the ways in which displaced East Timorese now living in Indonesia have negotiated issues of identity and belonging, and how complex forms of official labelling have influenced the ways in which humanitarian and development assistance has been delivered to displaced people in Indonesian Timor. Petrin (2002: 7) has argued that 'managing the returnees is not always possible', and I would add that managing those who choose to stay and maintain their citizenship is not always possible either. But the fact that the Indonesian Government explicitly encourages East Timorese to live among their fellow Indonesians should be seen in a positive light. For example, former president Susilo Bambang Yudhoyono, the day before attending the inauguration in Dili of the newly elected president of Timor-Leste, Taur Matan Ruak, declared: 'By 2014, I want all existing problems solved. [The East Timorese] must have somewhere to live because they have lived in the area [West Timor] since 1999 with little money' (Jakarta Globe 2012).

Nevertheless, as I have pointed out, the 'will to improve' (Li 2007) the life of East Timorese among government and humanitarian agencies has been dominated by 'simplifications' (Scott 1998), depersonalisation (Malkki 1997; Harrell-Bond 1999) and successive misinterpretation of East Timorese identities. In early October 2013, I held a meeting with the East Timorese group in Naibonat camp. On this occasion, Mauricio

Freitas and Agusto da Costa, both of whom had served as speakers of the Baucau district parliament and were considered elders of the Baucau people, declared:

> Andrey, we want you to know that we have nothing but our dignity [*dignidade*] when we decided to leave our homeland in East Timor and stay here in West Timor. That is what we preserve and celebrate.

Silva (2010: 110), in her discussion of East Timorese social conflict, suggests that 'to have dignity' in an East Timorese context means 'to be recognised for occupying a hierarchical position of such importance as to deserve deference and obedience'. While I support this recognition of East Timorese sensitivity to hierarchy and social precedence,[9] I believe that what Mauricio and Agusto meant by East Timorese dignity[10] refers to more than just honour and status. They were emphasising that East Timorese are not 'objects' of state charity but fellow human beings in possession of their own identities, histories and experiences, and the autonomy to act and react in response to situations of disadvantage. To understand how these values are further articulated, it is appropriate to quote Basilio Araujo (2009: 7), the former spokesperson of the pro-integration East Timorese, reflecting on a decade of life in Indonesia:

> The Indonesian government deserved to know that we came to Indonesia not to beg for food or illegal shelter. Nor did we come to Indonesia to ask for a piece of land to stay. Ninety percent of our people were slaves who had served their masters for years and centuries, sometimes even without food for days and nights. This experience taught us that we are resilient people who will always survive. The government can cease all support. The government can force us to stay on barren land. Nevertheless, be assured that we will stay and prevail even with cassava and maize. All we need is for this country to recognise us as Indonesian citizens and treat us equally as fellow Indonesians [so that] we can maintain our identity as East Timorese in Indonesia.

---

9   For a discussion of the idea of precedence, see Fox (2006d).

10   The lack of attention paid to human dignity in refugee intervention programming is not exclusive to the East Timorese. An executive director of an Irish NGO who worked among African refugees said: '[D]ignity is the vital ingredient missing when basic physical needs are delivered in a mechanistic and impersonal way. Respect for human dignity is too often the first casualty of emergency responses to assist refugees' (Needham 1994). This expression helped me to bring out concluding points on dignity in this section.

4

Old track, old path

'His sacred house and the place where he lived,' wrote Armando Pinto Correa, an administrator of Portuguese Timor, when he visited Suai and met its ruler, 'had the name Behali to indicate the origin of his family who were the royal house of Uai Hali [Wehali] in Dutch Timor' (Correa 1934: 45). Through writing and display, the ruler of Suai remembered, declared and celebrated Wehali[1] as his origin. At the beginning of the twentieth century, the Portuguese increased taxes on the Timorese, which triggered violent conflict with local rulers, including those of Suai. The conflict forced many people from Suai to seek asylum across the border in West Timor. At the end of 1911, it was recorded that more than 2,000 East Timorese, including women and children, were granted asylum by the Dutch authorities and directed to settle around the southern coastal plain of West Timor, in the land of Wehali (La Lau 1912; Ormelling 1957: 184; Francillon 1967: 53).

On their arrival in Wehali, displaced people from the village of Suai (and Camenaça) took the action of their ruler further by naming their new settlement in West Timor Suai to remember their place of origin. Suai was once a quiet hamlet in the village of Kletek on the southern coast of West Timor. In 1999, hamlet residents hosted their brothers and sisters from the village of Suai Loro in East Timor, and many have stayed. With a growing population, the hamlet has now become a village with its own chief asserting Suai Loro origin; his descendants were displaced in 1911.

---

1   In formal speech, it is known as Wewiku-Wehali or Wesei-Wehali, but I choose to use the abbreviated form, Wehali.

Wandering around the village, you can hear the resounding of the waves of the Timor Sea, which is referred to as *Tasi Mane* ('male sea') in Tetun. You can appreciate the warm, friendly smiles of Timorese women as they chew their betel and areca nut on the verandahs of their stilt houses. As you walk barefoot along the leafy dirt road, you can feel the sandy, silty and clay soils massaging your feet—as if you were actually strolling through the village of Suai Loro. In all senses of lived experience, Suai village in Wehali is indeed a mirror of Suai Loro village in East Timor.[2]

Yet, there is another compelling element that has made Suai—and, more broadly, the land of Wehali—a favoured destination for displaced Tetun people from East Timor, and that is its cultural significance. As the head of Suai village (*kepala desa*) asked me when I met him in his office, 'Have you ever wondered why the East Timorese in this land of Wehali are considered returnees?' As he saw me smiling without any intention of responding, he continued: 'Because the Timorese came from one origin [*hun* in Wehali].' By way of further explanation, he said:

> Our ancestors all came from Wehali. Some of them then went to the east and carried the sacred sword to protect themselves. They let the scabbard remain in the west. The East Timorese, as descendants of the swordbearer, will always look for their brothers and sisters in West Timor as descendants of the sheathbearer. That is why the East Timorese in Wehali are not refugees, because they are returning to the land of their ancestors, the land of the sheathbearer, the land of Wehali, our mother and our father [*ina no ama* in Wehali].

Later that day, the head invited me to his house and related the following expression (in the local language, Tetun) about the Wehali people meeting the East Timorese on their arrival in 1999:

Ami mai hola hika nahon no leon	We came back to the place where we belong
Iha ina no ama Wesei Wehali	To the mother and the father, Wesei Wehali
Ami hitin luan kbonan luan	The ones who hold and embrace us
Atu hodi kous hola hiti hola	To hold and embrace us
Tan funu no ledo	For it is war and conflict

---

2   Suai Loro has undergone significant recent landscape change for a planned gas refinery and hub.

Hoi mai taka tan hoku tan	That took us back to gather and reunite [with] mother Wehali
ina Wehali ama Wesei	and father Wesei
Sera hitin sera kbonan.	Please hold us and embrace us.

And the Wehali people replied:

Surik nuan surik isin	The sheath and the sword
Modi isin lao mela knuan	The sword went away, the scabbard remained
Kodi isin mai kaknua ba	The sword is reunited with the scabbard.

By emphasising Wehali as their mother and father, displaced East Timorese from Suai claimed Wehali as their ancestral land and understood their displacement as a journey of return to their land of origin. The previous displacement of East Timorese into the land of Wehali in 1911 was similarly perceived as a return to the land of their mother and father (Therik 2004: 49). This symbolic parentage category marks the pattern of relations between the incoming East Timorese and their hosts. In this ideology, Wehali is perceived:

> as the trunk and other societies are its flower and fruit. As the trunk, Wehali is the source of life and therefore deserves to be called 'mother and father' (*ina no ama*) while other peripheral societies are its daughters (*funan* = flower) and sons (*klaut* = fruit). (Therik 2004: 82)

The political significance of this symbolic category is that, by perceiving themselves as returning children of Wehali, the East Timorese legitimise the authority of their host, but at the same time claim belonging to the place in which they have just arrived.

In contrast to the labelling processes I discussed in the previous chapter, here, I explore the way the East Timorese 'label' themselves. In this self-constructed identity, I examine East Timorese processes of resettlement in West Timor and their representation of such notions as origin, place and exchange. Origin is a very common motif in the construction of social identity by the Timorese people and this is often expressed through botanical metaphors. Among origin narratives of the Dengka people of the neighbouring island of Rote, for example:

We men here are like a tree with one trunk but three roots; the main root is our father of birth. The second root, our mother's brother of origin, the third root our mother's mother's brother of origin. As long as a person lives, these three roots cannot be done away with for they are our path of life. (Fox 1980b: 118)

In a similar vein, the Meto people of West Timor describe their founding/ origin ancestor as the 'trunk' and their progeny as the 'twigs', 'tip' and 'flowers' (McWilliam 2009: 111). What is clear from these Timorese (and Austronesian) botanical metaphors is the idea that ancestral origin remains a significant feature of belonging.

Since the 1990s, the discussion of people, place and identity has been dominated by the view that, in the context of globalisation, or 'global space' (Gupta and Ferguson 1992), the idea that identity is defined by a physically demarcated territory has lost its significance. This is marked by what Appadurai (1990: 304–5) dubbed 'deterritorialised ethnicities', whereby identities are constructed through the experiences of a diaspora and imagined homelands and articulated through the media, separatist movements or nations without states. While I recognise the phenomenon of deterritorialisation in many displaced communities around the world, in the case of East Timorese in West Timor, I would argue that territorially based identity remains a significant modality of attachment. For the East Timorese, territory matters, and by this I am not referring so much to fixed physical boundaries. Rather, I prefer to think of the idea of territory as a series of interconnected places that form discursive/mythic ancestral pathways. In approaching this view, I am informed by Fox's *Poetic Power of Place* (2006c), in which it is argued that central features of emplacement and belonging among Timorese, and Austronesian societies in general, are the notions of origin, mobility and return. In the context of the East Timorese, a comparative analysis of *Land and Life in Timor-Leste* by McWilliam and Traube (2011: 5) offers a framework for the 'different ways that Timorese people assert attachments and claims to place and landscapes of memory and belonging in the contemporary world'.

I contend that East Timorese ideas of resettlement revolve around two seemingly contrary trends. One is the possibility of constructing and reconstructing a collective identity based on an origin narrative. As the above discussion has exemplified, Tetun-speaking people from Suai district in East Timor confirm and maintain their foundational ideology in Wehali and therefore articulate their experience of displacement as a process of reconciliation and reunification rather than one of loss and separation. The second trend is the evident possibility of a hybrid identity based on the colonial experience, the independence struggle and integration within Indonesia. Yet despite attempts to incorporate Indonesian nationalist views of colonial oppression, many East Timorese in this area have imagined their colonial struggle as a process of reconnecting broken ancestral paths and revitalising an ancient political structure. These trends arguably serve as a disjuncture between the realities of Timorese ethnolinguistic mobility, on the one hand, and their official membership of and integration within the Indonesian (and Timor-Leste) nation-state, on the other. This disjuncture is illustrated in this chapter by a comparative discussion of three major ethnolinguistic groups—Tetun, Bunaq and Kemak—all of which experienced displacement and migration from East to West Timor. In drawing on case studies of different settlements in Belu and Malaka districts, I demonstrate the significance of the conception of origins, land and locality in the 'reemplacement' process among different East Timorese groups within the mythic ancestral land in West Timor.

The Tetun 'returnees'

Among the Tetun-speaking people of Timor, their perspective of their collective origin has always revolved around the central position of Wehali. Wehali's great influence on both sides of the island was documented as long ago as 1522 in the report of Antonio Pigafetta, who landed on the northern coast of Timor and wrote of the existence of four kings on the island, one of them the king of Oibich domain, representing the Wewiku-Wehali domain (Therik 2004: 49). While this depicts an image of the significant authority of Wehali, there is a considerable lack of consensus on the way this apical authority operated. Two major political disruptions that occurred within Wehali territory might have played a role in this situation. The first was reported in 1642, when the Portuguese *fidalgo* (nobleman) Francisco Fernández led a small troop of men from their newly established settlement and trading post in Lifau (present-day Oecussi) on the northern coast, across the island to attack the Wehali centre, burning it to the ground. This event was of major symbolic significance, with many constituent Timorese domains distancing themselves from Wehali and realigning their allegiances towards the Portuguese (Boxer 1947; Hägerdal 2012). Another account, however, demonstrated the restored power of Wehali following the destruction in

1642. In the so-called Contract of Paravicini signed in 1756 by the Dutch and the rulers of Timor and its surrounding islands (Roti, Savu, Sumba and Solor), a sovereign ruler of Wewiku-Wehali of Timor, Hiacijntoe Corea, signed on behalf of the Timorese population across 29 domains. In an attempt to trace the location of these domains, Therik (2004: 57) found that more than half are in present-day Timor-Leste, including Liquiçá, Manatuto, Kova Lima, Same, Bobonaro and Ermera. In other words, the putative realm of Wehali in the past extended over a large area of both West and East Timor.

Nearly three-and-a-half centuries later, in 1906, Wehali's authority was challenged again, this time by the Dutch. During their coercive pacification efforts in the western part of the island, the Dutch launched an extensive military campaign across the area and control was eventually assumed over Wehali territory. The Dutch established a military post in Besikama, 12 km west of Laran. These incursions on Wehali (Francillon 1980) challenged their hegemonic power on both sides of Timor. And, indeed, there has never been any official recognition of Wehali's central authority and not all Tetun speakers, let alone other East Timorese language groups, see their collective origins as being in Wehali (Kehi and Palmer 2012). Nevertheless, Wehali's influence across the island persists. This cannot be separated from the fact that, in early 2000, after the flood that swept across most of Wehali land and took the lives of many displaced East Timorese, elders and representatives from different East Timorese communities in West Timor offered their tribute to the Wehali sacred house of earth and sky (*ai lotuk*) in the village of Laran. For the East Timorese, the flood was more than a natural phenomenon; it was a symbolic assertion of Wehali's position as the land of origin that holds spiritual authority over the newly arrived East Timorese. The tributary ritual was performed to recognise and receive this spiritual authority and secure access to and accommodation into Wehali land.

The Tetun-speaking people of Suai origin are aware that Wehali's spiritual authority cannot be separated from its origin narrative, and they announce this by affirming Wehali as their land of origin. According to their version of origin narratives:

> In the beginning, the entire world is covered with water. The first place to dry is Marlilu. In Marlilu, there were two brothers—namely, Loro Tuan Fatu Isin as the elder ('the flesh of the stone') and Loro Tuan Wehali as

the younger.[3] One day they decided to have a competition to determine the rightful leader of the land. The competition was to grow paddy rice. As time went by, Loro Tuan Fatu Isin produced more rice than that of his brother, Loro Tuan Wehali.

Marlilu lies on high ground to the south of Betun. Its upland position is central to the Wehali origin narrative. In their mythical conception, Marlilu is Marlilu Haholek, 'the place where the first dry land emerged and the first human beings lived' (Therik 2004: 197). The Tetun of Suai recognised its importance and used Marlilu to claim a shared origin place as the Wehali people.

Loro Tuan Fatu Isin and Loro Tuan Wehali are dyadic symbols representing an important cultural model of unity among the Tetun people. But the narrative also concerns the nature of the relationship between the two and describes them as being in an oppositional, agonistic relationship with each other. As in other Austronesian societies, here, the classic rivalry of brothers is often articulated in the origin narrative and is central to the notions of order and precedence.[4] Loro Tuan Fatu Isin managed to produce more paddy rice, legitimising precedence over Loro Tuan Wehali. The competition, however, was not yet resolved:

> Both men also tried to keep birds away from their plants. Loro Tuan Wehali called the people to stand and hold hands around his rice plants but the birds were still able to eat the rice. Loro Tuan Fatu Isin only sat on the top of Marlilu hill and weaved his *tais* while singing Tetun chants. The birds did not even get close to his rice plants.

The way Loro Tuan Fatu Isin protected his paddy rice from the birds bolsters his claim for precedence over Loro Tuan Wehali. The narrative continues:

> As the winner of the competition, Loro Tuan Fatu Isin was entitled to the leadership. However, to avoid conflict with his younger brother, he decided to delegate the leadership role to Loro Tuan Wehali and then went east to find new land to settle. As he was leaving, he took the sacred sword, leaving the scabbard in Wehali [*Taha Nuan Iha Wehali// Taha Isin Iha Lorosa'e*].

---

3   For the Wehali version, see Therik (2004: 49, 66, 84–99).
4   This rivalry between brothers is a classic origin narrative among the Austronesian people. See Fox and Sather (2006) for comparison.

Later, Loro Tuan Fatu Isin has three sons who rule over the entirety of East Timor. The eldest, Loro Mane Ikun, also known as Nai Loro Di Loli Taek Rai Litis, ruled over the eastern domains of Alas, Same, Viqueque, Los Palos, Baucau and Dili. The second son was Loro Mane Klaran, also known as Nai Loro Farata Rai Mia Nain, and he ruled the central domains of Zumalai, Cassa Ainaro, Ermera and Aileu. The youngest, Loro Manek Kawa'i, also known as Nai Loro Nubatak Suai Nain, ruled over Suai, Fatumean, Illiomar and Bobonaro.

The origin and ritual narratives generated by the Tetun people of Suai illustrate their displacement in the Wehali lands of West Timor in a different light. They consider displacement as a passage of reconciliation and reunification. The content of this origin narrative as well as its use as the basis for claiming belonging and authority vary according to whether it is told by the Tetun people of East Timorese origin or the local Tetun people of Wehali. In my discussions with Tetun *adat* (customary law) historians from Wehali, they expressed strong reservation with regard to the kin relationship between Loro Tuan Fatu Isin and Loro Tuan Wehali. In their version, Loro Tuan Fatu Isin did not originate from the land, but was an outsider. He was someone who 'came out from a fortress'. They also disagreed with the voluntary nature of Loro Tuan Fatu Isin's departure from Wehali land. For them, in contrast, Loro Tuan Fatu Isin was 'expelled' from the land because he dared to challenge the authority of Loro Tuan Wehali. As an ousted member of society, Loro Tuan Fatu Isin's existence should never have been acknowledged. In these terms, then, the Tetun in Wehali claimed their precedence over the return of the Tetun people from Suai who sought to revive their connection through Loro Tuan Fatu Isin.

In spite of this variation, both groups agree on the association of the complementary categories of sword and scabbard. In the Wehali version, political and spiritual centrality is defined because they are the holders of the sheath and therefore symbolically female. The sword is categorised as male and located in the periphery. These symbolic coordinates speak to order and authority in the land of Wehali. The male from the periphery functions as the protector (*makdakar*) of the female centre. In return, the female centre channels fertility and life to the periphery (Therik 2004: 76).

Tetun people from Suai share this idea of order and authority. They recognise that Wehali as female and sheathbearer is the place where peace and stability are maintained. Suai, as male and wielding the sword from the periphery, is the place where disputes and conflicts occur. Here, the violent conflict that erupted in Suai is conceptualised in relation to the sword that was carried by their ancestor Loro Tuan Fatu Isin, when he left his homeland in Wehali. But the sword also represents the role and responsibilities of the bearer/defender of the periphery to protect their source of life in Wehali.

Taking this view into the context of historical and more recent East Timorese displacement and emplacement in Wehali land has been revelatory. The domain of Wanibesak in the present-day village of Lorotolus was carefully selected as the settlement location for the Tetun returnees from Suai in the early twentieth century due to this categorical purpose: to protect the central Wehali village of Laran from the threat of Meto warriors from the domains of Amanuban and Amanatun in the west. On the eastern side of Laran, the initial Tetun returnees were settled in the villages of Kamanasa, Kletek, Suai and Fahiluka with a similar purpose. The displacement of the Tetun people from Suai in 1999 follows this returnee trajectory set out by their predecessors.

History in the present among the Fohoterin origin

In 1999, about 500 households from the Fohoterin area of Suai arrived in Wehali. Unlike other places in West Timor, where displaced East Timorese were housed in temporary barracks, the displaced Tetun of Fohoterin origin knew exactly where to seek accommodation. Their destination was Sukabiwedik, a hamlet in the village of Kamanasa. Kamanasa comprises seven hamlets and, as the village of Suai, is named in remembrance of people from Camenaça in East Timor who took refuge in Wehali land during the anti-tax rebellion of 1911. Therik (2004: 85), in his observations of these events, wrote:

> According to the oral history narrated in the area, the people of these hamlets were originally refugees from a Portuguese colony in the eastern part of Timor. Indeed the name of the village is often mentioned as Suai Kamanasa. The term Suai denotes a domain of origin in as much as the Kamanasa people claim that originally they came from Suai, a Tetun speaking area across the former international border between East and West Timor.

As expected, the local people welcomed their arrival. Thus, unlike other places, in Sukabiwedik, there were no camps. Instead, the displaced Tetun people of Fohoterin origin were accommodated in local people's houses. 'We come from one origin' is the common phrase used by local people to describe the basis of this support. It was this shared origin that also led locals to offer their land for the incoming East Timorese to settle. From the Wehali perspective, land is an appropriate gift from the female centre. The idea that land has a unifying influence among Tetun people is culturally encoded as an inevitable consequence of the symbolic representation of Wehali as the land of origin (*rai hun*). In Wehali, the concept of *rai hun* extends well beyond the areas around their ritual centre in the village of Laran. In another categorical sense, *rai hun* is perceived as the place of the light (*rai kroman*) and the earth itself (*rai klaran*) and therefore extends without limit (Therik 2004: 71; Fox 2006b: 247). In a complementary way, Suai is ritually expressed as the land of the darkness (*rai kukun*), the land of the dead (*rai matebian*). As the narrative goes:

Wehali: Atu simu ema moris iha rai klaran	Accept the living people in the bright land
Suai: Atu simu ema mate rai kukun.	Accept the dead people in the dark land.

The idea of unity between the Tetun people from Suai and the Tetun people of Wehali is also conceptualised in the symbolic representation of Wehali as Suai's source of prosperity. Another narrative about the living ritual of Nai Loro Nubatak, one of the sons of Loro Tuan Fatu Isin who ruled Suai, exemplifies this relationship:

One time during his leadership, Nai Loro Nubatak was very keen to make a ritual to offer thanks to God for the goodness extended upon the people of Suai. The essential instruments to conduct this ritual were betel and areca nut [*bua abut*]. Betel and areca nut, however, were not found in Suai area at that time so Nai Loro Nubatak made an appeal to Liurai Wehali to provide the seeds of betel from Wesei [*Takan Wesei Oan*] to be planted in Suai.

Liurai Wehali approved the request and gave the betel seeds delivered by a couple from Wehali. The name of the man was Klau Firak and the woman, Dahu Firak. This couple lived among the Suai people and together they planted the betel and areca nut in Weafou, Mota Masin and Wetaeboko.

Here, the ideology of unity between Suai and Wehali and the nature of their relationship are symbolically categorised as seedbed and plantation. As elsewhere in eastern Indonesia, in Wehali, betel and areca nut are the essential elements of ritual. The expression *Takan Wesei Oan* refers in ritual terms to the heir of the domain, the son of the *liurai*, the one who holds the authority. Thus, the association of Wehali as the source of betel and areca nut implies its central role in the ritual life of the Tetun people in Suai—symbolically, the source of life. As Wehali maintained spiritual authority, Suai is perceived as their cultivated land, the land that can grow and prosper. In this social paradox, Wehali as the centre becomes poor and Suai as the periphery becomes rich; Wehali becomes weak and Suai becomes strong (Fox 2006d; Therik 2004: 76–7).

Shared ideas of origin offer a crucial insight into Tetun people's understandings of displacement and emplacement. By revealing their origin, the Tetun people retrace the foundation of their existence with reference to the starting point of their ancestors' rite of passage that led them to their present situation. In this respect, origin serves as the basis for their claim as founders or first settlers and hence to entitlement by association. The shared recognition of Wehali as their land of origin, moreover, confirms an imagined unified identity as one people for the Tetun people from East Timor and West Timor. This, at the same time, legitimises the claim of the Tetun people from East Timor of belonging in West Timor by articulating their displacement culturally as a process of returning to one's land of origin.

Paths of return

The origin narrative depicts the Tetun people as returnees when they left Suai inside the East Timor border for the Wehali land on the western side. This does not mean they have completely detached themselves from Suai. For them, Wehali—with its representation as the mother and the father, the female and the centre, the land of origin and the earth—accommodates but does not constrain; Wehali embraces but does not confine; it receives but also gives away. The idea is based on a different narrative in Wehali, which conceptualises mobility as the key characteristic of the Tetun people. Mobility in Tetun narratives is categorised symbolically as the departure of Wehali's men to the land of the morning sun and the land of the setting sun. This is made explicit in the following segment:

Na'i Taek Malaka married Hoa'r Na'i Haholek and had six boys and one girl

The first born was Na'i Saku Mataus, then Na'i Bara Mataus, Na'i Ura Mataus, Na'i Meti Mataus, Na'i Neno Mataus, Na'i Leki Mataus.

The last born was a girl named Ho'ar Mataus, entitled Ho'ar Makbalin Balin Liurai [lit., the one who was in charge of appointing rulers or *liurai*]

Na'i Saku Mataus and Na'i Bara Mataus were given away to sit in the land of the rising sun

Na'i Ura Mataus and Meti Mataus were given away to sit in the land of the setting sun

Na'i Leki Mataus and Na'i Neno Mataus were left in Wehali

Ho'ar Mataus, the one who appointed the *liurai* sits in the house of the earth and sky to look after Wesei Wehali. (Therik 2004: 81–2)

While the Tetun people in Wehali depict the sending out of Na'i Saku Mataus and Na'i Bara Mataus to the eastern side of Timor, the Tetun people of Suai origin recount a slightly different version of this departure. For them:

Na'i Meti Mataus was sent out to lead the people of Suai Uma Rat.

Na'i Leki Mataus was sent to lead the people of Raimea Uma Loro.

Na'i Ura Mataus was sent to lead the people of Manufahi Oma Loro Rai Lor.

Na'i Suri Nurak was sent to lead the people of Suai Kamanasa.

Despite these differences, a shared ideology is found in the Wehali as female category sending away her men to rule the surrounding areas. For many Tetun people from Suai, moreover, the narrative serves as a foundation for their return to their land in Suai. And this is what happened to the displaced people of Fohoterin origin in Sukabiwedik in 1999. With the warm reception and gift of land from the Tetun people, one would expect the displaced people to eventually settle in Sukabiwedik. However, in late 1999, 400 households decided to return to Suai, followed by another 20 households between 2001 and 2003. At the time of writing, about 40 households remained in Sukabiwedik. For these returnees, Wehali has always been home, but another home should also be looked after. An elder in Kamanasa village once told me:

If everyone stays here, who is going to maintain the path of our ancestors and maintain the house and the land in Suai? You may not believe this, but in fact we encouraged them to go back for those purposes.

The Bunaq integration narrative

Like Tetun-speaking people from Suai, Bunaq-speaking people from East Timor have their own narrative to explain their origins and displacement. But while the Tetun considered the breakdown of their unity to be the result of internal disputes, the Bunaq emphasised the role of 'outsiders'—the Dutch and Portuguese colonial powers specifically—as antagonistic forces that destroyed the unity of Timorese. Appadurai (1996: 183) has noted that 'all locality building has a moment of colonization, a moment both historical and chronotypic'. For the Bunaq, this locality building is expressed in the story of the European colonisation of Timor, which transformed their identity from a shared origin into a shared colonial experience and struggle. It is this transformation that brings the Timorese into the realm of Indonesian nationalism. The following narrative, offered to me by the leader of the Bunaq people in Belu, the *loro* of Lamaknen, Ignasius Kali, was recited during the visit of El Tari, then governor of NTT, to the displaced Bunaq people in the camp at Sukabiren village in Belu district in early 1976. The narrative was spoken in Bunaq language in a form of parallel speech as follows:

Meten no, hahu no	In the beginning and origin times
Nai Giral Kere, Nai Gepal Owen	The One-Eyed King and One Ear
Pan hini hono, muk hini hati	Created the sky, provided the land
Gie ketemete, gie dairai	Made goods and wares
Mila lubu gutu, en lubu gutu	With the lives of slaves and human beings
Gini tetuk biel, gini nesan biel	In their wholeness and perfection
Homo dalas uwen, homo betak uwen	In their pieces and incompleteness

Siawa Mugiwa gene, Kanua Maliama gene	From Siawa Mugiwa and Kanua Maliama
Sinamutin gene, Malaka gene	In Sinamutin and in Malaka
Nei nei tata, nei nei bei	Our male and female ancestors
Biruk mo gie, ro meti gie	With watercraft and boat
Meti nagi man, mo dugun man	Sail and dive approaching
Riso none nere, teten no pir	Into the land
Riso gomo nobel, teten gemel nobel	The uninhabited land
Orel goi na pous, jon gio na pusen	Apart from the monkeys and wild boars
Dege rasa biel, dege sail beil	So they clean the land and clear the land
Hono ditimik, hono dalai	To emplace and settle down

It is at this stage that the process of settlement in Timor began. Originating from the same ancestors, the mythical society grew and developed through various kinds of relationships. They also migrated to the eastern and western sides of the island, but always recognised each other as brothers and sisters. This segment of the narrative is as follows:

Dege talik hoon, dege kait hoon	They started to create relationships
Talik kau kaa, kait hulo lep	Elder//younger relationship, relationship of bamboo flute
Talik malu ai, kait das arak	Wife-givers and wife-takers relationship
Talik guni sai, kait mil sai	Connect to outside and release from within
Talik dele rese, kait dele dene	Relations are diverged and shared
Dese hot taru, dese hot topa	Share to the morning sun and to the setting sun
Golo tama loi, gua res loi	To stay and remain there
Maligele ni, laktol ni	Without a ditch, without a gulf
Dege dubewiti, dege danaran	And then identify themselves [in reference to their place of living]

Lakulo Samoro gol, Lutarato *Jopata gol*	Children of Lakulo, Samoro, Lutarato, Jopata
Obulo Marobo gol, Sibiri *Kailau gol*	Children of Oburo Marobo, Sabiri Kailau
Ro Ikun Ro Wulan gol, Ton ba *Ton wai gol*	Children of Ro Ikun Ro Wulan, Ton ba Ton wai
Manuaman gol, Lakan gol	Children of Manuaman Lakan
Wesei gol, Wehali gol	Children of Wesei Wehali
Molo o Miomafo, Kupang *Amarasi*	Children of Molo Miomafo, Kupang Amarasi
Ambenu Amfoang, Nuba Taek *Natu Taek*	Children of Ambenu Amfoang, Amanuban, Amanatun
Sana Taek, Boki Taek, Ti Mau *Sabu Mau*	People of Insana Beboki, Rote Sabu
Hulo rese na bai, lep dene na bai	These are our brothers and sisters, our youngers and elders
Gasasi gaal ni, ganaran gaal ni	For those who have not been mentioned
Dagar na sala, tais na hone …	Please forgive us …

Another sequence of the narrative concerns a new chapter of history, when the white men from across the sea arrived, conquering and eventually dividing Timorese society. The Portuguese established their first base on the island of Solor, north of Timor, in 1562. In 1641, they began their first military expedition into the interior of Timor. Over the next decade, until 1650s, they established a permanent port at Lifau (present-day Oecussi) on the northern coast of Timor. The Dutch made their first visit to Timor in 1613, but only 40 years later, in 1653, did they establish their permanent base in Kupang. In spite of these colonial encounters, Timor remained independent under the control of the so-called black Portuguese[5] and their native allies for the next 200 years. As Fox (2003: 11) notes:

---

5   The black Portuguese were also known as the *topasses* of Timor—an ethnically mixed Portuguese group who dominated politics in Timor in the seventeenth and eighteenth centuries (see Boxer 1947; Hägerdal 2012).

[O]nly in the nineteenth century, through a process of relentless intrusions by military force, were the two colonial powers able to exert their influence on the interior of Timor. The Portuguese claimed to have pacified their territory by 1912, the Dutch theirs by 1915.

Timorese people from both sides of the island struggled to gain independence from their colonial oppressors. Yet only the west succeeded, by dispelling the Dutch. Success on the western side of Timor was then followed by the formation of the independent state of Indonesia. In this sense, Indonesia was inherently a transformation of the mythical ancestral paths in the western side of Timor. These lines of the narrative follow:

Betak uwen teni, dalas uwen teni	Then came the new chapter in our history
En gira look, en giwi belis	When the white people
Portugal uwen, Olandes uwen	The Portuguese and the Dutch
Meti iti gie, mo noet gie	From across the sea
Nie pan no neti, nie muk no dege	Conquered our land and sky
Gopil neta ni, gebel a ni	We were not able to fight back
Nei nese none, nei nake	They separated and divided us
Waen ewi guju, waen ewi belis	Into the black part and the white part
Ewi guju Olandes, ewi belis Portugal	West Timor to the Dutch and East Timor to the Portuguese
Betak uwen teni, dalas uwen teni	Then came the new chapter in our history
Nei nei kau, nei nei kaa	[When] our brothers and sisters
Hot topa gene, hot halu gene	On the western side [of Timor]
En giwi belis, en Olandes	Pushed and dispelled the Dutch
Dege gesesu, dege gururu	The white people, the coloniser
Dege pan ukon, dege muk baru	And governed themselves
Pan gobewiti, muk ganaran	And formed their own state
Pan Indonesia, muk Indonesia	Which was called Indonesia
Det pan hota, det mugi gaul.	An independent and sovereign one.

After the formation of Indonesia, the plight of those on the eastern side of Timor was revisited. Describing their suffering under Portuguese colonial rule, the narrative goes on to outline the option of self-determination offered by the Portuguese. Having claimed Indonesia as the transformation of their ancestral path, the narrative evokes an association with the Apodeti political party and declares the land in the east to be an integral part of Indonesia:

Nei hot taru, nei hot sae	We [the Timorese] on the eastern side
En giwi belis, en Portugal	The white people, the Portuguese
Nai neje dina-dina, nei derik han-han	Colonised and oppressed us
Gopil heta ni, gebel a ni	We were not able to fight them
To uwen no, to tut no	[But] some time ago, not long ago
En giwi belis, en Portugal	The white people, the Portuguese
Nei nege wese, nei nege ne	Separated us and divided us
Nei nini poi, nei nini hek	Asked us to make a choice and elect
Niba teo na none, hik teo na gene	Which way we are going to take
Ata helekere, ata houla	And we have agreed
Nei dini kere, dini Apodeti	We become one and become Apodeti
Hiba kere poi, hik kere hek	And uphold the foundational conviction
Pan Indonesia, muk Indonesia	The sky of Indonesia, the land of Indonesia
Gutu na dini kere, gutu na dini uwen.	Becoming one and only.

Finally, after declaring their intention to integrate within the Indonesian nation-state, the narrative returns to the continuing colonial oppression in East Timor. This was part of their attempt to emphasise their shared colonial experience and therefore legitimises their claim for integration within Indonesia. The concluding lines of the narrative are:

En giwi belis, en Portugal	The white people, the Portuguese
Hola dotole, hila dakbilan	Deluded themselves
Dojul tebe belo, ipos tebe a	Broke their promises
Hila gimil wel, hila gotok sae	And wreaked their anger
Notol suli bilik, notol su lela	They mobilised their armies
Nete nesesu, niep nururu	To fight us
Ata nelelan, ata nawawu	And confiscate our possessions
Gopil heta ni, gebel a ni	We were not able to fight them
Baa gie na he, baa gie na los	That was why we took refuge
Pan Indonesia, muk Indonesia	The sky of Indonesia, the land of Indonesia
Nita dosun taa, nita dot es	To protect and secure us
Nei poi o si, nei nek o si	And therefore we have chosen and decided
Holo lep halolo, kau kaa halolo	Based on our elder//younger relationship, a relationship by oath
Nei mete hini toek, nei mete hini lal	We declared today
Nei nei pan, nei nei muk	Our territory
Hot sae gene, hot taru gene	On the eastern side of Timor
Pan Indonesia piu, muk Indonesia bital.	Became an integrated part of Indonesia.

Just like the Tetun, the Bunaq people of East Timor articulate their displacement in West Timor as a process of reaffirming their origins. Moreover, they have additional sequences that lead to another possibility of identity based on colonial experience and their independent struggle. Politically, this implies an accommodation to Indonesian national identity, but culturally, the Bunaq imagine their belonging in Indonesia as the process of reconciling the broken ancestral paths as well as revitalising their mythic political order. In other words, displacement from East Timor to West Timor is inherently an expansion of traditional forms of alliance in the Indonesian part of Timor. Of course, not all Bunaq people in East Timor shared the origin and alliance narrative I have outlined here. It was the Bunaq of Aiasa domain in Bobonaro district who shared their origin and alliance narrative with the Bunaq of Lamaknen in Belu district. In what follows, I illustrate how this shared origin and alliance facilitated the resettlement of the displaced Bunaq from Aiasa in a Bunaq village in West Timor in 1999.

Emplacement and alliance in Dirun

In September 1999, the displaced Bunaq people from Bobonaro arrived in Dirun, a predominantly Bunaq-speaking village and one of eight regions forming the traditional domain of Lamaknen. Dirun is 36 km east of Atambua, the capital of Belu district. On their arrival, the displaced Bunaq camped in a flat area of Weluli hamlet. While in this temporary site, the newly arrived Bunaq—under the coordinating efforts of Fernando Dos Santos—approached local Bunaq elders to discuss a potential location for their permanent settlement. The displaced Bunaq were recognised not as strangers or outsiders, but as family members. 'We welcomed them in our land', recalled Yohanes Lesu, the head of Dirun village, about the arrival of the displaced Bunaq from Bobonaro district in 1999. 'We tried to find a place for them to stay here because they are our family.' In explaining what he meant by family, Yohanes emphasised the rooted kinship categories that have always been upheld and embodied by the Bunaq people in building alliances: 'In Bunaq, we call this relationship *malu-ai ba'a* [wife-giver//wife-taker]. They [the Bunaq from East Timor] were the wife-givers and we were the wife-takers and vice versa.'

After several negotiations, in 2004, the local Bunaq agreed to give away 2.5 hectares of land in the hamlet of Besak Lolo to become a permanent settlement for their Bunaq relatives from East Timor. This was formalised by a written agreement that was signed by the traditional elders as well as the elected village authorities. The agreement read as follows:

> Based on the consensus between the village authorities and the traditional elders in Dirun, herewith we give away the village land in the hamlet of Besak Lolo to the displaced East Timorese who are temporarily camped in the hamlet of Weluli. We give away this land in sincerity and without any time limit.

As with the Tetun people, the Bunaq considered land not as a commodity, but as a catalyst for exchange and alliance building. Sharing land with displaced kin was viewed as an obligation; that is the way kin should be treated. In so doing, the local Bunaq also recognised the significance of mobility in their social life. As outlined in the later part of the agreement:

However, if [later on] the displaced people decide to return to East Timor or move somewhere else, the land should be given back to the community through the village authorities.

Although traditional elders and village as well as subdistrict authorities signed the agreement, it was not considered culturally legitimate until the act of commensality. As Yohanes explained:

> The agreement is valid because after we signed it, we ate and drank together. We shared the local gin [*sopi*] to bind the agreement, which at the same time binds our relationship.

Currently there are about 600 Bunaq people from East Timor living among their fellow Bunaq of West Timor in the village of Dirun.

Cementing Kemak's new settlement

In contrast to the displaced Tetun and Bunaq who uphold the collective recognition of their shared foundational narrative and try to maintain their unity through their mythical ancestral paths, displaced Kemak stressed their origins in East Timor. A. D. M. Parera, a government officer who travelled around Belu district in the early 1960s, wrote:

> When the Kemak people were displaced and emplaced in West Timor, [they] brought along their wives, children, livestock and ancestors' sacred regalia. Upon their arrival [in West Timor], they [acquired land on which to settle] and maintained their [distinct] social organisation, language and culture although they have married other people here. (Parera 1971: 56)

In this section, I contend that Kemak people conceive of their 'displacement' in West Timor not in terms of separation from their land of origin in East Timor, but as a process of cementing their new settlement in West Timor.

Just like their predecessors, the Kemak people who arrived in 1999 understand that access to land is crucial to their resettlement. While the Tetun and Bunaq did not recognise land as a commodity and therefore chose to undertake symbolic land exchange to maintain their ethnic unity, the Kemak, in their process of emplacement, chose a different path. From a Kemak cultural perspective, West Timor is not their land of origin and for this reason any attempt to build new settlements in the west should be undertaken with authority of ownership over the new land on which they settle. This is exemplified in the case of Kemak people from the villages of Carabau and Cota Bo'ot in Bobonaro district. In 1999, they arrived at the hamlet of Siarai in the border village of Maunmutin, 52 km east of Atambua. The Kemak people in Siarai were originally from the Balibo area on the border. Mikael Berek, a Siarai elder, shared his story with Olkes Dadilado, an officer of CIS Timor, during his visit in 2005:[6]

> In the past, there was this so-called War of Manufahi. Our ancestor named Sulis Leo Mali led some warriors from Siarai and joined the warriors of Carabau under the leadership of Dom Asa Mali to fight the people of Manufahi whose leader was known as Dom Boaventura. Sulis Leo Mali did not just fight for Carabau, but he also took a Carabau woman named Sose as his wife. When the war was coming to an end, Sulis took his wife and men back to Siarai. Halfway along the return journey, they rested to bake taro as their lunch. All of a sudden, a Manufahi warrior named Lulito came out of the bush ready to attack. Sulis and his men did not have a chance to grab their weapons and so they surrendered. But Sose's presence was not noticed by Lulito. She moved quietly to get the firewood that was still burning and stabbed Lulito. She hit him right in his chest and cut through to his heart. Lulito died instantly. Sulis stood up immediately and decapitated Lulito. They then took Lulito's head back to Carabao and celebrated their victory with parties for three nights long. The ruler of Carabao then gave horses and some of his men to accompany Sulis, his wife and his men back to Siarai. And that was how we [the people of Siarai] established a relationship with the people of Carabau. We are the male and they are the female. We are *mane heu* [*mane foun*: wife-takers] and they are *uma mane* [wife-givers]. (Dadilado 2005a: 3–4)

A kinship relation between the Siarai people and the Carabao people is expressed in their ritual language as *hosi Balibo–Marobo//to'o Carabao–Cota Bo'ot*. The expression points to the unity of people from Balibo–Marobo and people from Carabao–Cota Bo'ot. The displaced Kemak of Carabao and Cota Bo'ot origin who arrived in Siarai in 1999 recognised the significance of their kinship and union with the Siarai people. And, since early 2000, they have approached the local people for land for settlement and cultivation purposes. Organised by Abilio de Araujo, a retired army officer who acted on behalf of 105 households, the newly arrived Kemak initially secured land for cultivation, which they attained without any obligation to share the harvest with locals. All they were required to do was pay the annual land tax for the land under cultivation. In 2004, an agreement was reached with the Siarai people for a settlement site.

6   Dadilado wrote this story, which was published in the August 2005 edition of the *Lorosae Lian* bulletin.

For this site, each household agreed to contribute about IRD500,000 (A$80) in the form of *bua malus* (betel nut). Betel nut from the new arrivals and land from the earlier settlers constituted a symbolic form of exchange between wife-takers and wife-givers. With land secured, the Indonesian Ministry of Public Works built 6 m x 6 m houses for 105 households. The site was later named (Carabao) Cota Bo'ot settlement to remember their place of origin in East Timor. There are currently nearly 500 East Timorese of Kemak Carabao–Cota Bo'ot origin living alongside their fellow Kemak in Siarai hamlet in West Timor.

About the same time, this ancestral alliance was also recognised in the neighbouring hamlet of Lesuaben in the village of Maumutin. In Lesuaben, about 1,000 newly arrived Kemak people from Bobonaro, Maliana, Cailaco and Balibo approached their Kemak kin and managed to secure land for a settlement. In a similar fashion, they used their position as wife-givers (*uma mane*) and were gifted 13 hectares of land by the Kemak, who considered them as wife-takers (*mane heu*). The land was exchanged for betel nut representing IRD500,000 (A$80) submitted by each resettled household. An elder from Lesuaben commented on the exchange: 'In our tradition, they [the newcomer Kemak] should gift us the betel nut and the woven cloth. And in return we gave them the water buffaloes.' The Kemak newcomers and their Kemak kin agreed to modify the practice—which was usually undertaken in the context of marriage exchange—for settlement purposes. The betel nut is symbolically represented by money; the water buffalo is symbolically represented by land. After securing the land, the Kemak approached the government and two settlements (Derok Aitous and Derok Sosial) were built in Lesuaben in 2004. At the time of writing, over 900 newcomer Kemak in Derok Aitous and nearly 300 newcomer Kemak in Derok Sosial are living alongside their Kemak kin.

Similar land acquisition processes took place between newcomer Atsabe Kemak and their Kemak kin in Kabuna village on the outskirts of Atambua. In mid-February 2013, I visited Sali Magu, a resettlement area that housed about 500 Kemak households, mostly from the Atsabe district in East Timor. Initially inclined to name their new settlement 'Atsabe' in remembrance of their land of origin in Ermera, East Timor, after careful consideration, they agreed to identify the area as Sali Magu—a Kemak expression meaning 'handshake'. 'Sali Magu is not our origin land,' one of the elders explained, 'but it is part of our ancestral landscape.' An established Kemak group who migrated to West Timor in the early twentieth century owned land in Kabuna. The newly arrived Kemak used this shared ethnic identity to purchase land on which to settle. Sali Magu resettlement site covers 13 hectares and is now one of the largest such areas for displaced Kemak in Belu district.

Plate 4.1 SALIMAGU Gallery, a cloth-weaving (*ikat*) business initiated by the Atsabe Kemak in Belu district
Source: Andrey Damaledo.

Conclusion

In the introduction to his discussion of Austronesian conceptions of land and territory, Reuter (2006: 14) argues:

> no matter how much displacement they might experience, their relationship with the land, their place of origin and their place of residence are matters of utmost importance to all people, and no less so to a people on the move.

The corollary of this statement is the strong sense of attachment to a particular locality or homeland. For the Tetun and the Bunaq, their homeland is not bounded within a particular national territory. Rather, it is where their ancestors have undergone a mythical passage of kinship and alliance building. By deciding to settle among their kin who migrated to West Timor prior to 1999, the newly arrived Tetun and Bunaq perceived their displacement not as a single event but as a process of reconnecting ancestral pathways. As a process, mobility will always be celebrated and accommodated.

In contrast to the Tetun and the Bunaq, the history of Kemak displacement and resettlement in West Timor has been shaped by a distinctive origin narrative. Despite this apparent difference in the conceptualisation of origins, the Kemak share a common pattern of mobility-based identity with the Tetun and Bunaq. The Kemak's origin narrative 'demonstrates the significance of place and local geographic features in the formulations of group identity as well as in narrating complex histories of human migration and group relations' (Molnar 2011: 99). In one of their narratives, the Kemak of Atsabe claim their origin to be Darlau Mountain in East Timor, but the mobility of their ancestors has included parts of West Timor as well as the surrounding islands of Alor, Flores, Kisar and Ambon (Molnar 2011: 104). Considering West Timor as part of their ancestors' pathway, the Kemak's displacement in West Timor is not perceived as detachment from the homeland. Rather, it is a form of cementing their distinct identity in their ancestral pathways. Cementing their distinct identity in West Timor can only be undertaken when the Kemak have full ownership over their new settlements. This is why they insisted on paying off their new land rather than relying on kinship exchange mechanisms.

Plate 4.2 Atsabe Creative House, a computer and internet business initiated by the Atsabe Kemak in Belu district
Source: Andrey Damaledo.

Another factor that makes Tetun, Bunaq and Kemak displacement distinct is recognition of shared origin by the host community in West Timor, which has led to supportive resettlement processes. This understanding challenges two prevailing views about the East Timorese in Indonesia. First, it is conceptually problematic to label the East Timorese in West Timor 'refugees', 'ex-refugees' and/or 'new citizens' when in practice they are able to claim entitlement to the land of their habitual residence based on their origin narratives and traditional alliances. It is also problematic to confine East Timorese in West Timor to members of a single nation-state, when in fact their cultural identity is based on constant mobility across the border between Indonesia and Timor-Leste.

5

New track, new path

The resettlement site of Sulit—a word that in the Indonesian language means 'difficult'—was indeed not easy to find. We had to make a real effort to reach the site in the village of Kereana in Belu district. Kereana is 53 km from Atambua. After more than an hour of motorbike riding along the main road from Atambua to Betun (via Halilulik), we had to turn west and ride downhill over a loose and stony dirt road towards the village market. From there, we turned south and crossed several creeks. We then rode uphill again before finally reaching Sulit resettlement site. The journey might have been difficult, but it was worth the effort when we reached the site. Surrounded by hills and on the edge of the We Mer forest protected area, the large shady trees of the resettlement provided a peaceful environment. Its remoteness and limited access meant it received few uninvited visitors. It was in this place that the Mambai people from the Holarua region of Manufahi district in East Timor had settled. Rosario Marcal, a former member of the Sasarus team, a Holarua-based militia that operated during the 1999 referendum, explained:

> The Indonesian Government built our resettlement. However, our arrival at this place would not have been possible without the marriage of one of our sons to the daughter of local people here. In their [local people's] terms, we are their *fetosawa* [wife-takers] and we are part of them now. After the wedding, they advised us about this place. The land on which we have settled forms part of the gifts they gave us; we now belong here.

In the previous chapter, I examined the significance of origin narratives among East Timorese groups who have previous experience of migration to West Timor. For the Tetun, the Bunaq and the Kemak peoples, displacement and resettlement in West Timor were understood not as separation, but as return to and reunification with their ancestral land of origin. In this chapter, I examine what happened to other East Timorese groups who shared few migratory and ethnic relationships with West Timorese prior to 1999. I discuss case studies of displacement and resettlement processes for two East Timorese highland groups, the Mambai and the Idate. I argue that the notion of a land of origin remains a significant feature of belonging among these East Timorese groups. What differentiates them from the Tetun, Bunaq and Kemak is their understanding that displacement and resettlement are not a reunification with one's land of origin; rather, they represent the expansion of that origin land.

This process of expansion is exemplified in two forms: first, through the building of alliances with local people by integrating into existing cultural categories; and second, through the rebuilding of one's subsidiary symbolic cultural identities to represent the significance of the land of origin. To explain this argument, I divide this chapter into two parts. The first examines modes of social integration among the Mambai. I begin by continuing the story of Rosario Marcal and his fellow Mambai of Holarua origin in the Sulit resettlement site, who were accommodated by the Tetun of Fialaran as wife-takers. The following narrative discusses another marriage perspective and practice, among Mambai people of Maubisse, who took on the symbolic role of a returning male ancestor when engaging with the Tetun people in Wehali. Moving from integration into local cultural categories, the second part of this chapter examines how cultural authority is restored outside the ancestral land of origin. Here, I use the example of the resettlement of Idate people and the reconstruction of their sacred houses in West Timor, along with the restoration of their sacred leader.

Mambai of Holarua

Earlier I noted how a group of Mambai people from Holarua (Manufahi district) married into a local Tetun group and secured land.[1] Comprising more than 200 households, these people arrived in Belu district in mid-September 1999. They immediately camped in the Sukabitetek and Naitimu areas of West Tasifeto, 30 km south-west of Atambua. After remaining in the camps for nearly four years, in 2003, under the coordinating effort of Julio do Carmo from Naitimu camp, they attempted to find land on which to settle.[2] This effort was initiated in part because the local people no longer considered them 'outsiders'. Although coming from different ethnic stock, the Tetun people of Fialaran—their hosts—perceived the displaced Mambai as insiders because one of their members, Francisco Araujo de Jesus, had married Christina Dahu, the daughter of Nimrot Fahik, a traditional leader of the neighbouring village of Dubesi. More than a civil union, the marriage of Francisco and Christina was seen in cultural terms as the integration of Mambai people into the realm of the Dubesi Tetun people.

Traditionally, Dubesi and its surrounding lands were part of the ancient domain of Naitimu. According to their oral narratives, Naitimu was made up of four subdomains led by the *sasekin hat, tatanen hat*—a metaphorical expression of house-based alliance that means 'the four supports, the four base supports' (lit., the four roasters, the four containers). These four leaders (*temukung*) were named as Leki Fahik in Seo, Ek Fatu Tabene in Maktaen, Kadus Nanaenoe in Halilulik and Balau in Haliserin. In their traditional political order, Naitimu was known as Timu Mauk, one of the four 'sons' from the western side of Tasifeto. Their three kindred domains were Lidak (Lida Mauk), Mandeu (Reu Mauk) and Jenilu (Lilu Mauk). This form of alliance is expressed in the following narrative:

---

1 Practising wife-takers are not exclusive to the Mambai of Holarua origin. I noted a similar arrangement among the Mambai of Hatu Builico, one of whose son married a Bunaq woman and who were subsequently gifted land for settlement in Lakekun village in Malaka district. East Timorese living in the eastern area of Kupang district experienced similar arrangements when one of their men married a Meto woman. Some 55 households from Viqueque and Dili were gifted land in Nekon village and 53 Fataluku households from Lautem village in Luro received land in Oebelo village. While this sort of incorporation provides access to land and other resources, it is important to recognise that such access lasts only as long as the alliance and exchange obligations are maintained.

2 This story of Mambai people in Naitimu camp was reported by Dadilado (2006: 3–8).

Oan natar hat, oan laluan hat	Four groups of children, four stables of children
Basa isin hat, kaer kadu hat	Four taps on the body, four pulls on the teat
Taka ulu hat, sabeo ulu hat.	Four heads covered, four hats on the head.

These four groups traced their origin to the larger domain of Fialaran, which encompasses both the eastern and western sides of Tasifeto in Belu. By acknowledging their roots (*husar kotu*: lit., 'cut from the same navel') in Fialaran and Naitimu domains, they followed Fialaran patrilineal tradition—in contrast with the neighbouring south Tetun people in Wehali, who are resiliently matrilineal. There are two kinds of preferred marriage alliances among the Naitimu people. The first is called *inuk tuan*//*dalan tuan* (lit., 'the old track, old path'). This is a kind of endogamous alliance whereby members of an established *umamane* (wife-giver) clan and *fetosawa* (wife-taker) alliances form a union. But, as Francisco is a Mambai, the marriage to Christina was recognised by the northern Tetun people as *inuk foun*//*dalan foun* (lit., 'new track, new path'), meaning an initial marriage or new alliance—in this case, with outsiders. During the gift exchange rituals, which are an essential part of the marriage process, the *fetosawa* group usually offers livestock and money to the *umamane* lineage or extended agnatic group representing the bride. In return, the *umamane* offers gifts of traditional male cloth (*tais mane*) and containers for men to store betel catkins (*koba mane*). In the case of Christina and Francisco, however, the Naitimu people, as the *umamane* group, offered their land to accommodate the displaced Mambai, who had been accepted as their *fetosawa* (wife-takers).

Initially, Nimrot Fahik, as the father-in-law and leader of the *umamane* alliance relationship, agreed to offer a parcel of land only to Francisco for his new family. But in June 2005, Nimrot gathered his whole family together for a discussion and they agreed to offer an additional 8 hectares to the displaced Mambai so they could all settle there. The land was given without reciprocal expectations and without any time limit, although there were two conditions: under no circumstances should the land be sold to outsiders and, if the Mambai people decided to return to Holarua, they should hand back the land to Nimrot and his group. Three months after receiving the land, nearly 30 Mambai households built their houses and moved on to the land. Here we can see that the gifting of land is provisional on the persistence of the alliance.

In addition to their house site, each household has access to an area of at least 1 hectare on which to plant their crops. These households were still living and working on the land when I visited the area in 2013. Despite their lack of a previous social relationship, the displaced Mambai people from Holarua have been able to integrate themselves among the north Tetun people through a key marriage. The marriage of Christina and Francisco had a domino effect for the remaining displaced Mambai from Holarua who were still camped in Sukabitetek, a neighbouring area of Naitimu. In late May 2004, Cornelis da Costa Marcal, the coordinator of the Mambai in Sukabitetek, approached Herman Besin Luan, the local landowner, to sound out the possibility of acquiring some of his land. Although their village administration differs, Herman is a member of the house of Lisu Aman Fahik, which is led by Nimrot Fahik, Francisco's father-in-law. This association placed Herman in the de facto position of *umamane*—in a complementary way—to the displaced Mambai from Holarua as *fetosawa*. After a series of negotiations and clarifications, in early August 2004, Herman offered 1.8 hectares land as a settlement site to 13 displaced Mambai households from Holarua. As a form of exchange, Herman allocated his land on the condition that the displaced Mambai remain and work the land for a limited period of eight years (see Solvang 2005).

Herman and the local people also advised the displaced Mambai about evidence of pre-1999 Mambai displacement in Sulit, a hamlet at the edge of the We Mer-Kateri protected forest area. Rosario da Costa Marcal, the younger brother of Cornelis, followed up on the information and began his mission to trace the possible presence of their predecessors. 'The locals were scared of the site. They said it was haunted', Rosario explained of the situation in Sulit before he arrived. Without hesitation, Rosario hiked through the bushland before arriving at a hilly site where he found two unmarked graves. He confirmed with the locals the existence of the graves and they acknowledged that they belonged to 'the elders from Manufahi'. As Rosario recalled:

> When I arrived here [in Sulit], there was nothing but two graves. According to the locals, they were the graves of a couple of elders from Manufahi. They [the locals] were not sure when they [the elders] arrived in the area. What they knew was that the couple originally came from Manufahi and they came due to a violent conflict there a long time ago. This land was probably their campsite, which then turned into their settlement. As no other people lived nearby, I immediately built my camp and stayed here.

Moving beyond claiming to belong to the land in relation to the graves of his predecessors, Rosario began to negotiate the possibility of making the land a resettlement site for the rest of his people from Holarua who were staying in Sukabitetek camp. The locals who considered the Holarua people their *fetosawa* agreed to give away the land. Eventually, almost 10 hectares was offered and 50 households moved into Sulit in late 2004. Similar to their brothers and sisters in Naitimu, they were given a time limit to stay on the land—in this case, 15 years as a kind of probationary period. During these 'probationary' periods, the Mambai have rebuilt their livelihood towards making a permanent settlement. When I asked Rosario about the time limit, he calmly responded: 'We are their *fetosawa*. We also have our predecessors who lived, died and [are] buried here. We belong here.'

Plate 5.1 The Mambai from Holarua in Kereana village, Belu district
Source: Andrey Damaledo.

Accepting the male host: The Mambai of Maubisse

The idea of marriage was articulated in a different fashion by the Mambai of Maubisse origin during their resettlement among the Tetun people in Wehali land. In 1999, 160 East Timorese households from Maubisse,[3] a predominantly Mambai-speaking area in the Ainaro highlands, arrived in the Wehali area and immediately camped around We Malae, near Betun. Mambai is one of the main Austronesian languages of East Timor and shares linguistic similarities with Tetun and Kemak. Geographically, Mambai are inhabitants of the East Timorese districts of Aileu and Same and parts of Ainaro and Ermera, which makes them the largest ethnolinguistic group in East Timor. Although their population is significant, records of Mambai displacement into West Timor prior to 1999 are limited. There are, however, verifiable accounts of relations between Mambai and West Timor recorded in the time leading up to the 1911–12 rebellion. These accounts recognised an extensive kinship and alliance network between the Mambai people and the people of the surrounding areas. This included the Tetun people from Camenaça, an eastern domain that claimed origin from Wehali in Belu, West Timor. A former Portuguese military officer reported to Governor Filomeno da Câmara about this network, which exemplified the alliance of Dom Boaventura, the *liurai* of the Mambai domain of Manufahi:

> Turiscai, Camenassa and Tutuluro should not be trusted because of the intimate connections between their respective chiefs … Viqueque has kinship connections with Dom Boaventura (who is the nephew of the deceased *regulo* [of Viqueque], Dom Matues). [Dom Boaventura is] married to the niece of Nai-Clara, *regulo* of Aituto; the *regulo* of Alas also has kinship connections with the rebels … and while Bibisuco is not believed to have joined the rebellion nor to have kin connections with Manufahi, they are nonetheless on very friendly terms. (Davidson 1994: 263–6)

---

3   I adapted this story of the Maubisse people in Wehali from Olkes Dadilado (2005b: 3–6), an officer of CIS Timor, who recorded it for the *Lorosae Lian* bulletin. Lado wrote that these people's origin was the Ainaro subdistrict of 'Maubesi'. I tried to clarify this information during fieldwork, including having a further discussion with Lado himself, who eventually clarified that the spelling in the original was incorrect and should have been Maubisse.

This kinship and alliance network might not have worked effectively during the 1911–12 rebellion, but it was helpful during the displacement and resettlement of Mambai people in 1999. The surrounding area of We Malae in Betun was controlled by the Indonesian Government and was managed by the local police station at Betun. Settling on land owned by a state institution was disconcerting because of the uncertainty. 'At any time, additional housing for police officers could be proposed and would automatically mean relocation for us', recalled Romaldo Lopez, a member of the Indonesian army who had acted as the coordinator for displaced East Timorese camped at We Malae. For this reason, Romaldo and his group had been trying to find and negotiate for land they could purchase, own and eventually resettle on.

Having searched the area for some time, in 2003, Romaldo and Dominggus Mendoza—both of whom were considered elders able to represent the nine villages in Maubisse—approached the traditional (*adat*) leaders as well as the landowners of Fatisin hamlet in the village of Kamanasa. Kamanasa was named in reference to the Camenaça domain in East Timor from which most residents of Kamanasa village originated. Following the meeting, Romaldo and Dominggus approached Nikolas Nahak and his wife, Petronela, who had considerable landholdings in the area. To their surprise, the landowners had been expecting this approach. Nikolas disclosed that he had anticipated their move because the night before he had dreamt about a visit by ancestors from Maubisse who advised him that a group of Maubisse people who were searching for land on which to settle would soon approach him. The ancestors then asked Nikolas to give up his land because these people were members of his family. As members of the family, they deserved to stay on the land.

When Romaldo and Dominggus arrived at his house, Nikolas offered to gift his land to them. The notion of a kin relationship was further elaborated by Petronela, who stood by her husband to greet the expected families: 'We [the Tetun people in Wehali] are the female and our brothers and sisters from the other side [East Timor] represent the male side' (*Ami ne'e feto, mak husi raibelan ne'e ba nia mane*). For Nikolas and Petronela, and the Tetun people generally in Wehali, the giving away of land is seen as the reestablishment of a kinship alliance with the East Timorese. In this respect, an appropriate ritual treatment is necessary because the gift could be beneficial but could also cause harm to both the hosts and the newly arrived. When Romaldo and Dominggus asked about the price, Nikolas replied: 'If I put a price tag on it, I will be cursed by the ancestors' (*Kalo ha'u fa'an, ikus mai ha'u bele kona moruk tan ne'e lulik*). As a result, 2 hectares of land was given away to the Maubisse people.

In this exchange, the displaced Mambai from East Timor have been accommodated into Tetun cultural categories and mythic associations to meet their need to rebuild their lives on Wehali land. At the same time, the returning male 'category' has reconfirmed the symbolic and historical precedence of Wehali and (symbolically) restored the spiritual power of the land. By facilitating this reunification, Tetun people avoid the anger of the ancestors and, at the same time, expect, in return, blessings for the land. This process of accommodation is further related to the notion of a cosmological order and apical authority. A few weeks after the meeting, a ritual ceremony was performed to transfer the land. Under the shade of a banyan tree, representatives from the Maubisse applicants offered betel nut and betel to Nikolas and Petronela. While the ritual was proceeding, it began to rain, which was taken as an auspicious sign. Nikolas stated that the ancestors approved and had shown their blessing towards the land. There are now 153 Mambai households living in Fatisin hamlet.

The Idate in West Timor

Another variation of social integration among the East Timorese in West Timor is exemplified by a case of Idate displacement and resettlement. Idate is also an Austronesian language. It is closely related to Tetun Terik and is spoken by the inhabitants of the subdistrict of Laclubar in Manatuto. The Idate-speaking people were among the major supporters of the pro-autonomy option of East Timor remaining within Indonesia. Some claimed they had maintained a pro-Indonesia stance since their Idate kinsman José Osório Soares founded the Apodeti party in 1975. His younger brother, Abílio Osório Soares, had served two terms as governor of East Timor up to the time of the 1999 referendum (Bovensiepen 2011: 49). As the Soares family's position as proponents of Indonesia became cemented, their role in the social life of the Idate assumed a cultural dimension. Traditionally, Osório Soares was recognised as the sacred ruler (*liurai lulik*) of the Idate people whose sacred house in the Laclubar village of Manelima is located near Mount Liambau and called Ba Hera (Bovensiepen 2017: 156). The dominant political role of the Soares family during the Indonesian period encouraged many Idate-speaking people to join the Indonesian military and police or become public servants in the Indonesian administration of East Timor. A complex mix of history, ethnicity, politics, culture and economy led more than 3,000 East Timorese from Manatuto district—mostly Idate-speaking people— to leave their homeland in 1999 and settle in West Timor.

In April 2013, I visited the Idate resettlement site in the village of Oekfoho in Belu district and met a panel of elders, who told me:

> People may say that we decided to stay here in West Timor because we were afraid to return. But you know the destruction in Manatuto in 1999 was not as massive as [in] other areas in East Timor. In fact, the Mahadomi militia group was formed rather late because we got the news that the BMP [Besi Merah Putih] militia group from Liquiça as well as the Aitarak group from Dili were going to attack Manatuto if we did not immediately form our own militia. But, frankly speaking, we never had any involvement in taking people's lives. We do not have blood on our hands.

I asked: 'If your hands were clean, why didn't you just return? Don't you miss your homeland?' One elder replied: 'Of course we miss our homeland in Laclubar. And, yes, our land is there in Laclubar, but now our home is here in Oekfoho.' The elder pointed to the two decorated timber and thatch houses standing across from our meeting place. Explaining what he meant about the houses, the elder continued:

> Our [origin] house was there in Laclubar, but it is nothing but a physical house now. When we came to West Timor in 1999, we brought along all of our ancestral sacred regalia from the origin house. In addition, we brought along the one who has the proper authority to sit in and consecrate the ritual in that house, our sacred leader [liurai lulik]. With these in hand, we have built our new house of origin [uma lulik] here and therefore here is our new home.

The Idate people came to West Timor in two ways. Some joined the early evacuation effort that took place immediately after the announcement of the result of the independence referendum. Most, however, walked from Laclubar to Manatuto and then took a truck to Dili. From Dili, they embarked on a ship that eventually landed them in Kupang. Here, they initially camped in two major sites in Kupang district, Tuapukan and Naibonat. Mateus Alves, an Idate elder from the Manelima hamlet of Lakenu, recalled:

Upon our arrival, some of us were camped in Tuapukan. But my family joined the rest of our kin who were camped around Naibonat military station. After living in camps for more than three years, most of the Idate households joined the Indonesian Government resettlement program in Kupang district in 2002 and were resettled in Naunu village, in the subdistrict of Fatuleu. Others remained in camps until 2004 and 2005, when another resettlement site, in Raknamo village of Kupang district, was offered to the East Timorese. The Idate people who first moved into Raknamo resettlement area were retired military personnel. They joined the predominantly Tetun Terik–speaking people from Viqueque and the Makasae people from Baucau. A year later, my group joined another resettlement facilitated by the Indonesian Department of Public Works. Currently there are around 1,000 Idate-speaking people in Kupang district. We are dispersed in two main locations, about 150 Idate households in Naunu and more than 50 households here in Raknamo.

The first group of refugees arrived in Kupang by boat, while the rest came overland. By the end of 1999, almost all of the East Timorese evacuees who came across the border had ended up in Atambua, except for those who joined the military truck convoys that went through to Kupang. With no previous social relationships with West Timorese, settling in the border area was not an option for the East Timorese from the central regions such as the Idate. The most feasible sites for these people to build their camps were in the western area of Belu district. Here, there were two sites allocated to the Idate group, Tirta and Labur. Tirta camp is 3 km west of the Belu district capital of Atambua. In 1999, 3,000 displaced East Timorese people, mainly from Manatuto district and including Idate-speaking groups, were accommodated in Tirta. The rest of the Idate refugees were camped 20 km further west in a village called Labur. Numerically, Mambai settlers from the East Timor district of Aileu dominated Labur. In 1999, the site sheltered more than 2,500 displaced East Timorese.

Reconciling calamity

The displacement of Idate groups into West Timor was not only a physical shift, but also a spiritual one. It was spiritual because Idate elders in the group carried all of their ancestral sacred regalia into West Timor. These sacred heirlooms included a reputed manuscript (*manuscrito*) of the house of Ba Hera written in golden ink, a sacred golden dagger (*espada lulic*), a spear (*dima lulic*), an arrow (*rama lulic*), a sacred gong (*tambor lulic*), the flag of the house of Ba Hera (*bandeira lulic*) and a sacred sculpture called 'Estatua Rei Moises' (*Estatua Lulic–Ai Maior*). In her discussion of the spirituality of the internally displaced Idate people who returned to their origins in the Laclubar village of Funar, Bovensiepen (2009: 323) remarks that 'the returning villagers were keen to "re-inspirit" the material environment, restoring reciprocal relations with the spiritual realm and thus ensuring the economic and social benefits flowing from this'. These intentions and actions led Bovensiepen (2009: 323) to view the spiritual nature of the landscape hence:

> [T]he returning villagers are involved in a two-fold process aimed at achieving the right balance in their relationship with the spiritual landscape: attempting to restore and revitalise their reciprocal relations with it whilst also establishing a safe distance by detaching themselves from its threatening aspects.

Arguably, in a similar fashion to their brothers and sisters in Laclubar, the displaced Idate people in West Timor are also involved in a twofold process to claim the spiritual potency manifest in their ancestral sacred items—understanding their threatening aspects while restoring their authority.

The threatening aspects of the *lulik* unfold in many ways. Idate elders admitted that although the Mambai outnumbered them in Labur during the period 1999–2001, the Idate people were the ones who suffered the most from various illnesses. Their worst fear was realised when those recognised as the bearers of the ancestral heirlooms—Magdalena Soares, Mateus V. Soares, Mau Lequi, Jorge da Cunha, Eugenio Casimiro and Celestine Sibae—passed away, one after another, in 2001. In addition, many Idate people claim to be haunted by spirits of their ancestors through recurring nightmares. In his remembrance of the symbolic events surrounding the death of Raimundo Soares, Coli Mau recounted:

> The leaders of the house-group [*dato*] came and told me that they dreamed about the coming of a big flood that would sweep away the Idate people in West Timor. Others expressed different kinds of natural disasters such as tornadoes, drought and fire that led to the extinction of the Idate people. In addition to these disasters, some also depicted the death of the Idate people when in their dreams they saw a future where the people are not living on a fertile land but on human faeces. These signs of death were also exemplified by incidents of spirit possession whereby our people could no longer speak Idate but other languages such as Galole, Mambai, Tetun Dili, Makasae, Waima'a, Kemak and Bunaq. The situation was more frightening when some actually spoke out in Meto, Indonesian, Portuguese and even English.

The Idate thought these strange diseases, natural disasters, living in disgrace and losing one's identity were signs from their ancestors about a tragic future for their people. In response to this seemingly imminent catastrophe and to distance themselves from future threats, in early 2002, Abílio Osório Soares—then the *liurai lulik* of the house of Ba Hera—gathered the leaders of the eight *dato* that made up the traditional order of Ba Hera. The meeting resolved that ancestral sacred houses should be built immediately in West Timor to hold all the sacred items. As most of the Idate people were camped in Belu district, they decided to build the houses (*uma lulik*) in Labur. Although more Idate people were camped in Tirta, it was deemed culturally unsuitable because it also contained a public swimming pool and recreational area. In late November 2002, the ancestral sacred houses for the Idate in West Timor were constructed and a water buffalo was sacrificed to sanctify the houses during the ritual ceremony.

Restoring life

Idate people recognise two sacred houses, *ada Timor* and *ada Malae*. Neither house is designed as a residence, so no guardians actually reside there. They are similar in construction, with the exception of an additional layer of palm fibres (*ijuk*) in the thatched roof of *ada Malae*. Each house has only one entrance door made of a carved wooden panel. Like other Austronesian societies, the Idate pay much attention to the orientation of their houses. In this case, both Idate houses face east—ostensibly in remembrance of their origins in Laclubar. In another form of classification, *ada Timor* is also known as the upper house, the dark house and the older house. This is the place for the sacred leader of the Idate people and is designated only for sacred life and death rituals (*lisan mean* and *lisan metan*). To complement it, *ada Malae* is known as the lower house, the brighter house and the younger house. This is the place for the executive leader of the domain and the place where guests are welcomed (*uma makerek*).[4]

---

4   For a comparative discussion of the Mambai dual houses classification, see Traube (1980: 295–300); and for the Fataluku people, see McWilliam (2011). For other house categories among Austronesian societies, see Fox (2006a: 9–14).

Although both houses are similar in shape and size, they differ in purpose. *Ada Malae* functions as an office for the *liurai* of Ba Hera and is where the day-to-day matters of the people are attended to and where meetings of elders are held. Traditionally, the house also served as the court where people's disputes were resolved. *Ada Timor*, on the other hand, is designated for sacred rituals such as life-cycle rituals of childbirth (*tau naran moris foun*), marriage and particularly the arrival of a daughter in-law (*hasae feto foun*) and death (*hasae naran matebian*). *Ada Timor* is also the place for conducting rituals related to the agricultural cycle, such as corn and rice planting (*kuda batar–kuda hare*), harvesting (*hasau batar–hasau hare*), appeals for rain (*haturu wari dusu udan*) and refusal of rain (*hasae wari duni udan*). During conflict, *ada Timor* was also the place where Idate warriors conducted their rituals for immunity (*hasae biru*) before they went into battle and the place for purification rituals (*fodame malu*) following victory.

The newly built sacred houses were expected to take away death and bring life to the Idate people in West Timor, but this was not immediately the case. Narratives of death remained prominent among the people. The sacred houses' spiritual potency for life seemed to have faded. This was partly related to the crowded and limited land in Labur camp, which made a complete and regular tributary ritual in the houses impossible. The once consecrated sacred houses were now nothing but storage places for ancestral items. Reflecting on this situation, Idate elders began to search for a new place in which to settle. Between Tirta and Labur lies the hamlet of Oekfoho in the village of Naekasa. Oekfoho lies on a plain 16 km from Atambua. The majority of people in this hamlet speak Meto. Topographically, it is not a highland region—recalling Laclubar—but Oekfoho was appealing because of its proximity to various economic and social facilities in the Belu subdistrict of West Tasi Feto. The Idate people did not want to miss an opportunity and approached the Meto landowner. For this collective land acquisition effort, each household agreed to contribute IDR250,000 (A$25). After a series of negotiations, the Idate elders managed to seal the purchase of 2 hectares with a total payment of IRD20 million (A$2,000).

Four years after the initial modestly sized sacred houses in Labur were built, death threats still lingered in people's dreams. In 2006, after securing the land on which to settle, the Idate group was ready to conduct a culturally appropriate rebuilding of their sacred houses. In a sense, this reconstruction was perceived as a process of reclaiming the ancestral authority of life that had been missing since their arrival in West Timor. The process of sacred house reconstruction involved several stages.

- A coordination meeting was led by the sacred *liurai* of Ba Hera with the leaders of eight named houses called Besi Lisan Walu.[5] One of many, this meeting discussed the site of the house and the responsibilities of each descent group in each reconstruction phase. There were several restrictions imposed on the eight people assigned to seek the beams and building materials: they should not smoke cigarettes, they should not consume alcohol, they should not cut their hair or shave their moustache and beard, and they should not have sexual intercourse.

- After the meeting, the next stage was called *kasa air in*, which literally means 'hunting for the beam'. This involved a quest for housing materials, and eight people were assigned to this task. They were to be first blessed by the elders and then given some food and drink, as well as a dog to accompany them in their endeavours. The building materials should comprise only specified natural products such as timber, bamboo, *alang* grass for the thatch and rattan from the forest. The most important element is the central beam, which should only be taken from the Timorese white gum tree (*Eucalyptus urophylla* 'S. T. Blake'), or *ai ru*, as the Idate people call it. When they notice an *ai ru* tree, they will mark it by firing an arrow into the trunk. A sacrificial ritual is then conducted in which a dog is killed and its blood is spread around the tree. The tree will also be offered betel and betel nut and the dog's liver. For the Idate, eight is their sacred number—referring to the eight clans (*dato*) that made up the ancient house of Ba Hera. The significance of the dog is expressed in their classification of the eight clans as 'the dogs that guard the gate'.

- Following the sacrifice, they will cut the tree into eight pieces—four for the main posts and four for the adjoining posts.

- Another ritual is held to accept the beams and other housing materials on the reconstruction site. The 'accepting the beam' ceremony will continue in the carving of the post as well as in lining up the walls made from bamboo (*fafulu*).

---

5   These eight named houses are: Rin Besi Lalang, Rin Besi Hohon, Asutalin Ada Ina, Ada Telu, Lisu Hoho, Dole Walu, Suhu Rama Ahoti and Matan At. Each house has its designated roles and responsibilities during the ritual processes. The house of Ada Telu, for example, is the one responsible for cooking. The house of Asutalin Ada Ina deals with water provision.

- A ritual 'planting' of the four base pillars is performed following the 'accepting the beam' ceremony. Before each of the pillars is planted, the elders put eight gold coins as well as betel and betel nut in each hole.

- After the base pillars, there will be another ritual for planting the ridge-pole, with a similar process of first placing eight gold coins as well as betel and betel nut in the hole.

- There will also be a ritual for construction of the roof, which includes installing the door and sacred chamber (*laleur*).

- Although at this stage the house has been fully reconstructed, prior to the inauguration ritual, the house should be cleansed (*dasa foer*).

- The final stage is the inauguration of the house. In this celebration, each clan prepares eight water buffaloes, eight pigs, eight roosters, eight sacks of rice and eight jerry cans of local gin (*sopi*).[6]

The rebuilding process took almost a year to complete and, in early October 2007, the Idate ancestral sacred houses were finally inaugurated. People danced all night long in this celebration. Like the Meto ritual of cooling the house (*haniki*) (McWilliam 2002: 243), this celebration is designed to reclaim the authority of the ancestors to protect and provide an opportunity for the Idate to celebrate the abundance in their lives. After their sacred houses were built, the Idate people received support from the Indonesian Government to fund the construction of 93 residential houses around their sacred houses. For their livelihood activities, each household managed to secure from the Meto landowner a minimum of 1 hectare on which to plant their crops. This cultivated land was located along the border between Belu and TTU districts, some 3 km west of Oekfoho. It takes one hour from Oekfoho to reach their cultivated land on foot, but, as Raimundo proudly reminded me before I left, 'After we completed the reconstruction of our sacred houses, now we are feeding the local people with our abundant harvests of corn, beans and cassava'.

The selective and appropriate efforts to rebuild their sacred houses in West Timor convinced the Idate people to see their displacement and resettlement in a different light. For them, Laclubar had always been their land of origin. However, as their sacred houses were now standing in West

---

6   The costs are very substantial from the first stage to the final inauguration feast. With the influence of Abílio Soares, the Idate received support from the Belu district government and the Indonesian military.

Timor, a new point of origin had also been created. The strong emphasis of the role of the sacred house as a point of origin is a common feature among different East Timorese ethnolinguistic groups (Fox 2006a: 16; McWilliam 2005: 32). The neighbouring Mambai of Aileu, for instance, stressed the significance of their sacred houses as symbolic representation of their division and unity. As Traube (1995: 46) observes:

> Individuals belonged to male-ordered units known as houses, *fada*, a term that designated both a group and its dwelling. The socially significant dwelling was not an everyday residence, but a named ancestral origin house where the group's sacred heirlooms were stored. House members or 'people of one house' were scattered for most of the year, living in what Mambai represented as the 'outer realm of space' but they reconvened at their origin house on ritual occasions to re-enact their mythical unity.

Makasae-speaking people also express this idea of collective origin and unity through their concept of *ome bese* or 'big house' (Forman 1980). In a similar vein, Kemak-speaking people invoke the notion of a core house that binds dispersed Kemak groups into a shared origin and unity (Clamagirand 1980). If the reconstruction of the Idate sacred houses in Oekfoho has unified the dispersed Idate people living in the West Timor districts of Belu and Kupang, a second concern has coalesced around the relationship between these sacred houses and the ones left behind in Laclubar. Since independence there has been a widespread 'resurgence of traditions' (Hicks 2007: 14) across Timor-Leste. This cultural recovery is exemplified by the reconstruction and inauguration of sacred ancestral houses that were burned, destroyed and/or abandoned during the Indonesian occupation and post-referendum exodus. The Idate in Laclubar are no exception. For some time, the sacred houses of Ba Hera fell into disuse after most of its members were displaced into West Timor. With the support of the Government of Timor-Leste, the Idate finally managed to repair their sacred houses in Laclubar in 2010. However, various attempts to conduct rituals in the houses have failed, in part because the people who acted as sacred leaders are deceased or no longer present in the area. It is considered culturally inappropriate (*tidak layak*) for the community to sit in the houses because the real sacred leader and sacred ancestral heirlooms are held in West Timor.[7] Without their sacred leader and appropriate rituals, the renovated sacred houses are nothing but physical structures.

---

7   For a similar phenomenon among the Meto people of West Timor, see McWilliam (1999: 138).

To have their sacred houses in Ba Hera properly inaugurated, a delegation of elders was sent to West Timor to seek out suitable spokespeople (*futu lenso*). Among the Idate elders in Belu and Kupang, two prominent figures were first approached to be the spokespeople for the sacred houses: Manuel Saldanha or Nai Liurai Amanu, the guardian of *ada Timor*, and Francisco Cornelio Pinto Lequi or Nai Liurai Sico, the guardian of *ada Malae*. Although the guardians had no reservations about accepting the invitation to return to Timor-Leste, their ultimate decision was in the hands of their leader, João Sino Osório Soares, the younger brother of the former governor of East Timor Abílio José Osório Soares and the most senior ritual authority of the Idate community. João Soares had previously been head of the East Timor Department of Public Works and, at the time of the inauguration, was a civil servant in the Indonesian Ministry of Mining and Energy in the NTT government. He readily acknowledged:

> I never wanted to become the sacred leader of the Idate people because I actually know little about our traditions and rituals. But after the death of my older brother [Abílio José Osório Soares] in June 2007, the elders told me the ancestors had appointed me to be the *liurai lulik* of Laclubar. Sometimes you just can't escape your destiny.[8]

As their sacred leader, only João had the authority to sit in the sacred houses of Timor in Laclubar for its inauguration. In his words:

> They [the Idate from Laclubar] came and told me that Laclubar has lived in misery for the last 11 years. The land has lost its spirit. The body has lost its soul. Now they have renovated the sacred houses, but they always fail to conduct a proper ritual because the spirit custodian of the land has moved to West Timor. For this reason, they asked me and the elders to return to Laclubar for the house inauguration. I would not mind at all because they are also my people.

---

8   Among Austronesian societies, it is not uncommon for the leader 'to know nothing' because the succession counts on who the person is, not on what he/she knows. See Sudo (2006: 60) and Lewis (2006: 163) for comparison.

Plate 5.2 *Ada Malae* and *ada Timor* of the Idate people in Oekfoho village, Belu district

Source: Andrey Damaledo.

Plate 5.3 The author (in white T-shirt) with Idate elders in Oekfoho village, Belu district

Source: Andrey Damaledo.

In late 2010, João, the house guardians and a handful of Idate elders from West Timor returned to Laclubar for the inauguration of their sacred houses. They spent two weeks there to complete all the necessary rituals. João recalled people expressing their belief that 'the ancestors were blessing the land again after years of drought' when rain poured down following completion of the rituals. Although this was implicitly understood as an open invitation for the Idate people in West Timor to return and reside again in Laclubar, João and the elders decided to go back to West Timor after the rituals were completed. 'Laclubar has always been our origin, but they need to understand that now we also have our sacred houses in Oekfoho to be looked after,' João explained. Although they have rebuilt their new sacred houses in West Timor, the Idate people insisted there is only one origin that matters and it remains in Laclubar. According to their cultural understanding, the sacred houses in Oekfoho are recognised as *ada Kiik* or subsidiary houses to that of *ada Los* (the true origin house) in Laclubar. Through the reconstruction of their new sacred houses in Oekfoho, the Idate people in West Timor have kept alive their relationship with their ancestral land and relatives in East Timor. This phenomenon illustrates the typical Timorese idea of dispersion from the central origin (Traube 1986: 66).

Processes and results of integration

From a political point of view, the 1999 displacement of East Timorese into West Timor was seen largely as an exodus of pro-Indonesian loyalists. As such, these people are generally perceived as supporters of East Timor remaining a constituent part of Indonesia. But, as I have pointed out in this chapter, this integrationist idea is less obvious among the Mambai and the Idate, as exemplified in their displacement and resettlement processes. What is more obvious is 'integration' in a cultural sense whereby the Mambai have formed new alliances with the West Timorese and, at the same time, maintained their attachment to their land of origin in East Timor. They are doing this by embracing the Wehali 'male' category and becoming wife-takers to north Tetun people. There are two striking similarities in this process. First, the integration has taken the symbolic and actual forms of marital union and the Mambai are represented by the male category. This should be understood as being beyond a mythic or civic union because the Mambai concept of men marrying out is perceived as the initiation of a 'new path' or new alliance (Traube 1986: 87).

The second point is related to land. In both instances of alliance building, the gifting of land is the outcome. Edmund Leach (1951: 44), in his classic essay on marriage and alliance building, has argued that 'the procedure for acquiring land rights of any kind is in almost all cases tantamount to marrying a woman from the lineage of the lord'. In this view, land is categorised not as a commodity, but as a spiritual catalyst that brings people together. Land becomes a place of encounter between outsiders and insiders, newcomer and host, centre and periphery, wife-givers and wife-takers and unity and division. Extending this into ritual exchange obligations, however, the male category puts the Mambai in a subordinate status to the local people and causes them to strive to fulfil their alliance role. This includes working the land gifted to them and providing assistance and gifts to the local people.

The story of the Idate exodus exemplifies a common phenomenon. While the Idate are generally identified as major proponents of East Timor's integration within Indonesia, their knowledge of Indonesia remains vague. They know they are living in Indonesia, but it is attachment to their ancestral sacred houses and their sacred leader that seems to matter more. And when their sacred houses and sacred leader were not bound to a fixed locality, Laclubar remained just another possibility for the future. As many Idate told me:

> If one day our sacred leader orders us to take our ancestral heirlooms and return to our origin land, then Laclubar is where we go … besides, we have our original sacred houses there waiting anyway.

It was not my intention in this chapter to suggest that the Mambai and the Idate do not recognise Indonesian nationalist symbols. In fact, during my visit to their resettlements areas, I found many households still raise the Indonesian flag. In Sulit resettlement site, in particular, the flag was planted next to the tombs of their acclaimed predecessors. The Idate people have also kept the flag in their sacred houses. What I am considering is another perspective for understanding the nature of East Timorese ideas of belonging. In a political sense, they belong to Indonesia because of the political choices they made. However, in a cultural sense, they have always claimed belonging to a place of origin in East Timor and to their ancestral sacred houses and sacred leader as the principal sources of their identity. In this sense, their displacement and resettlement in West Timor are not about loss and separation, but about the expansion of their land of origin. As the Mambai of Aileu express this metaphorically: 'Its trunk sits there. The little pieces of its tip go out again and again. It has but one trunk. It is the bits of the tip that are many' (Traube 1986: 81).[9] In the next chapter, I will examine another form of East Timorese belonging by moving from this 'origin epistemology' (Fox 2008: 201) to the ideas of sacrifice, suffering, purity and silence among former militia and military personnel now living in Kupang, Belu and Malaka.

---

9   I note that in early October 2015, five Mambai from Holarua finally decided to return to their origin land in Timor-Leste. Many others who have managed to rebuild their lives were encouraged to stay in West Timor. They are the 'new paths' of Mambai people in West Timor.

6

To separate is to sustain

It was approaching Christmas 2012 when I was introduced to Bonifacio Ximenes, a Makasae speaker from the Quelicai region of Baucau. Boni, as he is fondly called, was in his late 40s when I met him. A civilian worker in the Indonesian military sector, Boni is best known by his fellow East Timorese as a specialist on religious issues due to his position as a parish elder of Naibonat camp, about 30 km east of the NTT capital. We lunched together in Boni's dining room while I explained my interest in the way East Timorese view their presence in West Timor. Our conversation began with Boni's description of East Timorese around Naibonat and the location of their settlements. There are approximately 4,500 Makasae speakers remaining in West Timor and most of them live in Naibonat and its surrounding villages, such as Raknamo, Manusak, Tuapukan and Noelbaki. As we moved on to stories of the relationship with Indonesia that forced them to flee East Timor, Boni started to draw on his own experience:

> I was 11 at the time Indonesia began to intensify its military operations into Baucau [in 1976]. I have nine siblings and I was the youngest [with] five sisters and four brothers. When the military advance started, all of my brothers fled into the jungle around the mountainous area of Venilale. My oldest brother, José, was our leader and he ordered the five of us to stick together. We regularly moved around the rough mountainous terrain just to get away from the Indonesian soldiers. In 1978 we were approaching the top of Larigutu Mountain and my oldest brother, José, signalled to us to take a rest.

Suddenly Boni fell silent. He bowed his head for a moment and when he looked at me, tears started to flow. 'Sorry,' I said gently. 'No, I just remembered my brothers,' Boni replied. After a while he moved on:

> We sat at Larigutu together and I can still remember my oldest brother, José, saying, 'We can't go on like this. We are moving too slowly and running out of water and food. We are all going to die if we stay like this.' As I was trying to understand what he was saying, he continued, 'For the future of our family, we have to separate.' He then asked my older brothers Joachim and Mario to continue their resistance with Fretilin and decided the three of us [remaining] should return and surrender. 'We should do this to look after one another,' he concluded. That was the last time I saw my two older brothers. Three of us surrendered and went back to our village in Quelicai.

I shared my sympathy with Boni and decided to put our conversation on hold. I asked him instead to walk me around his neighbourhood. Boni is one of thousands of East Timorese who decided to join the Indonesian military during the occupation. This decision often put them in a difficult situation, and for most of the time they have been widely recognised as Indonesian state collaborators. As collaborators, it was their duty to make sacrifices for Indonesia during the occupation. And, in the lead-up to and immediately after the referendum on autonomy in East Timor in August 1999, an estimated 6,000 members of the Indonesian military of East Timorese origin joined the evacuation and left for West Timor.

As members of the Indonesian military, they were directed into temporary shelters built around the army compound in Naibonat village. Most have remained there ever since. These personnel have also continued their service in various army squads throughout Indonesia and continued to draw salary and other employment benefits within the Indonesian security forces. Over time, they have also become eligible for pensions and retirement benefits under the Indonesian civil service system. The traumatic experiences of the East Timorese of violent colonisation, military occupation, resistance, family breakdown and separation have created numerous stories of sacrifice.

However, the existing literature has thus far emphasised narratives of sacrifice among East Timorese in East Timor. This chapter examines the way the notion of sacrifice is used to reclaim national belonging and entitlements. I focus my discussion on people such as Boni and his fellow East Timorese who were and remain involved with the Indonesian military. By involvement, I am referring to active and retired soldiers, active civilian employees within the military and former members of militia groups who were displaced and remained in Indonesian West Timor after the referendum.

Their stories deserve attention because this is the group of people often labelled traitors by their fellow East Timorese in East Timor because of their allegiance with Indonesia during the occupation. These stories are also important because they exemplify another striking feature of belonging among East Timorese in West Timor, in addition to the cultural ideas of origin and alliance building discussed in previous chapters.

I argue that stories of sacrifice such as those of Boni and his fellows evoke life histories and shared memories that, in turn, entail their intention to maintain an intimate relationship with their homeland in East Timor and ensure a better future for their society. My understanding of sacrifice, which I draw from a combination of classic anthropological analysis of ritual and contemporary discussion of sacrificial discourse, is central to my analysis and I discus this in the next section. I then go on to describe sacrifice in relation to national belonging, focusing on the ways in which retired Indonesian military officers of East Timorese origin make use of narratives of sacrifice in their process of resettlement in West Timor and reconciliation with Timor-Leste. In the final part of the chapter, I explore sacrifice from the perspective of former members of East Timorese militia groups and how they used this to negotiate their position in contemporary Indonesian state-building.

Rethinking the multiple understandings of sacrifice

The notion of sacrifice has been analysed by a number of anthropologists in their studies of religious practices (Tylor 1871; Robertson Smith 1889; Frazer 1890; Hubert and Mauss 1964; Evans-Pritchard 1965; Buordillon and Fortes 1980; de Heusch 1985) (for an overview, see Bloch 1992; Howell 1996; Milbank 1996; Mayblin 2014). While these studies have provided rich views on the meaning and role of sacrifice in a variety of contexts, they share a view that sacrifice is essentially a form of ritual with two prominent features. The first feature is the role and function of sacrifice, for instance, as a ritual exchange, such as a gift or payment of debt to ancestors or deities. Sacrifice has also been explained in terms of its role in fostering unity among members of a community or in relation to a deity. Other interpretations describe sacrifice as a way of gaining power from deities or of control of the violence inflicted by deities (Howell 1996: 2). The second feature is the process of sacrificing. In this view, sacrifice is defined as a sequence of ritualised acts comprising formal presentation, consecration, invocation, immolation and, finally, eating or commensality (Hubert and Mauss 1964; Evans-Pritchard 1965).

Seeing sacrifice as a ritual should begin 'by listening to what the people say, by understanding what they think of their practices' (de Heusch 1985: 23). This effort has shed light on the way hunting practices in eastern Indonesia are understood (McKinnon 1986: 348). It has also explained the significance of blood sacrifice during agricultural rituals (Seran 1996: 259) and how to communicate and maintain relationships with ancestors (Renard-Clamagirand 1986: 200). Despite the various interpretations, a common idea I found useful in the context of East Timorese displacement and resettlement in West Timor is the way sacrifice is made to renew life or ensure future wellbeing (Howell 1996: 24). Understanding Boni's story of sacrifice, however, also means examining sacrifice beyond the realm of ritual. This 'other side of sacrifice', as Mayblin and Course (2014: 313) put it, has a diverse meaning that 'emerges beyond the altar and becomes embedded in the full gamut of social life'.

Sacrifice and national belonging

Moving beyond religious and ritual processes, studies of refugee communities have demonstrated the significant role of stories of sacrifice in refugees' efforts to maintain attachment to their country of origin. Among Burundian refugees, for example, this effort is elaborated in the form of 'mythico-history', in which 'the refugee camp had become both the spatial and the politico-symbolic site for imagining a moral and political community' (Malkki 1995: 16). By living in a refugee camp, the Burundians engaged in a purification process to maintain their distinctive identity as one 'people' and keep alive the relationship with their homeland. Malkki's analysis shows how national identity is often constructed through the narrative of suffering.

Stories of popular suffering and sacrifice are certainly not distinct to Burundians. Such a narrative is commonly used to foster national identity in post-conflict societies. In Indonesia, for instance, popular suffering has been associated with the struggle for independence, and national identity is often reinforced through the idiom of 'the land where blood has spilled' (*tanah tumpah darah*) (Robinson 2014: 13). East Timorese national identity has also been associated with and contested through people's suffering and sacrifice during the resistance struggle (see Kent 2016). And, with their diverse and complex experiences during the occupation, sacrifice comes in many forms.

Among the Mambai people in Aileu district, for instance, sacrifice has been associated with unpaid wages, exemplified by former Falintil guerillas and civilians who risked their lives in the clandestine resistance and who gained few opportunities or benefits for themselves in the new nation-state (Traube 2007: 10–22). In Dili, Aitarak Laran people have also used their suffering during the resistance in their claim for the state-owned land on which they are residing (Stead 2015: 84). Stories of suffering have been used by other East Timorese groups to rebuild their lives after their violent and traumatic past as well as to inform the identity and cohesion of their group (for the Idate people, see Bovensiepen 2009; McWilliam and Traube 2011; for the Meto people, see Sakti 2013). Perhaps these multiple idioms of sacrifice are what led Benedict Anderson (2001: 236) to argue that during the occupation, 'the Indonesian government was unable to incorporate East Timor imaginatively, in the broader, popular sense'. Yet, if the Indonesian Government was unable to imagine East Timor as part of its national community, how can we explain the situation of East Timorese like Boni and many others who left East Timor and decided to stay in West Timor following the 1999 referendum?

Separation as sacrifice

The day after our emotional conversation, I returned to Boni's house. He was happy to continue his story and admitted that after the brothers' separation at Larigutu, he tried unsuccessfully to understand the decision of his oldest brother to 'split up and sacrifice [*berkorban*] for a better future'. Having returned to his home village, in the late 1980s, Boni decided to join the Indonesian military as a civilian worker and was appointed to the military post in the neighbouring district of Viqueque.

Here, he also maintained regular contact with his military colleagues in Baucau, from where they received information about their military operations. He wanted to make sure he was informed if or when an update on his two brothers came through.

Despite his efforts, no information was received about his two brothers when Falintil guerillas were caught by the Indonesian military. After almost 20 years of separation, early one morning in 1996, a messenger rushed into Boni's barracks in Viqueque. He advised Boni that the military had just been successful in taking down some of the Falintil combatants from Baucau. Among these resistance fighters, there was one who had been shot and was now in the army hospital in Baucau. The captive had not said a word except for the name of his home village. Because the wounded captive shared his home village, Boni joined the messenger and headed to the hospital in Baucau:

> As a loyal combatant, he did not want to say a word. He looked at me suspiciously every time I came to visit him. He always said, 'You were sent by the Indonesians to dig information from me.' But I never gave up because when he acknowledged his home village, he must have known something about my two brothers. So I visited him in the hospital every day for four days before he started to respond. I remember my first question to him was about his family. He replied that he had nine siblings. It was common for East Timorese to have large families, so I asked about the location of his house. I did not expect his answer to be the house of my parents. I trembled. My hands were shaky and I had to grip the bedside as my heart was beating so fast. 'Is he really one of my brothers that I have missed for nearly 20 years?' I asked myself. Without waiting any further, I called out both names of my parents to him, which startled him. Then I mentioned the name of all of our brothers and finally I said: 'I am Boni, the youngest.' He did not believe what he had just heard. But then a gentle voice from behind me confirmed, 'Mario, he is Boni.' It was the voice of my oldest brother, José, who had just arrived. My brother Mario did not recognise me because he was 13 when we separated. But he certainly recognised our oldest brother, José, who approached the two of us and we hugged each another tightly. We all cried together. I did not realise that the nurses had been watching us from the beginning and they cried for us, too. Later, Mario advised us that our other brother, Joachim, had been killed [*gugur* = fallen] in a battle in Aitana close to Dili in 1986. He died a martyr for the family and the nation.

The reunion with Mario reunited Boni's family. But for Boni, it was also a reminder of José's last message in Larigutu. Because of Boni's employment in the Indonesian military, Mario was subsequently granted amnesty and released after his recovery—a happy fate other Falintil fighters did not share. Boni continued his work with the Indonesian military in Viqueque until late 1999. When the result of the referendum was announced, Boni decided to join the military evacuation and was again separated from his brothers and sisters. Yet, they knew their purpose remained the same: to secure the future of the family.

For Boni, national belonging is imagined as a passage of sacrifice that involves not only a strong narrative of separation, but also one of salvation. Boni's strong emphasis on separation and salvation represents a distinct feature of an imagined East Timorese community in West Timor. It is distinct because it barely recognises the Indonesian national struggle against the separatist movement. Nor does it support East Timor's national struggle and resistance against occupation. Sacrifice for the nation mediates these two opposing views and creates a consolidation of a sense of belonging that accommodates both Indonesia and East Timor. It does so by recognising the shared experience of many East Timorese who struggled to secure the future of their family and their society during the violent conflict.

Boni is not the only East Timorese who expressed his belonging in terms of separation and salvation. Between the late 1970s and early 1980s, when the Indonesian military intensified its operations in East Timor, many people had to make strategic separations to keep their family alive. A former member of the Indonesian military admitted to me:

> When Indonesia came in, some members of my family ran into the jungle and joined the resistance. But I decided to stay and join the Indonesian military. I did this so that I could save East Timorese when they were captured.

The decision of families to separate was widely unpopular among East Timorese, but knowing it could potentially sustain their future and that of their society, many East Timorese elected to split up.

The decision to separate is not a new response by East Timorese; it has been their effective survival strategy since colonial times. During the brutal military campaigns of the mid-nineteenth century, for example, a Portuguese officer reported that East Timorese gave them 'men for the war, but [also] as many or more to their allies' fighting against the

Portuguese (Gunn 1999: 168). This frustrated the Portuguese because the East Timorese from these opposing camps often engaged in combat, but, as the officer noted, their kinship relationships prevailed and 'when it comes to the point of fighting each other they fire into the air' (Gunn 1999: 168), thereby avoiding harming their kinsmen. A similar strategy was applied during the Japanese invasion in World War II. A former militiaman living in Atambua, near the border, told me his father:

> was among the Kemak group who smuggled the Australian Special Forces out of East Timor in the Second World War. But my adopted father [godfather] was among the Kemak people who fought alongside the Japanese troops against the Australians. If they did not do that, I would not have been here to talk to you right now.

The notion of separation and salvation offers important insights into East Timorese ideas of national belonging. Separation serves as a link to integrate East Timorese with Indonesia, while salvation reconnects them with East Timor. In this sense, East Timorese national belonging is imagined not as an Indonesian integrationist ideology or the secessionist idea of a resistance group. Rather, it emerges through the shared historical experience of sacrifice and a common desire to sustain their society. With such experience and desire, East Timorese in West Timor remain deeply attached to their origin places in East Timor while moving on with their lives in Indonesia.

Service as sacrifice

We have seen the forward-looking nature of national belonging and what East Timorese such as Boni have highlighted to be essentially a life renewal process. This national identity is what Hobsbawm (1990: 8) defines as a:

> dual phenomena, constructed especially from above, but which cannot be understood unless it is also analysed from below, that is, in terms of the assumptions, hopes, needs, longings and interest of ordinary people, which are not necessarily national and still less nationalist.

In this light, Radcliffe and Westwood (1996), in their discussion of nationalism in Latin America, argue that ordinary people actively remake the idea of the nation constructed from above. In the case of East Timorese in West Timor, this process is manifest in their distinct stories of sacrifice, which represent a sense of belonging that transcends state boundaries and confirms people's ongoing relatedness and continuity of life in East Timor.

The day after my meeting with Boni, I went to see Francisco Ximenes, who was also living in Naibonat camp. Boni addressed Francisco as *compadre* because Francisco is the godfather to one of Boni's children. For other East Timorese in Naibonat, Francisco is simply known as Sico. A former member of *Tropas*, the Portuguese colonial army, Sico's last assignment in East Timor was in the enclave of Oecussi. When Indonesia occupied East Timor and took over Oecussi, Sico and his fellow *Tropas* surrendered to the Indonesian army. 'My knowledge of the Indonesian language put me as the interpreter', said Sico as he recalled the event when the Indonesian Government, represented by governor El Tari of NTT, arrived in Pante Makasar to claim Oecussi in 1975. With their military experience, Sico and his fellow *Tropas* were incorporated into the Indonesian military and served in stations across East Timor during the occupation. 'Wherever I was appointed,' Sico said, 'my mission was always to serve the society.' And indeed, during his service in Manatuto, 'we built a church together with the community'. When he was removed to Ende on the neighbouring island of Flores, he helped build a mosque with the community there. After his service in Ende, Sico was appointed to serve with the Indonesian military in Baucau, his home district. During the period leading up to the 1999 referendum, Sico and other East Timorese in Baucau received news that the notorious Besi Merah Putih—a pro-Indonesia militia formed in Liquiçá district in early 1999—was planning to advance on Baucau.

Almost immediately, the commander of Baucau military station gathered Sico and other Indonesian military personnel for an emergency meeting. Sico said the Indonesian soldiers of East Timorese origin made it clear they did not want the militia in Baucau. He recalled saying in the meeting:

> They [Besi Merah Putih] were formed to commit violence against the community and we won't let that happen in Baucau. If they claim that they want to defend and keep the community safe, then what are our three established groups, Railakan, Saka and Sera, here for?

Railakan, Saka and Sera were three established militia that supported the operations of Indonesian special forces in East Timor. Members of these groups were mostly former Falintil guerillas from Baucau who had surrendered and then joined the Indonesian military. Their representatives were in the meeting and all declared their rejection of Besi Merah Putih's presence in Baucau.

With no outside militia groups in Baucau, order was maintained in the lead-up to the referendum. But this situation changed dramatically after the result was announced. Indonesia started to evacuate all Indonesian military personnel and their families to West Timor. Observing the chaotic situation in Baucau, Sico came to realise that Baguia, his home subdistrict 60 km east of Baucau, had been overlooked in the evacuation effort not only because of its remote location and difficult terrain, but also because the road passed through one of the strongholds of Falintil guerillas led by Lere Anan Timor. Sico therefore made an unpopular decision to head back to Baguia. As he recalled:

> In my mind, armed engagement was inevitable if the military station in Baguia was left behind. So, on the morning of 9 September, I borrowed a Mitsubishi T-120 pick-up truck, the official car of the head of the subdistrict, and headed to Baguia on my dangerous mission. But I had always maintained good relations with people from different political persuasions so when I arrived in Laga I went to the local church of Don Bosco parish and met my long-time spiritual friend, Father João de Deus Pires, SDB. I told Father João about my mission and asked for his support to advise Lere and his men to make way for us.

> I arrived in Baguia late in the afternoon and everyone was surprised that I had been able to make it through. In quick order, we had a convoy of seven fully loaded Hino army trucks and I led this evacuation of all the military personnel and families out of Baguia. Prior to our departure, I briefed everyone that I had coordinated the departure and had Lere's agreement to make way for us as long as we kept our weapons locked. However, 'If the Falintil stop us', I emphasised, 'let me firstly get down and negotiate. But, you should remain on full alert because if I raise my right thumb, then it is an order for you to open fire on everyone that I am talking to.'

Without interruption, the Baguia convoy arrived safely at the evacuation point in Laga about 10 pm. While the people were camped along the seashore, waiting to be evacuated by warship, Sico continued his journey and joined his extended family in Baucau. The next day, they took part in a massive air evacuation by Indonesian airforce Hercules carriers, which took them to Kupang. In early 2000, Sico sent his parents and relatives back to East Timor. A year later, he sent his oldest daughter, a midwife, to serve in Dili. He continued his military career in Kupang and served as the officer in charge of a military post on Rote Island for two years before returning to Kupang, where he joined his fellow East Timorese in Naibonat camp. Sico officially retired from the Indonesian army in 2004, but he decided to stay on in Naibonat camp and lead the East Timorese there.

In spite of his emphasis on serving the nation, what is striking about Sico's story is its similarity with Boni's. In their view, national belonging is not bounded by political ideology. Rather, it is understood as a shared desire to serve and create a better future for their community. This shared memory and intention to serve the nation are what keep Sico, Boni and many other East Timorese connected to East Timor although they are residing in West Timor. A Baucau elder in his 80s who once led the Railakan militia force explained the meaning of serving one's nation:

> Those new militia groups believed that killing your own people, burning their houses and destroying their properties was their service to the nation? I would say they were all stupid! Serving your nation is about ensuring the future of your society. We joined Indonesia simply for that reason, and you can see the result: Baucau was relatively peaceful during the referendum and, although many of us decided to remain in West Timor, we always had good relationships with our brothers and sisters in East Timor. I have visited East Timor 10 times since 1999 and enjoyed every single trip.

Viewing the nation as a future project embraces the experiences of other East Timorese striving to maintain peace and sustainability amid the political division and physical devastation of newly independent Timor-Leste. Although the 'sacrifice' of East Timorese resettled in West Timor tends to be overlooked in the mainstream historical narratives, this shared aspiration has been effective in explaining, in so many cases, why many East Timorese have reconciled their relationship with Timor-Leste while retaining their presence in West Timor.

Rewritten history of sacrifice

Idioms of sacrifice among East Timorese in West Timor can undoubtedly account for the significance of maintaining belonging to East Timor as well as Indonesia. According to Anderson (1983: 15–16), members of a nation cannot possibly meet and know every other member, but they are imagined through a sense of sharing and belonging to a common national community. This imagined community is constructed through print culture, including newspapers, popular novels and the imposition of a national language, among other things. The result is that 'the nation is always conceived as a deep, horizontal comradeship' Anderson (1983: 15–16). Indonesia recognises the significance of shared sacrifice in the formation of national belonging. Sacrifice in the Indonesian nationalist ideology derives from the Arabic term *watan*, which is translated in terms of the Indonesian idiom 'the land where blood has spilled' (*tanah tumpah darah*), which 'encodes the notion of a common unity through connections to the soil, and spilled blood connotes shared sacrifice' (Robinson 2014: 13). Here, Indonesian nationalists seek to cultivate Indonesia's struggle for independence to reinforce national unity.

This idea was taken further by Suharto's New Order regime during its attempts to incorporate East Timor within Indonesia. In 1992, the Directorate General of High School Education in the Indonesian Ministry of Culture and Education published a senior secondary school textbook entitled *The History of the East Timorese Struggle* (*Sejarah Perjuangan Rakyat Timor Timor*). The textbook claims the East Timorese spirit to free themselves from colonialists was initiated in 1959 in Viqueque and is evident in plans to carry out a rebellion at the end of that year. Support for the plan was strong and spread to Aileu, Same, Ermera, Baucau and other areas. Meetings were held to plan the rebellion. These meetings resolved that the rebellion would be initiated on 31 December 1959. To position East Timorese in the Indonesian nationalist ideology, the book describes how:

> the leaders and the people who were involved in the rebellion had to drape red and white ribbons [the colours of the Indonesian flag] around their necks and wear red and white insignia.

This is a significant point because it indicates that, since 1959, some East Timorese have been willing to 'integrate' with Indonesia, essentially legitimising the subsequent military occupation. To reconcile these events, the book ends on a theme of sacrifice by outlining the fate of the leaders of the rebellion, who were eventually 'sent into off-shore prison exile in Angola, then a Portuguese colony in Africa'.[1]

Three elements of Indonesian nationalist ideology are embedded in this account of the East Timorese rebellion in Viqueque: the notion of struggle against colonisation, the use of the Indonesian nationalist symbols of 'Red and White' and the sacrifice of East Timorese rebels. Through this

1 For a comparative perspective, see Atkinson (2003).

account, the New Order regime identified the 1959 Viqueque rebellion as an early attempt by the East Timorese to integrate with Indonesia (Chamberlain 2007: 55; Gunter 2007: 35). Indeed, many East Timorese Naueti speakers from Viqueque (particularly Uato Lari and Uato Carbao subdistricts), now resettled in West Timor, returned to this version of 'history' when I asked them about their decision to remain in Indonesia.

But rather than emphasising the fictional Indonesian narrative of rebellion supporter Antonio Metan's heroic effort to raise the red and white flag in Uato Lari, these other accounts put greater stress on the loss of loved ones. For example, one elder from Uato Carbao told me: 'Our family was killed by the Portuguese in 1959 although they had nothing to do with the rebellion.' This suggests that some East Timorese, particularly from Uato Lari and Uato Carbao, conceive of their belonging to Indonesia in different terms. Their image of 'one people' is not based on the utilisation of Indonesian nationalist symbols from the 1959 revolt. Rather, it is shaped by the sacrifice of their families during Portuguese colonisation—a sacrifice they were forced to make again during the 1975 political upheaval when their family members who supported the politics of integration were killed by Fretilin supporters.

When the Indonesian military assumed control over most of East Timor in 1978, many East Timorese from Uato Lari and Uato Carbao claimed the reward of their sacrifice by assuming social, political and economic privileges from the Indonesian administration. The first head of the subdistrict (*camat*) of Uato Lari appointed by the Indonesian Government, for instance, was the son of Antonio Metan (Gunter 2007: 36). In 1999, these people tried to maintain their political alignment with Indonesia and left their homeland. Currently, there are about 1,500 Naueti speakers residing in West Timor.

Displacement and resettlement in West Timor have amplified their ideology of shared sacrifice, which includes their brothers and sisters still living in Timor-Leste. Furthermore, they view themselves as continuing to make sacrifices because they are living outside the land of their ancestors. For some, this sacrifice has been compensated for by the continuation of their careers in the Indonesian military or as civil servants, which will eventually entitle them to a government pension. For others, however, it seems a return to be reunited with their ancestors in Timor-Leste will be the ultimate reward.

Silence as sacrifice

Among East Timorese such as Boni, Sico and other active and retired army personnel, it is common to hear narratives of sacrifice that are directed towards reconciliation and future aspirations. However, in East Timor's long and complex military occupation and resistance struggle, diverse narratives of sacrifice are inevitably at work. For some East Timorese, particularly former militiamen, sacrifice is not about reconciliation, but about reconstruction of their identity. For them, sacrifice is not defined by whether people remain in West Timor or return to Timor-Leste. It is, rather, about maintaining silence in post-referendum and politically reformed Indonesia. Silence is a crucial marker of identity among the East Timorese. Culturally, silence is associated with the sacred (*lulik*) and is therefore understood as a source of potency (Therik 2004; Bovensiepen 2014: 121). In the political realm, this source of potency translates as an act of denial or partial recognition of the violence and human rights violations in East Timor during the occupation and, in particular, during and after the 1999 referendum.

East Timorese militia groups allegedly involved in such crimes choose to exclude the Indonesian military as the sponsor of their atrocities. This silence is considered a sacrifice because the East Timorese position themselves as a substitute for the Indonesian military. This view creates the conditions for what Anderson (1983: 44) has referred to as 'purity through fatality', where the national imagination is constructed through participation in collective sacrifice, regardless of its consequences.

Some former militiamen told me they are purely Indonesian because 'although we were not part of the Indonesian struggle to gain independence, we were part of the struggle to defend that independence by defending Indonesia's interest'. Joining pro-Indonesia militia was one such sacrifice. More importantly, it was in the aftermath of militia activity—involving killings and destruction in East Timor—that the sacrifice of the former militiamen was put to the test. By remaining silent about their actions during and after the referendum, these former pro-Indonesia militiamen claim they are continuing to defend Indonesia's national interest. Silence here has a sacrificial value because it is performed for a national cause. And, in so doing, the hope is to confirm the militiamen's imagined belonging within the Indonesian nation-state.

The rhetoric and reciprocity of sacrifice

Staying silent has transformed former militiamen into loyal nationalists, but such a transformation can only be maintained as long as there is some compensation for their suffering. When compensation fails, the flipside of silence emerges: public rhetoric. This is clearly exemplified by former members of the Mahidi (*Mati Hidup dengan Indonesia*), a militia group formed in Ainaro subdistrict in Cassa, currently living in Malaka district near the southern border of Cova Lima. In late 2011, these predominantly Bunaq speakers broke their long silence by drafting an open letter to more than 30 relevant parties, including the Pope, the presidents of Indonesia and Timor-Leste, the UN Secretary-General and the President of the United States.[2] The 50-page document began with the public rhetoric of their version of history. Unlike the Naueti speakers of Viqueque, however, the Bunaq speakers' version omitted the 1959 rebellion and started instead with the political situation in 1975.

Another significant difference was the language they used to describe events. Rather than seeing Indonesia's action in East Timor as integration, it was framed as invasion and annexation—idioms considered taboo by supporters of Indonesia. The notion of sacrifice was mentioned frequently in relation to repressive military operations, the exclusion of East Timorese and appointment of people from other parts of Indonesia to lead military and government departments, as well as control of economic resources by the military. The narrative moved on to describe the 1999 referendum that led these people to become displaced to West Timor. Here, the language of sacrifice was expressed through the sentiment of exclusion from humanitarian and development assistance, disputes with local communities and the longing to reunite with their families in East Timor.

The public rhetoric contained in the letter took ideas of sacrifice in a different direction from previous narratives. Sacrifice, according to the former Mahidi group, was invested with the idea of reciprocity. Indeed, as explained to me by one of the main authors of the letter, Indonesia had broken its promise to secure the lives of former Mahidi militia in West

---

2   One of the main authors of the letter told me: 'If God had a residential address, He would certainly be included in the list of recipients.'

Timor. 'They promised to give us houses and secure our livelihoods, but did otherwise by letting us stay in camps and working on local people's land,' he stated.

Former members of the Mahidi group living in West Timor spoke with a united voice in telling their narrative of sacrifice and articulating their expectation that the Indonesian Government would reward them. And they were not alone in this view. Other former members of militia groups have expressed the view that 'the Indonesian military encouraged us to love the nation [*cinta tanah air*],[3] but how can we maintain our love for this nation when there is no land [for us] and no water to drink?' This clearly suggests the narrative of sacrifice is about not just commemoration, but also remuneration. This cultural idea of reciprocity offers a lens through which to understand the exchange value of sacrifice. This different understanding of sacrifice articulated by the Mahidi group was a consequence of growing feelings of abandonment felt by some East Timorese in response to what they perceived as their unreciprocated patriotic service to Indonesia.

Songs of sacrifice

Having concentrated my fieldwork around the border area, in May 2013, I was invited by Boni and Sico to return to Naibonat camp and observe a gathering between the provincial army commander (*Komandan Korem 161 Wirasakti*) and active and retired army personnel of East Timorese origin. As an active member of the Indonesian army, Boni was assigned to liaise with retired East Timorese personnel. Sico, as an elder of Naibonat camp, was appointed to host the event. The collaboration of Boni and Sico resulted in a novel gathering in the camp that day. Along the narrow dirt track to the camp, a line of woven palm leaves tied to the wooden fence provided a decorative entrance. It was a decoration similar to that used in East Timorese marriage exchange rituals when the wife-takers are welcomed by the bridal affinal group.

A shower of rain the previous day had freshened the appearance of the camp. Around the chapel, where the event was going to take place, a group of East Timorese women dressed in their finest pink *kebaya* lined up with

---

3   In Indonesian, 'homeland' is expressed as the composite phrase *tanah* + *air*, which literally means 'land and water'.

their small drums around their arms, set to perform the *Likurai* dance. About 10 am, the brigadier general arrived and the women welcomed him with their drums, singing:

> Welcome to the camp, Provincial Military Commander
> We usher you with joy and pride
> You come to serve the nation
> We accept you with pure heart
> We have sacrificed our body and soul
> For the Red and White
> We have sacrificed our body and soul
> For the Red and White

As they ushered him to the chapel, the women repeated the chorus:

> We have sacrificed our body and soul
> For the Red and White
> We have sacrificed our body and soul
> For the Red and White.

Plate 6.1 East Timorese women in Naibonat camp prepare to usher the provincial military commander into the chapel

Source: Andrey Damaledo.

Plate 6.2 Boni (wearing tie) and his big family in Naibonat, Kupang district
Source: Bonifacio Ximenes.

The so-called social communication event was attended by hundreds of active and retired soldiers of East Timorese origin, so it was not surprising the theme of sacrifice immediately resonated. The factor of occupation—working within the Indonesian army—provided a framework that enabled East Timorese to recall their memories of sacrifice. Another factor was age. Narratives of sacrifice are popular among the older generation of East Timorese because they have experienced different struggles during the different periods of colonisation and occupation. But what surprised me was the statement Sico made when given a chance to speak. He stood and declared that the East Timorese sacrifice was not yet over. After receiving a round of applause from the audience, he continued, stating that the East Timorese presence in West Timor demonstrated that their continued sacrifice for the nation and recent history should not be forgotten by Indonesia. In other words, Sico implied that the presence of East Timorese in West Timor should be understood as a living historical legacy for Indonesia.

Here the political nature of East Timorese sacrifice is considered in material form. The Indonesian national memory of East Timor has been commemorated most notably at the Seroja Cemetery—a specific monument—which remembers the soldiers who fell during the invasion and occupation.[4] For many East Timorese, Seroja commemorates the

---

4   Seroja Cemetery is in Atambua, West Timor, near the current airport.

past. Their future lies in their continuing presence in West Timor and their memorial materialises not in built form, but in the existentiality of collective individuals. As Sico explained to me after the event: 'We hope our sacrifices presented a meaningful lesson for Indonesia to deal with its citizens.'

Sico was referring to the state's violent responses to issues of separation and disintegration in contemporary Indonesia. On other occasions, many East Timorese often commented, 'We are here, look at us', in response to continued oppression of citizens in other parts of Indonesia. From this perspective, the presence of East Timorese in West Timor constitutes a living historical monument—one that symbolically displays their national belonging in two interrelated ways. First, as a reminder that military occupation in East Timor forced many people to be separated from their families and homeland. Second, and introspectively, a lesson that repressive military operations are not effective in bringing peace to society.

Conclusion

The discussion thus far suggests there are 'multiple sides of sacrifice' (Lambek 2014: 432) among East Timorese in West Timor. But whether emphasising separation, service, silence, reciprocity or commemoration, these ideas share a common underlying inspiration—namely, the sustainability of East Timorese society. For this reason, let me draw three points by way of a conclusion. First and foremost are the related East Timorese concepts of a cultural code of reciprocity and public rhetoric of sacrifice. It is clear that sacrifice is understood as an exchange process and, therefore, when it is performed for a national cause, it must be rewarded. This understanding mirrors the policy of compensation and reward that has been implemented in Timor-Leste towards former resistance fighters (veterans).[5] In Indonesia, these concepts should not be underestimated, in part, because they are in line with contemporary Indonesian nationalist ideas of defending the nation (*Bela Negara*). If an imagined Indonesia is based on a simplistic idea of defending the nation regardless, it would seem that East Timorese rhetoric of sacrifice remains influential and their claims for compensation remain valid for as long as this takes.

---

5   For further discussion of this compensation policy in Timor-Leste, see Wallis (2013: 143).

The second point is related to the idea of reconciliation. Sacrifice among East Timorese in West Timor is reconciliatory in nature, but the idea of reconciliation is not about forgiving and forgetting. It is about forgiving and learning to make sure that future generations will not suffer similar consequences. This learning process applies to both Indonesia and Timor-Leste. For Indonesia, the existence of East Timorese in West Timor demonstrates that repressive military responses towards issues of secession across Indonesia will not be effective in bringing about a peaceful and just society. Instead, such repressive responses lead to a breakdown in family relationships and cause long-term suffering for the whole society. For Timor-Leste, their common enemy—the so-called pro-autonomy East Timorese—now remain in West Timor. Although the possibility of return still exists, most have decided to remain in West Timor and consider their separation from their homeland as a kind of sacrifice. In so doing, they hope people in Timor-Leste are no longer focused on the past. Rather, they should be united towards the future, which means joining efforts to combat their new common enemies: poverty and inequality.

The final point I want to make is that by asserting their sacrifice, East Timorese in West Timor mediate the divisive political ideologies and obscure state boundaries by reintegrating all East Timorese into an imagined shared future project.[6] The success of such a project is yet to be determined, but evidence so far suggests it is proceeding along the right path. Many East Timorese in Timor-Leste have sent their children to be looked after by their own parents (the children's grandparents) who now live in West Timor. With the role of carer comes the transmission of memories. But, as I have pointed out, the violent and dark past is now being internalised by the grandparents. In its place they have discovered a new narrative—one that is still based on sacrifice but that will bring a better future for all East Timorese regardless of their political allegiance.

For East Timorese, a shared, better future is not possible without reproduction. 'We are separated but we need to continue to reproduce so there will be East Timorese everywhere' is a common answer I received whenever querying the large number of children in East Timorese families. A baby boom is common in many post-conflict societies; however, the emphasis on future East Timorese population expansion also points to a process of intergenerational memory transmission. The retired solders

---

6   For a comparative perspective, see Anderson (1999).

and older generation of East Timorese in West Timor seem to have isolated their dark and violent past within themselves and now transmit a shared desire for reconciliation and a brighter future to the younger generation. As many East Timorese elders said to me:

> We [the old generation] were 'conflict people' and lived in the past. The future is in our children. They had nothing to do with the conflict and they are the future of all East Timorese.

This idea of reproduction helps to explain why East Timorese representatives from both sides of the border are present at every life-cycle ritual and celebration. In mid-September 2013, Boni invited me to his daughter's wedding. He insisted I come because he wanted to present me with something special. As someone born and raised almost entirely in West Timor, I had attended many wedding parties, but that of Boni's daughter was one of the largest in terms of people, food and general excitement. These elements, however, were not what Boni wanted me to witness. Rather, he wanted me to understand that this wedding was not merely a life-cycle celebration; it was another fruit of the stories of sacrifice and separation he had recounted to me almost a year before. And nobody could understand his feelings better than his older brother José, who came from Baucau to attend the wedding.

Throughout the wedding ceremony and celebration, Boni shared his seat with his older brother and the tears running down Boni's face during the family photo session spoke of their shared sacrifice and aspirations. In early 2018, Boni contacted me about his youngest daughter's university graduation. Big brother José came again from Baucau and joined Boni to witness his daughter walking to the stage, marking the emergence of a highly educated generation within their family. What is clear from Boni, and by extension many East Timorese who have opted to live in West Timor, is that their decision to join Indonesia was one made not just to save themselves, but also to save their families and, beyond that, the future of East Timorese society.

Plate 6.3 Francisco (Sico) Ximenes (in brown *batik* shirt) attends Boni's daughter's graduation party

Source: Bonifacio Ximenes.

Plate 6.4 Boni celebrates his daughter's graduation

Source: Bonifacio Ximenes.

7

The struggle continues

If the cultural elements of sacrifice and popular suffering provide insights into an East Timorese sense of belonging that spans national boundaries, it is through the dynamics of their political mobilisation that their belonging and citizenship are performed. By perform, I am not referring to an individual action. Rather, my focus is on East Timorese collective action manifest in community and political associations and activism. I am interested in the way this collective action has rebuilt and transformed East Timorese political activities through long-term engagement in the complex politics of occupation, migration and democratisation.

Studies of political activities among conflict-affected communities show that institutions in the host country provide opportunities for refugees or IDPs to channel their political interests. Scholars (Tarrow 1996: 54) interpret the host institution as a 'political opportunity structure', which they define as a 'consistent—but not necessarily formal, permanent, or national—signal to social or political actors which either encourages or discourages them to use their internal resources to form social movements'. According to this view, the political activities of immigrants or newcomers tend to grow when the state's political system provides avenues for the free expression of dissenting opinions. These opportunities, however, often place protesters in a reactionary position against government policies.

In this chapter, I explore the character of East Timorese political mobilisation, and the ways in which Indonesian citizenship has been exercised in response. East Timorese in West Timor are often considered demanding and sometimes ungrateful and stubborn citizens because they continue to demand government assistance despite the ongoing housing and livelihood projects delivered to them since their chaotic arrival in late 1999. I challenge this assumption by examining East Timorese political mobilisation to shed light on how they have transformed the political landscape in contemporary Indonesia. To explain the changing nature of their civic participation, I draw on Engin Isin's (2009: 380) idea of an 'activist citizenship', which goes beyond participation in political processes to explicit engagement in resistance and oppositional work to create 'a break, a rupture and a difference'. For the East Timorese in West Timor, 'making a break' does not refer to secessionist activity or resistance against the nation-state. Rather, it is directed to a separation of the past from a vision of future renewal.

It has been widely recognised that pro-Indonesia East Timorese associations were formed and directed by the Indonesian military to demonstrate their allegiance to Indonesia during the occupation and referendum. But, on their arrival in West Timor, these people changed their political direction and mobilised around a new agenda of struggle to make the state more accountable to its citizens. Many have said to me, 'Our struggle continues but in a different direction now'. This narrative of change from collaborating with to challenging the state makes East Timorese political mobilisation distinctly potent. Once we see the ongoing demands of East Timorese for state responsibility as more than simply the action of stubborn citizens, we can consider citizenship practice in a new light. The confrontational character of East Timorese public rallies and demonstrations then becomes not so much an interruption to service delivery as a catalyst for remedial policy and accountability. As my focus is restricted to East Timorese politics within Indonesia, I will not discuss political unions and associations formed during the Portuguese decolonisation process in East Timor. Rather, my point of departure is the political change following the Indonesian invasion and occupation. In this section, I situate East Timorese associational life in the context of Indonesian politics during the New Order regime. The section discusses continuity and change within East Timorese associations and how these associations were mobilised for political activity and active citizenship. Beyond this, I discuss the notion of citizens' struggle and the way East Timorese transformed their rights as citizens after they migrated to West Timor. I will then move on to explore East Timorese alliances with established Indonesian associations. The final part of the chapter discusses the changing perspective of citizen activism.

Era of political reticence

As soon as the Indonesian military invaded and occupied East Timor, radical changes were instituted, including severe restrictions on political activities. Although Indonesia's constitution guarantees citizens' the right and freedom to associate, the New Order regime imposed the so-called *organicism* ideology, uniting state and society in an organic form. This ideology, combined with the idea of the 'floating mass' (*massa mengambang*), allowed Indonesian citizens to express their political rights in elections every five years, but did not permit oppositional political activities in the intervening period (Beittinger-Lee 2009: 43–4; Fernandes 2011: 25). As a result, citizens' associations had to comply with government categorisations and function in accordance with government edicts. Associations that did not comply were dissolved, through coercive measures if necessary. Although some associations such as NGOs remained active during the 1970s and 1980s, their interests were directed mainly towards community development. A focus on active citizenship and political mobilisation was not permitted (Acciaioli 2001: 17; Beard 2003: 22).

In East Timor, throughout the late 1970s and early 1980s, political associations, unions and political parties formed during the decolonisation process were dissolved and their activities integrated into three mainstream Indonesian political parties, the Party of the Functional Groups (Golongan Karya, or Golkar), the Indonesian Democratic Party (Partai Demokrasi Indonesia, or PDI) and the United Development Party (Partai Persatuan Pembangunan, or PPP). Indonesia's coercive attempts to curb East Timorese political activities were not limited to political parties. East Timorese traditional alliance structures were also coopted and manipulated for the purpose of integration within the unitary state of Indonesia. Just as had occurred under the Portuguese, the former *dato* and *liurai* who were aligned with Indonesia were installed as official leaders of administrative units in the village (*desa*), subdistrict (*kecamatan*) and district (*kabupaten*). Others served in the Indonesian military, police force and government offices. Their followers were recruited by the Indonesian military and trained to function as village-based vigilantes (known as Babinsa or Hansip) or armed paramilitary groups (Perlawanan Rakyat-Wanra and Rakyat Terlatih-Ratih). Formation of vigilante groups was a common practice across Indonesia and was known as the 'universal people's security system' (*Sistem Pertahanan Keamanan Rakyat Semesta*), but it was subject to greater intensification in East Timor than elsewhere and formed up to the village level.

Regardless of such government restrictions on association, East Timorese traditional alliances remained active and functioned in a clandestine way to support the resistance movement. In March 1981, defeated and near-extinguished Fretilin supporters and Falintil guerillas consolidated their organisation and established the Revolutionary Council of National Resistance (Conselho Revolucionário de Resistência Nacional, or CRRN) with Xanana Gusmão as their president and the commander in chief of Falintil. The CRRN linked armed guerilla activities in the mountainous areas with clandestine activities in residential areas and operated as a shadow opposition to the Indonesian-installed administrative structure. East Timorese kinship alliances were utilised to develop a network of resistance that spanned the occupied territory, with each village possessing a 'nucleus of popular resistance' (Núcleos de Resistência, or Nurep) and every hamlet a community cell (Célular da Comunidade, or Celcom) (McWilliam 2005: 35).

In 1985, the Indonesian Government enacted Law No. 8 on Civic Organisations, which forced all civic associations to accept the state's ideology of *Pancasila* ('five principles')[1] as their sole foundation and to adopt it in their statutes. This law incorporated community associations within state functions and directed their activities in accordance with state interests. In East Timor, such associations included the Union of Military Wives (Persatuan Istri Tentara), which ran a maternity clinic in the Dili neighbourhood of Colmera, and the Union of Public Servants' Wives (Dharma Wanita), focused on family welfare activities. The regime also worked with the East Timorese Students and Youth Association, which organised sports and youth events, and the Indonesia-wide youth Scout movement. Village shadow organisations such as Nurep and Celcom, regardless of their fragmentation, were classified as prohibited organisations (*organisasi terlarang*) as they were considered agents of resistance. This labelling legitimated Indonesian military efforts to curtail Nurep and Celcom activities.[2]

---

1   The five principles of *Pancasila*, as outlined in the Indonesian constitution, are: belief in one God, just and civilised humanity, Indonesian unity, democracy under the wise guidance of representative consultations and social justice for all Indonesians.

2   In spite of the state's effort to prohibit organisations, Nurep cells, which were mostly 'motivated by family ties' (Budiardjo and Liong 1984: 179), continued to grow—reaching 1,700 cells across East Timor (Cristalis 2002: 57). In Indonesia, parallel growth occurred in the establishment of NGOs (Beittinger-Lee 2009: 64).

Until the mid-1980s, almost all East Timorese associations were formed inside East Timor. Many solidarity groups and movements existed overseas, but none was yet established in other parts of Indonesia.[3] It was in June 1988 that a group of nine East Timorese students in Bali formed a student association under the banner of the National Resistance of East Timorese Students (Renetil). Clandestine Renetil cells later formed in various cities in Java (Bexley 2009). On 1 November 1988, president Suharto visited Dili to open the Indonesian National Assembly of the Youth Scout Organisation and addressed delegates from across Indonesia on the importance of youth participation in national development. The next day, the president inaugurated major construction projects and declared that development in East Timor had moved in step with that in other Indonesian territories. On his return to Jakarta, Suharto issued Presidential Decree No. 62 to lift travel restrictions and open East Timor to foreign visitors. This not only opened East Timor to foreign observers, but also provided an opportunity for greater political mobilisation.[4]

Era of political openness

The late 1980s were also marked by a growing demand for political reform and democratisation in other parts of Indonesia. 'Magazines, newspapers, seminars, public meetings and television talk shows dealt almost incessantly with topics such as democracy and the 1945 Constitution, democracy and Indonesian culture, and democracy and globalisation' (Bourchier and Hadiz 2003: 185). President Suharto recognised the mounting debates in his state address to commemorate 44 years of independence. He said:

> [B]oth in Indonesia and in the world more generally, we are witnessing the end of an era that began in 1945 with the end of the Second World War. As the twenty-first century approaches, we are entering a new era in the history of human kind; new perspectives, new aspirations, and new forces are emerging everywhere … let us regard the recent voicing of political proposals and aspirations with calm hearts, clear heads and a great feeling of responsibility. (Cited in Bourchier and Hadiz 2003: 192–3)

---

3   For a discussion of solidarity movements overseas, see Fernandes (2011: 91–100).
4   At the time this policy of opening up East Timor was implemented, the resistance organisation CRRN underwent structural changes, and changed its name, first, to the National Council of Maubere Resistance and, later, to the National Council of Timorese Resistance.

Exactly one year later, and also at independence commemorations, the president reflected: '[S]ome time ago I stressed that we did not have to worry too much about the diversity of viewpoints and opinions in society.' Having considered the mounting demands for democratisation, Suharto said:

> [D]emocracy indeed requires a lot of consultation, discussion, exchanges of views and dialogue, both between the government and the society and between various groups in society. We should see differences of opinion as the very source of life's dynamism. (Cited in Bourchier and Hadiz 2003: 195)

With this clear signal of political openness (*keterbukaan*) in Indonesia, more dissenting groups emerged to express their critical views of the regime (Bourchier and Hadiz 2003: 192; Beittinger-Lee 2009: 65). This situation resonated in East Timor, with more frequent mass mobilisations, student rallies and peaceful demonstrations. Increasing numbers of youth and student associations were formed to organise these efforts,[5] which reached a crisis in November 1991 when the Indonesian military opened fire on East Timorese students participating in a funeral march at the Santa Cruz Cemetery in Dili. Hundreds of participants were shot and killed, and the massacre was broadcast around the world. The events shattered Indonesian assurances about the situation in East Timor and encouraged the formation of solidarity groups around the world and also within Indonesia.[6]

To counter the growth in clandestine activities, in 1995, the Indonesian military stepped up their counter-resistance efforts by forming East Timorese youth associations (which were in fact militias) called Young Guards Upholding Integration (Garda Muda Penegak Integrasi, or Garda Paksi). Members of Garda Paksi 'appeared to be drawn largely from

---

5   In the early 1990s, such organisations included the East Timor Catholic Youth Organisation (Organização da Juventude Catolica de Timor-Leste, or OJECTIL), which later became the Organisation for Youth and Students of Timor-Leste (Organização de Jovens e Estudantes de Timor-Leste, or OJETIL); the Always United Front of Timor (Frente Iha Timor Unidos Nafatin, or FITUN); and the Popular Organisation of East Timorese Women (Organização Popular Juventude Lorico Ass'wain Timor-Leste, or OPJLATIL).
6   Within East Timor, these associations included: OPJLATIL; Movimento Buka Dalan Foun (MOBUDAN); the Apodeti Youth Union (Persatuan Pemuda Apodeti, or PPA); the Front of East Timorese Students (Frente Clandestina Estudantil de Timor Leste, or FECLETIL); the Sacred Family (Sagrada Familia); and the Association of Anti-Integration Youths and Students (Himpunan Pemuda, Pelajar, dan Mahasiswa Anti-Integrasi, or HPPMAI) (see Nicholson 2001; Babo-Soares 2003; Leach 2012). More specific organisations, such as the East Timorese Human Rights and Legal Aid Foundation (Yayasan HAK), were formed in 1994.

unemployed East Timorese youth' and their main role was 'to infiltrate the underground resistance and provoke disturbances among East Timorese' (Robinson 2010: 75–6).

In the late 1990s, after the resignation of president Suharto and the process of political reforms leading up to the East Timor referendum, the Indonesian military-backed Garda Paksi groups were transformed into fully fledged militia groups called the Integration Fighters Force (Pasukan Pejuang Integrasi, or PPI), which organised intimidation and extrajudicial killings of pro-independence supporters. Other Indonesian supporters were integrated into three additional groups: East Timor People's Front (Barisan Rakyat Timor-Timur, BRTT), Forum for Unity, Democracy and Justice (Forum Persatuan, Demokrasi dan Keadilan, or FPDK) and the Timorese Alliance (Aliansi Orsospol Pendukung Otonomi).[7]

An era of political opportunity

On 23 June 1999, with referendum day approaching, the East Timorese political groups in favour of the option of special autonomy within Indonesia came together as the United Front for East Timor Autonomy (Front Persatuan Pendukung Otonomi, or UNIF). When the result of the referendum—rejection of continued autonomy within Indonesia in favour of independence—was announced, members of the four factions making up UNIF were displaced into West Timor. But as early as January 2000, UNIF leaders gathered in Kupang for three days of discussion— and dispute (the conference venue was moved three times). The '*biti bot Timoris*' (lit., 'Timorese large mat') congress agreed to dissolve UNIF and its four foundational organisations. In response, UNIF members formed a new organisation, called Union East Timorese in Indonesia (Uni Timor Aswain, or UNTAS).

The transformation of UNIF into UNTAS was arguably the most ambitious political project of the East Timorese in West Timor. Two striking features of the UNTAS manifesto distinguished it from previous East Timorese associations. First, its rejection of the referendum result clearly indicated that it had been formed to deal with political issues not

---

7   During this period, another resistance association formed under the banner of the Student Solidarity Council was their organisation wing, called the Young Women's Group of East Timor (Grupu Feto Foin Sa'e Timor Lorosa'e, or GFFTL).

only in the homeland (East Timor) and the receiving society (Indonesia), but also at an international level (at the United Nations). Second, it suggested that East Timorese who previously supported Indonesia had started to express dissenting opinions towards the state that formed them.

The Indonesian Government, however, did not buy into UNTAS's demands. Instead, president Abdurrahman Wahid, during a visit to Dili, acknowledged the result of the referendum—a move that was followed by formal recognition in the Indonesian national parliament. The Indonesian military also dissolved vigilante groups formed during the occupation and referendum and confiscated their weapons. Without the support of the Indonesian Government, UNTAS's political activism lasted only until late 2000.

The departure of UNTAS from the political stage resulted in the formation of a growing number of new East Timorese associations.[8] An attempt to crowd out these associations occurred in 2005 when the Indonesian Government announced the end of humanitarian and development assistance for displaced East Timorese.[9] Again, however, more associations emerged in response.[10] Since 2000, more than 10 East Timorese associations have formed in West Timor to represent their interests. Some were established to bring together people from the same origin in East Timor, while others pursued social welfare, human rights and social justice issues. Regardless of their seemingly fragmented relations, all associations acknowledged that they had grown out of UNTAS. In 2010, the younger generation of these East Timorese manoeuvred to organise a congress to wrest the leadership of UNTAS from the older generation. The latter responded by deeming this plan illegal, reporting it to the

---

8   In subsequent years, various new groups emerged to represent the voices of East Timorese in West Timor, such as the National Committee of East Timor Political Victims (Komite Nasional Korban Politik Timor Timur, or KOKPIT); Front of Indonesia Defenders (Front Pembela Bangsa Indonesia, FPBI); Front of Red and White Defenders (Front Pembela Merah Putih); East Timorese Community Association (Masyarakat Komunitas Timor Timur, or Makasti); and the Union of Displaced East Timorese (Persatuan Pengungsi Timor Timur). These associations, however, did not have clear associational platforms and faded away with time. Only KOKPIT remains active.

9   The theory of crowding out is inspired by de Tocqueville's classic work *Democracy in America* (1835–40). In this view, state intervention acts in opposition to community organisations and consequently works to undermine it (for a discussion of this theory in the context of immigrant organisations, see Bloemraad 2005; Caponio 2005; Hooghe 2005).

10   The following year, various associations, including the Atsabe Family Union (Himpunan Keluarga Atsabe, or Hikbat), the Association for the Protection of Indonesian Timorese Community (Lembaga Perlindungan Masyarakat Timor Indonesia, or LPMTI), the Forum for the Defenders of Justice (Forum Pembela Keadilan, or FPK), the Baucau Indonesia Union (Persehatian Oan Timor Baucau Indonesia, or POTIBI) and the Humanitarian Forum, emerged to represent East Timorese in West Timor.

police and asking the authorities to dissolve it. The congress went ahead and eventually elected a leader from the younger generation, signalling an end to the monopoly of authority by the older representatives.

Plate 7.1 Banner for Arnaldo Tavares, the chief of UNTAS in Belu district
Source: Andrey Damaledo.

The first political mobilisation of the younger generation saw them reclaim the political mission of UNTAS and renew their focus on social and welfare issues affecting East Timorese. This contrasted with the agenda of the older generation, who had viewed UNTAS as a forum for East Timorese solidarity and communitarianism. Since 2010, East Timorese political mobilisation and demonstrations have been represented by the younger generation of UNTAS. In late January 2013, I was invited to be an observer in the annual working assembly of UNTAS in Kupang. During his opening address to the assembly, notorious former militia leader Eurico Guterres, the chief of UNTAS, declared that 'UNTAS [was] a *house* that united all East Timorese in Indonesia as one family'. He indicated that the UNTAS assembly was a symbolic representation of all East Timorese associations that had transformed their citizenship practices in contemporary Indonesia. In late January 2017, I attended the inauguration of UNTAS's central committee in Kupang. Guterres retained his position as UNTAS's top leader. However, this time, I noted significant differences with the congress I had attended four years earlier. There were more politicians from Indonesian mainstream political parties attending the event, including top Indonesian politicians from Jakarta. Guterres also changed his tone from an inward-looking plea for unity to an outward-looking appeal for more government attention to East Timorese civic engagement and their struggle to perform their citizenship in Indonesia.

Integrating mainstream political parties

For the East Timorese, adapting their civic engagement to contemporary Indonesia meant integration into Indonesian mainstream politics. When I asked a senior East Timorese politician about this, he replied:

> Having an association like UNTAS is great, but in order to make it effective we also have to become active members of Indonesian political parties and play the game of governance, decision-making and resource allocation. By doing so, we can sustain our struggle, and our voices and demands will be heard.

The process of mainstreaming politics began as early as mid-2003 in the lead-up to the 2004 Indonesian general election. During this period, East Timorese politicians began to consolidate and mobilise their networks within Indonesian mainstream political parties.

This tactic proved fruitful, with one of their senior politicians, Armindo Mariano (Golkar), elected to the NTT parliament. The East Timorese tendency for fission, however, has led many to decline the opportunity to unify their voice through Mariano and undertake their own political manoeuvres. For example, Arnaldo Tavares, son of former top militia leader João Tavares, chose to join president Susilo Bambang Yudhoyono's Democratic Party (Partai Demokrat, or PD). An East Timorese legal practitioner, João Meco, joined general Wiranto's Hanura Party. Ali Atamimi, who was a representative from East Timor in Indonesia's People Consultative Assembly between 1997 and 1999, maintained his allegiance to the PPP.

Plate 7.2 Campaign poster for East Timorese politician Fatima Ferrao, from the National Mandate Party
Source: Andrey Damaledo.

A surprising decision was made by Eurico Guterres to join another quasi-Islamic party, the National Mandate Party (Partai Amanat Nasional, or PAN). Another significant change occurred in early 2009, when Prabowo Subianto—regarded by many East Timorese as their comrade due to his military service in East Timor—formed the Great Indonesia Movement Party (Gerakan Indonesia Raya, or Gerindra) as his political machine to run for the Indonesian presidency. Many East Timorese acknowledged a narrative of shared comradeship and struggle with Prabowo, which led them to join Gerindra. Armindo Mariano, for example, resigned from Golkar and aligned himself with Gerindra, securing the position of party secretary in NTT.

151

Plate 7.3 Campaign poster for East Timorese politician Agustinho Pinto, from Gerindra (who was elected to office)
Source: Andrey Damaledo.

Struggling citizens

In addition to their involvement in mainstream political parties, East Timorese have always been active in their own political rallies. Since early 2000, various East Timorese associations have organised rallies and demonstrations to challenge the way the Indonesian Government delivers services to them. These public demonstrations have become part of their life in West Timor. To attract media attention, they always seek to stage their rallies in prominent government spaces such as parliamentary buildings or the office of the governor and/or head of the district (*bupati*). If a rally targets a specific government agency—whose service provision is the subject of the protest—dramatic action may be performed, such as chaining the gate, blocking the entrance and shutting down the activities of that office. At some rallies, groups have performed a theatrical war dance.

Perhaps the largest rallies ever staged took place in Atambua (Belu) during 2006 in response to the allocation of compensation funds managed by the Indonesian Ministry of Social Affairs. According to the policy, each East

Timorese household would receive a total of IDR4 million (approximately A$400) to support their livelihoods in West Timor. In Belu district, it was reported that only 1,500 East Timorese households were entitled to this allocation. The majority of the East Timorese population in the district perceived this as discriminatory, as the total number of households far exceeded that figure, and, in their view, all East Timorese deserved compensation. Protest rallies were organised and a census was conducted to provide precise information about the number of resident East Timorese households. Finally, after nearly a year of rallies that culminated in the destruction of the Belu House of Parliament and detention of three East Timorese, the Indonesian Government agreed to meet their demands, although it insisted no additional budget allocation would be made. As a result, instead of receiving IDR4 million as promised, each East Timorese household in Belu district received just IDR503,000 (A$50). As one activist recalled:

> The amount was pitiful considering what we had done, including spending time in prison, but it was a worthy cause. We have shown that East Timorese are here and that our struggle continues.

Following the large rallies in Atambua, East Timorese held smaller protests on a regular basis throughout West Timor until 2012, when then president Yudhoyono issued a directive to provide housing for East Timorese in West Timor. To make this program more inclusive and consistent with mainstream Indonesian policy, the East Timorese were classified as people with low incomes (*Masyarakat Berpenghasilan Rendah*) and therefore eligible for public housing. The Indonesian Minister for Public Housing was assigned leadership of the project and Atambua was chosen as the place where the project would be launched.

However, like many previous housing projects, in this one, the quality of construction was poor and various East Timorese groups rejected their housing allocations and launched a strike to remain in their camps. One East Timorese elder who helped organise the strike in Atambua told me:

> The government said these houses were broken because we left them empty. We did not want to argue with them, so we invited them to come to the location and see for themselves. We ushered them into one of the houses that had just been completed. Once they were all inside and observing the rooms, we went outside and pushed the wall. The thin concrete walls immediately cracked and shook. Noticing that the house seemed to be on the verge of collapsing, the officers rushed outside.

Imitating the officers' expression of fear and outrage, the elder explained that they had not intended to treat the officers badly or to humiliate them. They were simply trying to demonstrate the problem and show them why they had chosen to remain in their camps. He said: 'Now that they had experienced it themselves, they knew firsthand how bad the house was, and hopefully they would change the way they delivered their services.'

East Timorese groups in the neighbouring district of North Central Timor (TTU) also responded negatively to the housing project and organised rallies around the office of the *bupati*. They demanded the local government pursue an inclusive social policy and treat them with respect. In Kupang district, different forms of protest were organised by East Timorese groups in the village of Naibonat. They refused to participate in the registration census or be included in the program.

This renewed struggle finally reached the office of the Indonesian National Commission on Human Rights (Komisi Nasional Hak Asasi Manusia, or Komnas HAM) in Jakarta and a team was sent to West Timor to investigate. After visiting some of the housing project sites and talking to East Timorese in Belu and TTU districts, the team confirmed, in October 2013, that the housing was substandard (Kompas Online 2013). After a lengthy standoff, in early 2014, the Indonesian Public Prosecutor was called on to investigate allegations of corruption against the project contractors. Officials from the Ministry of Housing and the local government, together with the managing contractors, were charged with corruption in the special Indonesian court and a number were found guilty and sentenced to prison. The investigation was then expanded to cover all districts in NTT and, at the time of writing, other alleged offenders were still waiting to appear in court.

Many East Timorese expressed satisfaction that their struggles had eventually paid off. They were pleased that their efforts resonated across district boundaries and influenced other people in NTT. They have also demonstrated that corrupt officials who seek to gain from the displacement and suffering of East Timorese will be brought to justice. The cases have illustrated that the East Timorese in West Timor are not simply 'active citizens' who participate in civic life by casting their votes, paying taxes, and so on. Rather, they are 'activist citizens' who are prepared to challenge the state's authority and demand that it be more responsive and accountable for its actions. In this sense, the East Timorese have transformed themselves from agents of the state into champions of their own communities and in this role they are prepared to act in the interests of their fellow citizens. The transformation demonstrates that East Timorese political mobilisation in West Timor is not simply about serving their own agendas and securing compensation from the state. Their demands for state accountability confirm they are also playing a new role in demonstrating a willingness to embrace and support the Indonesian democratic reform agenda.

Plate 7.4 An East Timorese rally in front of the NTT governor's office, September 2017
Source: Kompas.com/Sigiranus Marutho Bere.

Alliances with established associations

East Timorese struggles and political mobilisation have so far been influential because they have managed to form alliances with established associations in West Timor. 'As we have lived here [in West Timor]', some declare, 'we should not just build our own house, but also be part of local people's houses'. Here, the ideology of house dispersion or 'marrying out' is alluded to in their involvement with West Timorese associations, particularly local ethnic organisations. The United Timorese (Persehatian Orang Timor, or POT) is one such prominent organisation, and the largest association formed to accommodate and represent local

Meto-speaking West Timorese in NTT. East Timorese who have been members of this association since its early formation denounce the claim that POT is exclusively Meto. They argue that POT is an organisation for all Timorese regardless of their ethnolinguistic background and, with East Timorese support, some leaders of this association have been elected to office at the district and provincial levels.

Some East Timorese are also involved in Indonesian philanthropic organisations. The Wadah Foundation, a philanthropic group set up by Indonesian billionaire Hashim Djojohadikusomo, supports the active involvement of East Timorese. Recently, the foundation provided solar panels and a water pipeline for East Timorese groups in TTS district.[11] East Timorese are also active members of the Indonesian Farmers' Union and Indonesian Veterans' Association. But perhaps the most important alliance they have formed so far is with the Indonesian Retired Armed Forces Association (Pepabri). By virtue of their enduring sense of comradeship and shared military experience, the association keeps alive relations between East Timorese and former Indonesian army generals (and some active generals) who served in East Timor during the occupation. This relationship is a crucial political alliance considering most of these retired generals remain key players in contemporary Indonesian politics.

Religious-based organisations make up a second set of alignments. Many East Timorese are active members of the Indonesian Interreligious Communication Forum. They are often appointed to represent members of the Catholic Church in their respective districts and this is crucial because the forum is a nationwide organisation with offices at provincial and district levels. With such a well-established institutional structure and broad membership, leading members of this forum have a direct channel to political leaders such as the governor or *bupati*,[12] and therefore direct access to key decision-makers. Muslim East Timorese are also active in established Islamic groups in West Timor. Some mosques near East Timorese resettlement areas, such as those in Boneana and Reknamo villages in Kupang district, were built as a result of these associations.

---

11   Wadah is significant because of its link with one of Indonesia's largest political parties, Gerindra, and its chief patron, Prabowo Subianto.

12   East Timorese in Naibonat village in Kupang district, for instance, used the forum to approach the local *bupati* in their attempt to secure land for their church.

A third alliance that is beneficial to East Timorese involves human rights groups and grassroots activists in West Timor. Although few East Timorese are active members, these organisations have promoted East Timorese displacement as a human rights issue in West Timor and therefore represent an active voice promoting their interests. A final association relates to East Timorese involvement with a local disaster management group. West Timor has long been known for its severe droughts and frequent floods and a multi-stakeholder group has been formed to respond to these events. Some East Timorese have become focal points for their respective districts in support of this group, which is linked to national and global climate change and disaster risk reduction programs. Members have their mobile phone numbers registered as part of an early warning system, and when destructive events are predicted East Timorese are able to immediately report their situation to the emergency response agencies.

This diverse and multilayered participation demonstrates that associations play an important role in East Timorese social life and the practice of citizenship in Indonesian Timor. They have formed their own associations to express their views and interests, but they make these views and interests more relevant and powerful by building coalitions with established organisations. Putnam (2000: 338), in his study of community associations in the United States, argues that when citizens form associations, 'their individual and … quiet voices multiply and are amplified'. Taking this view in relation to the East Timorese in West Timor, I suggest the voices of newly resettled communities are multiplied and amplified not simply when they form associations, but also when they pursue causes that matter to the wider society. Rather than seeking financial compensation for their displacement and suffering, East Timorese political activism has sought to broaden their impact as citizens by engaging in diverse issues such as human rights, climate change, anticorruption and religious plurality and tolerance.[13]

---

13   The political mobilisation of East Timorese refugees in Sydney gained momentum and influence when they broadened their links with global interests (Wise 2006: 72).

Conclusion: Changing perspectives on citizen activism

In the debate over citizen participation, researchers have attempted to identify associations formed and transformed by institutional or individual agency. Institutions in the host country provide opportunities for citizens to channel their political interests. This view, however, has placed participants in a reactionary position against government policies. Personal agency offers another approach to explain citizens as active political actors who engage in activities to overcome poor service delivery and associated policy practices.

In this chapter, I have endeavoured to apply both ideas to the context of East Timorese in West Timor. In so doing, I have considered the changing Indonesian political system in relation to East Timorese associational life. The result, however, suggests a need to look from a different perspective rather than to reengage with earlier debates. Indonesia's reformed political system offers more spaces for East Timorese to form associations and pursue their diverse political interests, but their idea of struggling citizens provides insights into the way associations are established, consolidated and mobilised.

In nearly two decades, East Timorese in West Timor have shown that associations play a pivotal role in fostering political involvement and civic virtue.[14] Scholars have argued that, for refugee or conflict-affected communities, the structure of conflict in their country of origin frequently serves as the determining factor in their choices. Some associations are oriented towards politics in their homeland while others focus on adaptation to and integration into their host society. This structure of conflict leads others to explain various political mobilisations among newcomers as revolving mostly around ideas of maintaining ethnic relationships with the homeland and adaptation to their new place (Rex 1987: 10; Bloemraad 2006: 162).[15]

---

14 Hamidi (2003: 318–19), in her study of North African immigrant associations in France, asks: 'Are associations places of democratic socialisations and of politicisation? Are they places where people learn to take care of other people's interest, where people develop broad solidarities and where they learn how to discuss issues in a spirit of communication and tolerance? Are they places that develop civic virtues?'

15 The Greek Cypriot population in London, for instance, formed their associations specifically to maintain their ethnic group and preserve distinctive Greek Cypriot culture (Josephides 1987: 42).

Korac (2009: 33) neatly summarises the role of such organisations, writing:

Refugee and immigrant organisations are considered not only important for keeping the sense of continuity with past lives and identities through maintaining ties with the society of origin, but also for establishing links with mainstream society and for overcoming social isolation and marginalisation'.

Similarly, Wise (2006: 76–7) has amply demonstrated in relation to East Timorese associations in Sydney, Australia, that these were forged from solidarity groups that were focused mostly on political activism for East Timor's independence while assisting newly arrived East Timorese refugees to settle in. Their efforts included networking among their ethnic group, facilitating access to government welfare services, learning English, finding accommodation, children's education and employment (Wise 2006: 76–7).

East Timorese associations in West Timor are not simply about generating social capital and effective adaptation. They are also driven by the continued political mobilisation to claim their due rights as Indonesian citizens. This is exemplified in their successful efforts to send their own representatives to the local parliament in three consecutive elections in West Timor. An East Timorese is also running in the election for district head (*pilkada*) in 2018. This is a milestone in their political mobilisation; however, many East Timorese elders have expressed their frustration with ongoing division. One elder told me that 'if you look at our growing population, we could actually win more seats if only we were united'. In a similar vein, another elder said:

If we look at the ballot paper, we'll always find East Timorese candidates in all the parties. We tried to advise them to unite our voice, but nobody listened. How could we elect more [East Timorese] representatives if we always campaign against each other?

Indeed, in the 2009 general election, most major political parties had East Timorese candidates in their teams. This dispersion has proven successful, with three East Timorese politicians elected to the Belu district parliament, one representative elected to the Kupang district parliament and one to the NTT parliament.[16] This division continued into the 2014

---

16 Armindo Mariano was reelected to the provincial parliament. At the district level, the late Mauricio Freitas was elected to the Kupang district parliament. In Belu district, Arnaldo Tavares (Demokrat), Ali Atamimi (PPP) and Antonio dos Santos (Indonesia Sovereign Party: Partai Kedaulatan Bangsa Indonesia, or PKBI) were elected.

general election, with similar results. There were three East Timorese representatives elected to the Belu district parliament and one to the Kupang district parliament, as well as two to the NTT parliament.[17] Since 2009, many East Timorese from these electorates have run for the national parliament, but have encountered the same problem—no single candidate wins enough votes to represent East Timorese in Jakarta.[18] The successful participation of East Timorese in three consecutive elections in Indonesian West Timor has shown they have the capacity to adapt, reproduce and expand in new sociopolitical settings. However, their endless infighting and tendency for fission lead them to stagnation and frustrate their political mobilisation.

In spite of this ongoing division in their political ambition, the idea of 'struggling' citizens deserving of government support has taken East Timorese citizenship practice in a new direction. Having operated as state agents during the violent conflict in East Timor, they are now becoming agents of their own communities by seeking accountability from the Indonesian Government. From their initial mobilisation for compensation, East Timorese associations in Indonesia have progressively expanded and diversified their activism into larger issues on the national and international stages. This demonstrates that East Timorese in West Timor have been more politically active than when they were still in East Timor. The concept of struggling citizens also signifies that East Timorese are not passive recipients of government policies or interventions. More importantly, it illustrates how the majority of East Timorese in West Timor have reconciled with their confrontational past and are moving on with dignity in Indonesia.

---

17   In Belu district, three East Timorese were elected: Agostinho Pinto, Fernando Pareira (Gerindra) and Manuel da Conseçãio (PPP). In Kupang district, Tomé da Silva (Gerindra) was elected. In August 2016, Edjido Manek (Gerindra), a former leader of the Laksaur militia group, was appointed to Malaka district parliament, replacing a West Timorese representative who had run for the *bupati*. At the provincial level, Armindo Mariano, who has controlled the East Timorese electorate in Belu and TTU districts for a decade, was defeated by Angelo da Costa, Guterres's assistant from PAN. Another East Timorese elected to the provincial parliament was Antonio Soares, a son of former governor Abílio Soares, who stood for Gerindra. In January 2017, Antonio resigned from his political activities after being caught by Indonesian police for using drugs. A West Timorese eventually took his seat in the parliament.
18   In 2014, Eurico Guterres (PAN) was challenged by Mario Vieira and Octavio Soares (from Gerindra), with the result that none of them was elected. After more than a decade and two terms as its chief in NTT, Guterres resigned from PAN in October 2017.

8
Divided loyalties

In this book, I have explored how displacement, belonging and citizenship are perceived and articulated among East Timorese who decided to remain in Indonesian West Timor after the 1999 referendum. East Timorese who supported Indonesia might have lost the referendum, but, as I have argued, their cultural identity as East Timorese was something they never relinquished. These East Timorese might have seen Indonesia as their destination when they first left East Timor following the referendum, but they have managed to retain an abiding sense of national belonging and cultural attachment to East Timor. This is a significant feature of their lives that has made East Timorese society one of more than just winners and losers. For those who fled East Timor after the defeated vote on autonomy, their collective struggle, sacrifice, inspiration and aspirations illustrate their refusal to be easily defined as refugees/IDPs, ex-refugees or new citizens. This means that an understanding of East Timorese displacement, belonging and citizenship in Indonesia must be placed in the context of their continuing attempts to negotiate diversity, navigate complexity and live with dignity.

The connections between displacement, belonging, citizenship and living with dignity that are drawn by East Timorese living in West Timor indicate the emergence of a 'trans-Timor citizenship' phenomenon. This multiple citizenship phenomenon is not new. Scholars have argued that the dynamics of global capital flows, violent conflict and migration have changed the way we understand citizenship. Ong (2006: 15), for example, has argued that 'contemporary flows of capital and of migrants have interacted with sovereignty and rights discourses in complex ways to disentangle citizenship claims once knotted together in a single territorial mass'. It has also been widely documented that in this new perspective of multiple belongings, newcomers are engaging in 'transborder citizenship' to maintain relationships with their place of origin. Simultaneously, they also work 'to protect themselves against discrimination, gain rights, or make contributions to the development of that state and the life of the people within it' (Glick Schiller and Fouron 2001: 25). What make the notion of trans-Timor citizenship different are the diverse and complex ways in which East Timorese continue to negotiate their lives across national boundaries. In the preceding chapters, I have sought to offer insights into the diverse ways these attachments and connections are realised and reinvigorated. But to illustrate the point another way, let me share some other accounts of my encounters with East Timorese in Belu and Kupang.

Mateus Guedes, a former member of the Aitarak militia group, assisted me in gathering information about East Timorese in Belu over a period of nearly 12 months. In September 2013, I arrived at Mateus's shelter in the temporary settlement of Tenu Bot to bid him farewell. He had just finished his afternoon task of drawing water from the well across the street. The sun had set and we were busy discussing local politics. As this would be our final meeting, I offered to buy him dinner. Happily, Mateus agreed and we rode a motorbike to the Beringin, a restaurant that served spicy Padang cuisine, near the main mosque in Belu.

We collected our food, returned to his shelter and sat around a small table. As we were about to enjoy our meal, I saw Mateus give one portion of the fried chicken to his wife, who took it outside. As far as I know, there was nobody waiting outside. A minute later, his wife returned and Mateus immediately said, '*Avo sira, maun alin sira, uma inan sira, mai ita ha hotu*'.[1] 'Is that some kind of a Tetun dining invocation?' I asked him. 'No,' he answered. 'It is just my expression to acknowledge and invite all of the family in East Timor to join in our dinner.' The fried chicken his wife took outside constituted an offering to his family and ancestors in East Timor. The fried chicken was put on a stone at the front corner of his shelter, orientated towards East Timor.

---

1   Meaning 'all grandparents, brothers and sisters, mother and father [in Timor-Leste], let us share this meal together'.

Mateus explained that they always remembered their families and ancestors in East Timor whenever they enjoyed a special meal: 'They are in the East and we are here in the West, but we are still united.' As we were finishing our meal, Mateus looked at me and said:

> Andrey, my friend [*kolega*], when Indonesia decided to let East Timor go, I joined Aitarak to defend Indonesia, but if one day, Indonesia has another offer to let West Timor go, then, I want you to know that I will fight to remain in Timor because I am a Timorese.[2]

Mateus's compelling and profound sentiment clearly suggests there are East Timorese who perceive West Timor to be the vehicle for the rediscovery of their Timorese identity. For them, locality matters and therefore their displacement and resettlement are more than simply physical movement or relocation; they are part of their attempt to maintain a cosmological unity. By remaining in West Timor, Mateus negated the political division of East and West Timor by assuming a unified cosmic integration of Loro Monu (the land of the setting sun) and Loro Sa'e (the land of the rising sun).

Mateus is not alone in emphasising the significance of this dual classification to an East Timorese sense of belonging. In my last meeting with East Timorese groups in Kupang district, they also expressed support for this east and west cosmic unity. In their words: 'If this [West Timor] was not Loro Monu, we would have been left hungry and would have died.' In another mythologised formulation, an elder from Baucau recalled:

> When we arrived here, this was a barren land full of thornbush. But when the first seeds of corn were planted, more than 20 springs emerged, and they have never dried up. This land recognised us, this land is Loro Monu.

---

2   In October 2017, I returned to Atambua only to find that Mateus had moved out of Tenu Bot. He is now settled permanently in his own house in the neighbouring village of Kuneru. He took his offering stone with him and put it at the corner of his new house, orientated towards Timor-Leste, as always.

Plate 8.1 The new generation of East Timorese casting their vote during the 2013 election for NTT governor
Source: Andrey Damaledo.

While their decision to support Indonesia resulted in them leaving East Timor, the maintenance of their sense of cultural unity with their homeland is what connects them to their East Timorese origins. This is why the proposal to relocate all East Timorese to an island beyond Timor on their arrival in West Timor in late 1999 was highly unpopular and overwhelmingly rejected before it was even discussed. This also explains why many East Timorese who relocated beyond the island of Timor subsequently resettled in West Timor. In other words, by remaining in West Timor, East Timorese are politically displaced but remain culturally and—in a real sense—physically connected.

The significance of the cosmological orientation is inextricably linked to complex ideas about land (*rai*). Land has always been the primary mode of attachment to place. But it is also an enduring metaphor for living. I have often heard East Timorese proclaim Indonesia as their 'land of life'. Most were East Timorese who worked in the Indonesian public sector during the occupation and were able to maintain their positions in various Indonesian government and public sector agencies. Yet they also emphasise East Timor as their land of origin. In cultural terms, this 'land of life' (*tanah kehidupan*) is often symbolically referred to as their 'cultivated house' (*rumah kebun*). In practice, the cultivated house should always pay tribute to the 'sacred ancestral house' (*rumah leluhur*)—the land of origin. With continuing salary and welfare benefits from Indonesia, many public servants of East Timorese origin have sent money and their children to be educated in Timor-Leste. In turn, they have also looked after East Timorese who are studying and travelling in Indonesia.

In addition to land, another East Timorese metaphor of belonging is the idea of expansion from a central origin. Some East Timorese groups develop this idea by forming new alliances with West Timorese through symbolic and/or physical marriage. Others have done this by reconstructing their new 'sacred house' (*uma lulik*). These new alliances and sacred houses are not simply representations of East Timor in Indonesia. They are subsidiary expressions of the ancestral origin that connects East Timorese who do not want to return to Timor-Leste with their hosts in West Timor and with their relatives in their homeland in Timor-Leste. In this sense, these people use Indonesian West Timor as a means of repositioning themselves to keep the relationship with their ancestral land and relatives in Timor-Leste alive and in balance.

While East Timorese maintain their Indonesian identity cards (Kartu Tanda Penduduk, or KTP) and have actively and successfully participated in three national elections and numerous local elections, they have done so with an understanding that East Timorese in West Timor are not one but many. And in this sense, West Timor is not just another place to seek refuge; it is a culturally and physically appropriate place to build a new life because it is always connected to the land of their ancestors in East Timor. Perhaps, as my friend Mateus has indicated, they are not really Indonesian citizens but trans-Timor citizens in Indonesia.

It is legitimate at this point to ask how these complex ideas of belonging and citizenship might play into the future shape of East Timorese society in relation to both Indonesia and Timor-Leste. To understand what the future could look like for the East Timorese in West Timor, we must first understand a major factor informing continuity and change within East Timorese communities—namely, demography. I have outlined the complexity of demographic trends in Chapter 1, but here I shall concentrate on the changing significance of intergenerational family composition. This is a significant phenomenon because, nearly two decades since the major exodus from East Timor, most East Timorese who joined the Indonesian military, police force and/or public administration in the early occupation period (the late 1970s) have now retired. The younger generation, who were recruited into the Indonesian public sector in the 1980s, are now entering their early 50s. As the retirement age in the Indonesian public sector is 58, this group will soon be joining their predecessors. This situation also applies to other East Timorese who were recruited by the Indonesian military to form vigilante groups such as Hansip, Kamra and Wanra. A slightly younger group, perhaps, exists among those East Timorese who were born during the period of Portuguese decolonisation. These people were in their mid to late 20s when the Indonesian special forces recruited them to form the Garda Paksi youth group, which was transformed into militia groups in 1999. Former members of this group in West Timor are now aged in their mid to late 40s. Intergenerational changes show that the future of East Timorese in West Timor will be largely dependent on the new generation. This generation has had little to do with the politics of decolonisation and/or occupation. And, as the older generation is retiring, it is likely East Timorese integrationist political ideology will slowly but surely fade away. The lack of enthusiasm and support for this goal by the Indonesian Government itself will ensure this occurs.

There are three major characteristics of this new generation. First, they were born during the Indonesian rule of East Timor, but grew up in Indonesian West Timor. Second, regardless of the difficulties faced in camps and resettlement sites, this generation grew up in a time when Indonesia itself had entered a period of radical political reform and democratisation. This is a generation that has grown up with an understanding that newly reformed Indonesia recognises Timor-Leste as an independent and sovereign state. Third, this generation has been educated in the Indonesian system and speaks the Indonesian language fluently. These features suggest the future of East Timorese in West Timor is likely to take on new sociopolitical forms and agendas.

Plate 8.2 Pro-autonomy East Timorese in Raknamo, Kupang district, performing a traditional dance, wearing the scarf of Timor-Leste
Source: Father Jefri Bonlay.

Plate 8.3 The new generation of East Timorese in Naibonat camp (one is wearing a Fretilin t-shirt) have accommodated symbols of resistance in their identity
Source: Andrey Damaledo.

The emerging trend among those who have finished their university education is to move to Timor-Leste for work, usually drawing on extended family connections. This indicates that a sense of unity among East Timorese on both sides of the border will continue to grow while sensitivities around the international border that separates them will decline. The future is likely to see a marked improvement in access and movement across the border. Over time, this may grow into a shared national consciousness that even imagines Timorese territorial reunification. So far, in terms of national security, this is seen as a potential threat, given Indonesia's traumatic history of disintegration and concerns about the illegal movement of people and criminal activity such as fuel smuggling (which is driven by marked price differentials between the two countries). In response, more military posts have been built along the border,[3] although this would not be effective enough on its own to stop reunification given the strong relations between East Timorese in West Timor and those in Timor-Leste.

For this reason, I would argue that the East Timorese desire for a unifying cultural identity should be seen as a potential opportunity—an opportunity for greater reconciliation as people continue to negotiate their lives and belonging in both countries.[4] For those who have been able to make peace with their past, increased mobility could be seen as their ultimate return. Between 2011 and 2017, almost 200 East Timorese gave up their Indonesian citizenship and returned permanently to Timor-Leste.[5] For many others who have been able to come to terms with their displacement and resettlement in West Timor, visits to Timor-Leste are recognised as a return to the homeland. Increased reconciliation and cross-border contact means more social and economic networks. In recent years, growth in the number of transport businesses jointly initiated by East Timorese on both sides of the border clearly indicates that East Timorese are becoming more entangled in a surprisingly mutual way. And this mutual collaboration is what will inform and contribute to improved bilateral relations between Indonesia and Timor-Leste. The Indonesian language will also play a pivotal role in the future of island-wide interaction.

---

3   I note that the expansion of military posts is occurring in other parts of Indonesia, too. An increase in newly recruited soldiers in recent years played a role in this expansion.

4   Many East Timorese told me that they prefer their traditional *Nahe Biti Bo'ot*, or grass-root reconciliation (and justice) process compared to the formal elite-level meetings. See Babo-Soares (2004) for a discussion of the *Nahe Biti Bo'ot* process.

5   See Thu (2015) for a discussion of the return of the Waima'a people in Baucau village of Caicua.

This leads to my second point about the potential mutual partnership. Officially, a bilateral partnership between Indonesia and Timor-Leste was initiated in July 2002 through the signing of a joint communiqué on diplomatic relations and the establishment of a joint commission for bilateral cooperation. This partnership was taken further in late 2004 with the initiation of the joint Commission of Truth and Friendship (CTF), which provided a basis for both countries' further cooperation in the name of a 'forward looking, inclusive and non-discriminatory' framework (CTF 2008: 288). This was recognised by president Susilo Bambang Yudhoyono in his address to the Timor-Leste parliament in early April 2005: 'In the heart of the Indonesian people, the people of Timor-Leste have always been our close relatives. We are two nations and we are two states.' In line with his two predecessors, Yudhoyono sent a clear message that territorial ambition had been Indonesia's motivation in the past, but the newly reformed Indonesia respected and recognised the sovereignty of Timor-Leste. He further outlined that Indonesia is 'committed to develop a mutual partnership [with Timor-Leste], so that the two nations can rise up together towards a brighter future' (Yudhoyono 2005: 291–2).

This message was echoed by former Timor-Leste prime minister Xanana Gusmão when he visited Indonesia in early May 2008, just a month after the CTF finished its work. He said:

> Our future relations must be built around a strong partnership that promotes peace and security, as well as new opportunities of prosperity, freedom, justice, tolerance and democracy for our neighbouring and friendly countries … Let us reinvent new partnerships, formulating serious cooperation proposals, as a way to defend the freedom of our brother countries. Our common history is made by our two peoples. Let us create the conditions for friendship and solidarity among them to grow stronger and stronger. (Gusmão 2008: 6–12)

In January 2016, during his state visit to Dili, Indonesian President Joko Widodo pledged to enhance the close friendship between the two countries and reaffirmed Indonesia's commitment to be the main partner in the development of Timor-Leste. This partnership has been manifested in various sectors apart from the judicial work of the CTF. In the trade sector, for instance, both countries have since mid-2003 signed various agreements, memorandums of understanding and letters of intent to boost the exchange of goods and services. The results of these agreements have so far been satisfactory, with a total trade value of US$580 million in 2017—a significant increase from US$175 million in 2010. Indonesia's main export commodities to Timor-Leste are groceries, office supplies, vehicles, palm oil, cement and tobacco. Timor-Leste, meanwhile, has exported coffee, water buffalo, candlenut and timber. These trade activities have also been followed by increased investment in Timor-Leste by the Indonesian private sector. To date, there are about 400 Indonesian businesses operating in Timor-Leste, including nine major state-owned companies, with a total investment of nearly US$600 million.

Other sectors have followed the positive trend of trade. In education, for example, since 2005 there have been commitments by some universities in Indonesia—particularly in East Java province, such as Airlangga in Surabaya and Brawijaya in Malang—to provide scholarships for East Timorese students who want to pursue higher education in Indonesia. According to the Indonesian Ministry of Education, as of May 2017, about 2,100 East Timorese have made use of this opportunity. Other accounts estimate the number to be about 5,000, with a large number of students studying at universities in Kupang, Bali, Yogyakarta and the capital, Jakarta.

In the security and defence sector, 100 officers of Polícia Nacional de Timor-Leste (PNTL) have received training in Indonesia in criminal investigation, traffic policing and intelligence. In early 2005, an East Timorese police officer joined Indonesia's exclusive education program for promising police leaders (SESPIM (Sekolah Staf dan Pimpinan, or Staff and Leaders School of the Indonesian Police Force)). The Indonesian army and the Timor-Leste Border Patrol Unit regularly hold joint patrols and meetings along their shared 269 km land border. Recently, Timor-Leste expressed interest in strengthening this security and defence partnership by purchasing Indonesian-made weapons. To promote better cultural understanding, an Indonesian cultural centre has been operating in Dili, offering language and art courses as well as regular information sessions on Indonesian higher education scholarships.

This growing relationship among institutions has been followed by a growing network of person-to-person relationships. During my visit to Timor-Leste, I frequently heard the expression, 'We rejected the Indonesian military regime, not the Indonesian people'. As a result, in 2007, more than 2,000 Indonesians lived and worked in Timor-Leste (KBRI Dili 2013). As of 2016, the Indonesian Ministry of Foreign Affairs estimated that nearly 9,000 Indonesians had made Timor-Leste their second home (Kemlu RI 2016). Indonesians in Timor-Leste come from different parts of Indonesia and are working collaboratively for their shared interests. Indonesians from NTT, for example, are now serving as nuns and pastors in various Catholic convents and churches in Timor-Leste. Others are working in car or motorbike repair shops. With NTT's proximity to Timor-Leste, migrants from the province are also working in other sectors, such as construction, travel businesses, retail and pharmacy.

Indonesians from South Sulawesi living along the Rua Campo Alor (Kampung Alor) have been effectively working with East Timorese traders to sell household products to people in remote areas of Baucau, Lautem and Viqueque. Indonesians from Java are well known in Dili for their furniture-making, carpentry and construction skills. Indonesians from Java, Padang and North Sulawesi have been successful in their culinary businesses, employing both Indonesians and Timor-Leste citizens. Partnerships between Indonesians and citizens of Timor-Leste have been more intimately exemplified in 'cross-marriage' (*kawin silang*). Thousands of Indonesians married East Timorese during the occupation and after the referendum and their families are key to Indonesia and Timor-Leste's future relationship.

Timor-Leste and Indonesia appeared to remain intricately entwined at social, political, cultural and personal levels (Bexley 2009; Bexley and Nygaard-Christensen 2013; Nygaard-Christensen 2013; Peake et al. 2014). With Timor-Leste gearing up to become a member of the Association of Southeast Asian Nations (ASEAN), much freer movement across members' borders will be guaranteed. This could significantly increase the flow of people, goods and logistics between Timor-Leste and Indonesia. In this sense, Indonesian and East Timorese social networks across national boundaries are an enduring asset that could significantly contribute to mutual cross-border management and constructive partnerships between both countries in the future.

The East Timorese in West Timor are at the forefront of the renewed partnership between Indonesia and Timor-Leste. Trans-Timor citizenship as a vernacular form of belonging and entitlement could help us understand a wide range of interactions between and networks among Indonesians and Timor-Leste citizens. It shows the significance of a messy, complex and detailed sociopolitical allegiance of people whose lives have been overturned by extraordinary events. The devastating setbacks inflicted by the referendum on East Timorese who supported Indonesia were followed by their struggle to rebuild their lives and maintain their dignity and identity. Rather than simply tales of being uprooted from their homeland, stories of East Timorese in West Timor are accounts of connection, of abiding commitment and of divided loyalties. In the future, this will provide a more nuanced understanding of how people conceptualise their changing ideas of citizenship and national identity. Perhaps we should not take for granted the national boundary between Indonesia and Timor-Leste, because many people continue to negotiate their lives and families across that border.

Bibliography

Acciaioli, G. 2001. 'Archipelagic culture' as an exclusionary government discourse in Indonesia. *The Asia Pacific Journal of Anthropology* 2(1): 1–23. doi.org/10.1080/14442210110001706015.

Achmad, J. 2003. East Timorese refugees in West Timor. In J. Fox and D. Babo-Soares (eds), *Out of the Ashes: Destruction and reconstruction of East Timor*. Canberra: ANU E Press, pp. 190–206. Available from: press-files.anu.edu.au/downloads/press/p68261/pdf/c12.pdf.

Aditjondro, G. 1994. *In the Shadow of Mount Ramelau: The impact of the occupation of East Timor*. Leiden: Indoc.

Agar, M. 1980. *The Professional Stranger: An informal introduction to ethnography*. San Diego, CA: Academic Press.

Akhmadi. 2006. *Studi Keluar dari Kemiskinan di Komunitas RW 4, Dusun Kuiteta, Desa Noelbaki, Kecamatan Kupang Tengah Kabupaten Kupang, Nusa Tenggara Timur* [*Study of Poverty Alleviation in Noelbaki Village of Kupang District*]. Jakarta: Lembaga Penelitian SMERU.

Amirthalingam, K and R. Lakshman. 2009. Displaced livelihoods in Sri Lanka: An economic analysis. *Journal of Refugee Studies* 22(4): 502–24. doi.org/10.1093/jrs/fep031.

Amnesty International. 1999. *Indonesia/East Timor: No end to the crisis for East Timorese refugees*. Document Index ASA 21/208/1999, December. London: Amnesty International.

Anderson, B. 1983. *Imagined Communities: Reflections on the origin and spread of nationalism*. London: Verso.

Anderson, B. 1999. Indonesian nationalism today and in the future. *Indonesia* 67(April): 1–11. doi.org/10.2307/3351374.

Anderson, B. 2001. Imagining East Timor. *Lusotopie* 2001: 233–9.

Anderson, R. and G. Anderson. 1962. Voluntary associations among Ukrainians in France. *Anthropological Quarterly* 35(4): 158–68. doi.org/10.2307/3316620.

Appadurai, A. 1990. Disjuncture and difference in the global cultural economy. *Theory, Culture & Society* 7(1990): 295–310. doi.org/10.1177/026327690007002017.

Appadurai, A. 1996. *Modernity at Large: Cultural dimensions of globalization.* Minneapolis, MN: University of Minnesota Press.

Aragon, L. 2008. Reconsidering displacement and internally displaced persons from Poso. In E. Hedman (ed.), *Conflict, Violence and Displacement in Indonesia.* New York: Cornell Southeast Asia Program Publications, pp. 173–206.

Araujo, B. 2009. Realitas Kehidupan WNI Eks Timor Timor Selama 10 Tahun di Indonesia [Reality of the lives of Indonesian citizens from East Timor after 10 years in Indonesia]. Unpublished ms.

Askland, H. 2014. 'It was all about independence': Loss, division and rejuvenation amongst the East Timorese in Melbourne. *The Australian Journal of Anthropology* 25: 321–36. doi.org/10.1111/taja.12107.

Aspinall, E. 2003. Modernity, history and ethnicity: Indonesian and Acehnese nationalism in conflict. In D. Kingsbury and H. Aveling (eds), *Autonomy and Disintegration in Indonesia.* London: RoutledgeCurzon, pp. 128–47.

Aspinall, E. 2008. Place and displacement in the Aceh conflict. In E. Hedman (ed.), *Conflict, Violence and Displacement in Indonesia.* New York: Cornell Southeast Asia Program Publications, pp. 119–46.

Ataupah, H. 1992. Ekologi, persebaran penduduk dan pengelompokan orang Meto di Timor Barat [Ecology, distribution and the grouping of Meto people in West Timor]. PhD thesis, Universitas Indonesia, Jakarta.

Atkinson, J. 2003. Who appears in the family album? Writing the history of Indonesia's revolutionary struggle. In R. Rosaldo (ed.), *Cultural Citizenship in Island Southeast Asia: Nations and belonging in the hinterlands.* Berkeley, CA: University of California Press, pp. 134–61. doi.org/10.1525/california/9780520227477.003.0005.

Azca, M. 2006. A tale of two troubled areas: Forced migration, social violence and societal (in)security in Indonesia. *Asia and Pacific Migration Journal* 15(1): 93–114. doi.org/10.1177/011719680601500105.

Babo-Soares, D. 2003. Political developments leading to the referendum. In J. Fox and D. Babo-Soares (eds), *Out of the Ashes: Destruction and reconstruction of East Timor*. Canberra: ANU E Press, pp. 53–73. doi.org/10.26530/OAPEN_459402.

Babo-Soares, D. 2004. Nahe biti: The philosophy and process of grassroots reconciliation (and justice) in East Timor. *The Asia Pacific Journal of Anthropology* 5(1): 15–33. doi.org/10.1080/1444221042000201715.

Badan Pusat Statistik (BPS). 2017. *NTT Dalam Angka 2017* [*NTT in Figures 2017*]. Kupang: BPS Provinsi NTT.

Barnes, S. 2011. Origins, precedence and social order in the domain of Ina ama Beli Darlari. In A. McWilliam and E. Traube (eds), *Land and Life in Timor-Leste: Ethnographic essays*. Canberra: ANU E Press, pp. 23–46. doi.org/10.22459/LLTL.12.2011.02.

Basch, L. with N. Click Schiller and C. Blanc-Szanton. 1994. *Nations Unbound: Transnational projects, postcolonial predicaments and deterritorialized nation-states*. Langhorne, PA: Gordon and Breach.

Bauman, Z. 2004. *Wasted Lives: Modernity and its outcasts*. Cambridge: Polity.

Beard, V. 2003. Learning radical planning: The power of collective action. *Planning Theory* 2(1): 13–35. doi.org/10.1177/1473095203002001004.

Becker, H. 1963. *Outsiders: Studies in the sociology of deviance*. New York: Free Press.

Beittinger-Lee, V. 2009. *(Un)civil Society and Political Change in Indonesia: A contested arena*. London: Routledge.

Bertrand, J. 2004 *Nationalism and Ethnic Conflict in Indonesia*. Cambridge University Press: Cambridge.

Bexley, A. 2009. Youth at the crossroads: The politics of identity and belonging in Timor-Leste. PhD Thesis, The Australian National University, Canberra.

Bexley, A. and M. Nygaard-Christensen. 2013. Engaging processes of sense-making and negotiation in contemporary Timor-Leste. *The Asia Pacific Journal of Anthropology* 14(5): 399–404. doi.org/10.1080/14442213.2013. 834959.

Bloch, M. 1992. *Prey into Hunter: The politics of religious experience*. Cambridge: Cambridge University Press.

Bloemraad, I. 2005. The limits of de Tocqueville: How government facilitates organisational capacity in newcomer communities. *Journal of Ethnic and Migration Studies* 31(5): 865–87. doi.org/10.1080/13691830500177578.

Bloemraad, I. 2006. *Becoming a Citizen: Incorporating immigrants and refugees in the United States and Canada*. Berkeley, CA: University of California Press.

Bourchier, D. and V. Hadiz. 2003. *Indonesian Politics and Society: A reader*. London: RoutledgeCurzon.

Bovensiepen, J. 2009. Spiritual landscapes of life and death in the central highlands of East Timor. *Anthropological Forum* 19(3): 323–38. doi.org/10.1080/00664670903278437.

Bovensiepen, J. 2011. Opening and closing the land: Land and power in the Idaté highlands. In A. McWilliam and E. Traube (eds), *Land and Life in Timor-Leste: Ethnographic essays*. Canberra: ANU E Press, pp. 47–60. doi.org/10.22459/LLTL.12.2011.03.

Bovensiepen, J. 2014. Lulik: Taboo, animism, or transgressive sacred? An exploration of identity, morality and power in Timor-Leste. *Oceania* 84(2): 121–37. doi.org/10.1002/ocea.5049.

Bovensiepen, J. 2017. Entanglements of power, kinship and time in Laclubar. In M. Nygaard-Christensen and A. Bexley (eds), *Fieldwork in Timor-Leste: Understanding social change through practice*. Copenhagen: NIAS Press, pp. 144–68.

Boxer, C. 1947. *The Topasses of Timor*. Amsterdam: Indisch Instituut.

Bradt, D. and C. Drummond. 2008. Delayed recognition of excess mortality in West Timor. *Emergency Medicine Australasia* 20(1): 70–7. doi.org/10.1111/J.1742-6723.2007.01048.x.

Breton, R. 1964. Institutional completeness of ethnic communities and the personal relations of immigrants. *American Journal of Sociology* 70(2): 193–205. doi.org/10.1086/223793.

Budiardjo, C. and L. Liong. 1984. *The War against East Timor*. London: Zed Books.

Buordillon, M and M. Fortes. 1980. *Sacrifice*. London: Academic Press.

Campbell-Nelson, B. with Y. Damapolii, L. Simanjuntak and F. Tadu Hungu. 2000. *Perempuan dibawa/h Laki-laki yang Kalah: Kekerasan terhadap Perempuan Timor Timur dalam Kamp Pengungsian di Timor Barat* [*Women under the Lost Men: Violence against East Timorese women in refugee camps in West Timor*]. Kupang: JIKPIT and PIKUL.

Caponio, T. 2005. Policy networks and immigrants' associations in Italy: The cases of Milan, Bologna and Naples. *Journal of Ethnic and Migration Studies* 31(5): 931–50. doi.org/10.1080/13691830500177891.

Chamberlain, E. 2007. *Faltering Steps: Independence movements in East Timor— 1940s to the early 1970s.* Point Lonsdale, Vic.: Ernest Chamberlain.

Chambers, R. 1986. Hidden losers? The impact of rural refugees and refugee programs on poorer hosts. *International Migration Review* 20(2): 245–63. doi.org/10.2307/2546034.

Clamagirand, B. 1980. The social organization of the Ema of Timor. In J. Fox (ed.), *The Flow of Life: Essays on eastern Indonesia.* Cambridge, MA: Harvard University Press, pp. 231–47. doi.org/10.4159/harvard.9780674331907.c5.

Commission for Reception, Truth and Reconciliation in Timor-Leste (CAVR). 2005. *Chega! Executive summary.* Dili: CAVR.

Commission of Truth and Friendship (CTF). 2008. *Per Memoriam Ad Spem: Final report of the Commission for Truth and Friendship Indonesia–Timor-Leste.* Available from: www.cja.org/downloads/Per-Memoriam-Ad-Spem-Final-Reeport-of-the-Commission-of-Truth-and-Friendship-IndonesiaTimor-Leste.pdf.

Connerton, P. 1989. *How Societies Remember.* Cambridge: Cambridge University Press. doi.org/10.1017/CBO9780511628061.

Correa, A. 1934. *Gentio de Timôr [Gentile of Timor].* Lisbon: Lucas.

Cristalis, I. 2002. *Bitter Dawn: East Timor, a people's story.* London: Zed Books.

Dadilado, O. 2005a. Karena Fetosawa-Umamane [Due to Fetosawa-Umamane]. *Lorosae Lian* L(August): 3–6.

Dadilado, O. 2005b. Mimpi Membawa Berkah [A blessed dream]. *Lorosae Lian* LI(September): 3–7.

Dadilado, O. 2006. Dubesi, Dulu dan Sekarang [Dubesi, past and present]. *Lorosae Lian* LXV(October): 3–8.

Davidson, K. 1994. The Portuguese colonisation of Timor: The final stage, 1850–1912. PhD thesis, University of New South Wales, Sydney.

de Heusch, L. 1985. *Sacrifice in Africa: A structuralist approach.* L. O'Brien and A. Morton (trans.). Bloomington: Indiana University Press.

de Tocqueville, A. 1835–40. *De la démocratie en Amérique [Democracy in America].* London: Saunders and Otley.

Djami, A. 2006. Awal Hidup Baru di Pucuk Gebang [The beginning of a new life at the edge of the palm tree]. *Lorosae Lian* LX(May): 12.

Dolan, C. with J. Large and N. Obi. 2004. *Evaluation of UNHCR's Repatriation and Reintegration Programme in East Timor, 1999–2003*. Geneva: UNHCR Evaluation and Policy Analysis Unit.

Duncan, C. 2005. Unwelcome guests: Relations between internally displaced persons and their hosts in North Sulawesi. *The Journal of Refugee Studies* 18(1): 25–46. doi.org/10.1093/jrs/18.1.25.

Duncan, C. 2008. Where do we go from here? The politics of ending displacement in post-conflict North Maluku. In E. Hedman (ed.), *Conflict, Violence and Displacement in Indonesia*. New York: Cornell Southeast Asia Program Publications, pp. 207–30.

Durand, F. 2011. Three centuries of violence and struggle in East Timor (1726–2008). *Online Encyclopaedia of Mass Violence*. Available from: www.sciencespo.fr/mass-violence-war-massacre-resistance/printpdf/3028.

Evans-Pritchard, E. 1956. *Nuer Religion*. Oxford: Clarendon Press.

Fentress, J. and C. Wickham. 1992. *Social Memory: New perspectives on the past*. Oxford: Blackwell.

Fernandes, C. 2011. *The Independence of East Timor: Multi-dimensional perspectives—Occupation, resistance, and international political activism*. Brighton, UK: Sussex Academic Press.

Forbes, H. 1884. On some of the tribes of the island of Timor. *The Journal of the Anthropological Institute of Great Britain and Ireland* 13: 402–30. doi.org/10.2307/2841556.

Forman, S. 1980. Descent, alliance and exchange ideology among the Makassae of East Timor. In J. Fox (ed.), *The Flow of Life: Essays on eastern Indonesia*. Cambridge, MA: Harvard University Press, pp. 152–77. doi.org/10.4159/harvard.9780674331907.c6.

Fox, J. 1980a. Introduction. In J. Fox (ed.), *The Flow of Life: Essays on eastern Indonesia*. Cambridge, MA: Harvard University Press, pp. 1–18. doi.org/10.4159/harvard.9780674331907.intro.

Fox, J. 1980b. Obligation and alliance: State structure and moiety organization in Thie, Roti. In J. Fox (ed.), *The Flow of Life: Essays on eastern Indonesia*. Cambridge, MA: Harvard University Press, pp. 98–133. doi.org/10.4159/harvard.9780674331907.

Fox, J. 2003. Tracing the path, recounting the past: Historical perspectives on Timor. In J. Fox and D. Soares (eds), *Out of the Ashes: Destruction and reconstruction of East Timor*. Canberra: ANU E Press, pp. 1–27. Available from: press.anu.edu.au/publications/out-ashes.

Fox, J. 2006a [1993]. Comparative perspectives on Austronesian houses: An introductory essay. In J. Fox (ed.), *Inside Austronesian Houses: Perspectives on domestic designs for living*. Canberra: ANU E Press, pp. 1–28. Available from: press.anu.edu.au/publications/series/comparative-austronesian-series/inside-austronesian-houses.

Fox, J. 2006b. Contending for ritual control of land and polity: Comparisons from the Timor area of eastern Indonesia. In T. Reuter (ed.), *Sharing the Earth, Dividing the Land: Land and territory in the Austronesian world*. Canberra: ANU E Press, pp. 237–52. Available from: press.anu.edu.au/publications/series/comparative-austronesian-series/sharing-earth-dividing-land.

Fox, J. (ed.). 2006c [1997]. *The Poetic Power of Place: Comparative perspectives on Austronesian ideas of locality*. Canberra: ANU E Press. Available from: press.anu.edu.au/publications/series/comparative-austronesian-series/poetic-power-place.

Fox, J. 2006d [1996]. The transformation of progenitor lines of origin: Patterns of precedence in eastern Indonesia. In J. Fox and C. Sather (eds), *Origins, Ancestry and Alliance: Explorations in Austronesian ethnography*. Canberra: ANU E Press, pp. 130–46. Available from: press.anu.edu.au/publications/series/comparative-austronesian-series/origins-ancestry-and-alliance.

Fox, J. 2008. Installing the 'outsider' inside: The exploration of an epistemic Austronesian cultural theme and its social significance. *Indonesian and the Malay World* 36(105): 201–18. doi.org/10.1080/13639810802267942.

Fox, J. and C. Sather (eds). 2006 [1996]. *Origins, Ancestry and Alliance: Explorations in Austronesian ethnography*. Canberra: ANU E Press. Available from: press.anu.edu.au/publications/series/comparative-austronesian-series/origins-ancestry-and-alliance.

Francillon, G. 1967. Some matriarchic aspects of the social structure of the southern Tetun of middle Timor. PhD thesis, The Australian National University, Canberra.

Francillon, G. 1980. Incursions upon Wehali: A modern history of an ancient empire. In J. Fox (ed.), *The Flow of Life: Essays on eastern Indonesia*. Cambridge, MA: Harvard University Press, pp. 248–65. doi.org/10.4159/harvard.9780674331907.c13.

Frazer, J. 1890. *The Golden Bough: A study in comparative religion*. London: Macmillan.

Glick Schiller, N. 2007. Transnationality. In D. Nugent and J. Vincent (eds), *A Companion to the Anthropology of Politics*. Malden, MA: Blackwell, pp. 448–67. doi.org/10.1002/9780470693681.ch28.

Glick Schiller, N. and G. Fouron. 2001. *Georges Woke Up Laughing: Long-distance nationalism and the search for home.* Durham, NC: Duke University Press. doi.org/10.1215/9780822383239.

Gunn, G. 1999. *Timor Loro Sae: 500 years.* Macau: Livros do Oriente.

Gunter, J. 2007. Communal conflict in Viqueque and the 'charged' history of '59. *The Asia Pacific Journal of Anthropology* 8(1): 27–41. doi.org/10.1080/14442210601177977.

Gupta, A and J. Ferguson. 1992. Beyond 'culture': Space, identity and the politics of difference. *Cultural Anthropology* 7(February): 6–23. doi.org/10.1525/can.1992.7.1.02a00020.

Gusmão, X. 2008. Redefining future relations between Indonesia and Timor-Leste: Speech by His Excellency the Prime Minister Kay Rala Xanana Gusmão on the occasion of his visit to Jakarta, 1 May 2008. Dili: Office of Prime Minister.

Hägerdal, H. 2012. *Lords of the Land, Lords of the Sea: Conflict and adaptation in early colonial Timor, 1600–1800.* Leiden: KITLV Press. doi.org/10.1163/9789004253506.

Halbwachs, M. 1992 [1950]. *On Collective Memory.* L. Coser (trans. and ed.). Chicago: University of Chicago Press.

Hamidi, C. 2003. Voluntary associations of migrants and politics: The case of North African immigrants in France. *Immigrants and Minorities* 22(2–3): 317–32. doi.org/10.1080/0261928042000244899.

Harrell-Bond, B. 1986. *Imposing Aid: Emergency assistance to refugees.* Oxford: Oxford University Press.

Harrell-Bond, B. 1999. The experience of refugees as recipients of aid. In A. Ager (ed.), *Refugees: Perspectives on the experience of forced migration.* London: Continuum, pp. 136–68.

Harrell-Bond, B. and E. Voutira. 1992. Anthropology and the study of refugees. *Anthropology Today* 8(4): 6–10. doi.org/10.2307/2783530.

Hedman, E. 2008. Introduction: Dynamics of displacement in Indonesia. In E. Hedman (ed.), *Conflict, Violence and Displacement in Indonesia.* New York: Cornell Southeast Asia Program Publications, pp. 3–28. doi.org/10.1111/j.1477-7053.2008.00257.x.

Hicks, D. 2004. *Tetum Ghosts and Kin: Fertility and gender in East Timor.* 2nd edn. Long Grove, IL: Waveland Press.

Hicks, D. 2007. Community and nation-state in East Timor: A view from the periphery. *Anthropology Today* 23(1): 13–16. doi.org/10.1111/j.1467-8322.2007.00484.x.

Hobsbawm, E. 1990. *Nations and Nationalism since 1780: Programme, myth, reality.* Cambridge: Cambridge University Press.

Hooghe, M. 2005. Ethnic organisations and social movement theory: The political opportunity structure for ethnic mobilisation in Flanders. *Journal of Ethnic and Migration Studies* 31(5): 975–90. doi.org/10.1080/13691830500177925.

Howell, S. 1996. Introduction. In S. Howell (ed.), *For the Sake of Our Future: Sacrificing in eastern Indonesia.* Leiden: CNWS Publications, pp. 1–26.

Hubert, H. and M. Mauss. 1964. *Sacrifice: Its nature and function.* W. D. Halls (trans.). London: Cohen and West.

Hugo, G. 2002. Pengungsi: Indonesia's internally displaced persons. *Asian and Pacific Migration Journal* 11(3): 297–331. doi.org/10.1177/011719680201100302.

Internal Displacement Monitoring Centre (IDMC). 2010. *Durable Solutions Still Out of Reach for Many 'New Citizens' from the Former East Timor Province.* Geneva: IDMC Norwegian Refugee Council.

Internal Displacement Monitoring Centre (IDMC). 2015. *Forgotten Displacement: Why it's time to address the needs of West Timor's protracted IDPs.* Geneva: IDMC Norwegian Refugee Council.

International Crisis Group (ICG). 2011. *Timor-Leste: Reconciliation and return from Indonesia.* Asia Briefing No. 122. Dili/Brussels: ICG, pp. 1–20.

Isin, E. 2009. Citizenship in flux: The figure of the activist citizen. *Subjectivity* 29: 367–88. doi.org/10.1057/sub.2009.25.

Jacobsen, K. 2002. Can refugees benefit the state? Refugee resources and African statebuilding. *The Journal of Modern African Studies* 40(4): 577–96. doi.org/10.1017/S0022278X02004081.

Jakarta Globe. 2012. SBY wants action on Timorese refugees. *Jakarta Globe*, 19 May.

The Jakarta Post. 2009. Former East Timorese settlers run amok over BLT. *The Jakarta Post*, 18 May.

Jolliffe, J. 1978. *East Timor, Nationalism and Colonialism.* Brisbane: University of Queensland Press.

Josephides, S. 1987. Associations amongst the Greek Cypriot population in Britain. In J. Rex, D. Joly and C. Wilpert (eds), *Immigrant Associations in Europe*. Aldershot, UK: Gower, pp. 42–61.

Kammen, D. 2016. *Three Centuries of Conflict in East Timor*. Singapore: NUS Press.

KBRI Dili. 2013. *Buku Saku Warga Negara Indonesia di Timor-Leste* [*Handbook for Indonesians in Timor-Leste*]. Dili: KBRI.

Kehi, B. and L. Palmer. 2012. Hamatak halirin: The cosmological and socio-ecological roles of water in Koba Lima, Timor. *Bijdragen tot de Taal-, Land- en Volkenkunde* 168(4): 445–71.

Kemlu RI. 2016. Indonesia–Timor-Leste terus dorong penyelesaian perundingan perbatasan: Siaran pers [Indonesia and Timor-Leste are to finalise border negotiation: Press release]. 20 September. New York: Permanent Mission of the Republic of Indonesia to the United Nations.

Kent, L. 2016. Sounds of silence: Everyday strategies of social repair in Timor-Leste. *Australian Feminist Law Journal* 42(1): 31–50. doi.org/10.1080/1320 0968.2016.1175403.

Kibreab, G. 1993. The myth of dependency among camp refugees in Somalia 1979–1989. *Journal of Refugee Studies* 6(4): 321–49.

Kibreab, G. 1999. Revisiting the debate on people, place, identity and displacement. *Journal of Refugee Studies* 12(4): 384–410. doi.org/10.1093/jrs/12.4.384.

Kok, W. 1989. Self-settled refugees and the socio-economic impact of their presence on Kassala, eastern Sudan. *Journal of Refugee Studies* 2(4): 419–40. doi.org/10.1093/jrs/2.4.419.

Kompas Online. 2012. Kondisi Rumah Eks Pengungsi Timtim Memprihatinkan [Housing conditions of ex-East Timorese refugees are concerning]. *Kompas Online*, 25 April. Available from: bola.kompas. com/read/2012/04/25/18080826/kondisi.rumah.eks.pengungsi.timtim. memprihatinkan.

Kompas Online. 2013. Komnas HAM Janji Selesaikan Masalah Warga Eks Timtim [The National Commission for Human Rights promised to solve issues of East Timorese]. *Kompas Online*, 23 October. Available from: regional. kompas.com/read/2013/10/23/1532453/Komnas.HAM.Janji.Selesaikan. Masalah.Warga.Eks.Timtim?utm_campaign=related&utm_medium=bp-kompas&utm_source=news&.

Korac, M. 2009. *Remaking Home: Reconstructing life, place and identity in Rome and Amsterdam.* New York: Berghahn Books.

Kunz, E. 1973. The refugee in flight: Kinetic models and forms of displacement. *The International Migration Review* 7(2): 125–46. doi.org/10.2307/3002424.

Kunz, E. 1981. Exile and resettlement: Refugee theory. *The International Migration Review* 15(1–2): 42–51. doi.org/10.2307/2545323.

Kymlicka, W. 1995. *Multicultural Citizenship: A liberal theory of minority rights.* Oxford: Oxford University Press.

Laguerre, M. 1998. *Diasporic Citizenship: Haitian Americans in transnational America.* New York: St Martin's Press.

La Lau, H. 1912. Ons Politiek en Militair Optreden op Timor [Our political and military action on Timor]. *Indisch Militair Tidjschrift* 43: 325–46.

Lambek, M. 2014. Afterthoughts on sacrifice. *Ethnos* 79(3): 430–7. doi.org/10.1080/00141844.2012.747552.

Leach, E. 1951. The structural implications of matrilateral cross-cousin marriage. *The Journal of the Royal Anthropological Institute of Great Britain and Ireland* 81(1–2): 23–55. doi.org/10.2307/2844015.

Leach, M. 2012. FITUN: A preliminary history of a clandestine movement. In M. Leach, N. C. Mendes, A. B. da Silva, B. Boughton and A. da Costa Ximenes (eds), *New Research on Timor-Leste: Proceedings of the Timor-Leste Studies Association 2011 Conference.* Melbourne: Swinburne Press, pp. 255–64. Available from: www.tlstudies.org/pdfs/TLSA%20Conf%202011/chp_37.pdf.

Lewis, E. 2006 [1996]. Origin structures and precedence in the social orders of Tana 'Ai and Sikka. In J. Fox and C. Sather (eds), *Origins, Ancestry and Alliance: Explorations in Austronesian ethnography.* Canberra: ANU E Press, pp. 154–74. Available from: press-files.anu.edu.au/downloads/press/p63701/pdf/ch0828.pdf.

Li, T. 2007. *The Will to Improve: Governmentality, development and the practice of politics.* Durham, NC: Duke University Press. doi.org/10.1215/9780822389781.

Lowie, R. 1963. *Social Organization.* New York: Holt, Rinehart and Winston.

McKinnon, S. 1986. Hot death and the spirit of pigs: The sacrificial form of the hunt in Tanimbar Island. In S. Howell (ed.), *For the Sake of Our Future: Sacrificing in eastern Indonesia.* Leiden: CNWS Publications, pp. 337–54.

McWilliam, A. 1999. From lord of the earth to village head: Adapting to the nation state in West Timor. *Bijdragen tot de Taal-, Land- en Volkenkunde BKI* 155(1): 121–44. doi.org/10.1163/22134379-90003882.

McWilliam, A. 2002. *Paths of Origin, Gates of Life: A study of place and precedence in southwest Timor.* Leiden: KITLV Press.

McWilliam, A. 2005. Houses of resistance in East Timor: Structuring sociality in the new nation. *Anthropological Forum* 15(1): 27–44. doi.org/10.1080/0066 467042000336698.

McWilliam, A. 2009. Trunk and tip in West Timor: Precedence in a botanical idiom. In M. Vischer (ed.), *Precedence: Social differentiation in the Austronesian world.* Canberra: ANU E Press, pp. 111–32. doi.org/10.22459/P.05.2009.05.

McWilliam, A. 2011. Fataluku living landscapes. In A. McWilliam and E. Traube (eds), *Land and Life in Timor-Leste: Ethnographic essays.* Canberra: ANU E Press, pp. 61–86. doi.org/10.22459/LLTL.12.2011.04.

McWilliam, A. and E. Traube. 2011. Land and life in Timor-Leste: Introduction. In A. McWilliam and E. Traube (eds), *Land and Life in Timor-Leste: Ethnographic essays.* Canberra: ANU E Press, pp. 1–22. doi.org/10.22459/ LLTL.12.2011.01.

Malkki, L. 1995. *Purity and Exile: Violence, memory, and national cosmology among Hutu refugees in Tanzania.* Chicago: University of Chicago Press.

Malkki, L. 1997. Speechless emissaries: Refugees, humanitarianism, and dehistoricization. In K. Olwig and K. Hastrup (eds), *Siting Culture: The shifting anthropological object.* London: Routledge, pp. 227–58.

Marcus, G. 1995. Ethnography in/of the world system: The emergence of multi-sited ethnography. *Annual Review of Anthropology* 24: 95–117. doi.org/ 10.1146/annurev.an.24.100195.000523.

Martin, A. 2005. Environmental conflict between refugee and host communities. *Journal of Peace Research* 42(3): 329–46. doi.org/10.1177/002234330505 2015.

Matza, D. 1969. *Becoming Deviant.* Englewood Cliffs, NJ: Prentice-Hall.

Mayblin, M. 2014. The untold sacrifice: The monotony and incompleteness of self-sacrifice in northeast Brazil. *Ethnos* 79(3): 342–64. doi.org/10.1080/ 00141844.2013.821513.

Mayblin, M. and M. Course. 2014. The other side of sacrifice: Introduction. *Ethnos* 79(3): 307–19. doi.org/10.1080/00141844.2013.841720.

Milbank, J. 1996. Stories of sacrifice. *Modern Theology* 12(1): 27–56. doi.org/
10.1111/j.1468-0025.1996.tb00079.x.

Molnar, A. 2011. Darlau: Origins and their significance for Atsabe Kemak
identity. In A. McWilliam and E. Traube (eds), *Land and Life in Timor-Leste:
Ethnographic essays*. Canberra: ANU E Press, pp. 87–116. doi.org/10.22459/
LLTL.12.2011.05.

Needham, R. 1994. *Refugee Participation, in Partnership: Issues of coordination
and participation*. Oxford: Refugee Participation Network 17, Refugees
Studies Programme.

Nicholson, D. 2001. The lorikeet warriors: East Timorese new generation
nationalist resistance, 1989–99. BA (Hons) thesis, University of Melbourne,
Melbourne.

Nygaard-Christensen, M. 2013. Negotiating Indonesia: Political genealogies
of Timorese democracy. *The Asia Pacific Journal of Anthropology* 14(5):423–37.
doi.org/10.1080/14442213.2013.834958.

Ong, A. 1999. *Flexible Citizenship: The cultural logics of transnationality*. Durham,
NC: Duke University Press.

Ong, A. 2006. *Neoliberalism as Exception: Mutations in citizenship and sovereignty*.
Durham, NC: Duke University Press. doi.org/10.1215/9780822387879.

Ormelling, F. 1957. *The Timor Problem: A geographical interpretation of an
underdeveloped island*. 2nd edn. Groningen, Netherlands: J. B. Wolters.

Pakereng, Y. 2009. What factors contributed to the increased roles of women in
community management: The case of East Timorese refugees in West Timor,
Nusa Tenggara Timur province, Indonesia. MA thesis, Van Hall Larenstein
University of Applied Sciences, Wageningen, Netherlands.

Parera, A. 1971. *Sejarah Pemerintahan Raja-Raja Timor* [*History of the Kings
of Timor*]. Jakarta: Pustaka Sinar Harapan.

Peake, G. with L. Kent, A. Damaledo and P. Myat Thu. 2014. *Influences and
echoes of Indonesia in Timor-Leste*. SSGM Discussion Paper 2014/8. State,
Society and Governance in Melanesia Program, The Australian National
University, Canberra.

Pero, D. 2008. Migrants' mobilizations and anthropology: Reflections from the
experience of Latin Americans in the United Kingdom. In D. Reed-Danahay
and C. Brettell (eds), *Citizenship, Political Engagement, and Belonging:
Immigrants in Europe and the United States*. New Brunswick, NJ: Rutgers
University Press, pp. 103–23.

Petrin, S. 2002. *Refugee Return and State Reconstruction: A comparative analysis*. Geneva: UNHCR Evaluation and Policy Analysis Unit.

Pos Kupang. 1999. Jumlah Pengungsi di NTT 12,186 Jiwa [Total number of East Timorese refugees in NTT is around 12,186]. *Pos Kupang*, 10 August.

Pos Kupang. 2015. Kami Bukan Ingin Menyusun Kekuatan Melawan Pemerintah Indonesia [We are not joining forces to fight against the Indonesian Government]. *Pos Kupang*, 29 July.

Putnam, R. 2000. *Bowling Alone: The collapse and revival of American community*. New York: Simon & Schuster. doi.org/10.1145/358916.361990.

Radcliffe, S. and S. Westwood (eds). 1996. *Remaking the Nation: Place, identity and politics in Latin America*. London: Routledge.

Raybeck, D. 1988. Anthropology and labeling theory: A constructive critique. *Ethos* 16(4): 371–97. doi.org/10.1525/eth.1988.16.4.02a00020.

Reed-Danahay, D. and C. Brettell. 2008. Introduction. In D. Reed-Danahay and C. Brettell (eds), *Citizenship, Political Engagement, and Belonging: Immigrants in Europe and the United States*. New Brunswick, NJ: Rutgers University Press, pp. 1–21.

Renard-Clamagirand, B. 1986. Sacrificing among the Wewewa of West Sumba: Dialogue with the ancestors, relations between the living. In S. Howell (ed.), *For the Sake of Our Future: Sacrificing in eastern Indonesia*. Leiden: CNWS Publications, pp. 195–212.

Reuter, T. (ed.). 2006. *Sharing the Earth, Dividing the Land: Land and territory in the Austronesian world*. Canberra: ANU E Press. Available from: press.anu.edu.au/publications/series/comparative-austronesian-series/sharing-earth-dividing-land.

Rex, J. 1987. Introduction: The scope of a comparative study. In J. Rex, D. Joly and C. Wilpert (eds), *Immigrant Associations in Europe*. Aldershot, UK: Gower, pp. 1–10.

Robertson Smith, W. 1889. *Lectures on the Religion of the Semites: The fundamental institutions*. 1st edn. Edinburgh: A. & C. Black.

Robinson, G. 2008. People power: A comparative history of forced displacement in East Timor. In E. Hedman (ed.), *Conflict, Violence and Displacement in Indonesia*. New York: Cornell Southeast Asia Program Publications, pp 87–118.

Robinson, G. 2010. *If You Leave Us Here, We Will Die: How genocide was stopped in East Timor*. Princeton, NJ: Princeton University Press.

Robinson, K. 2014. Citizenship, identity and difference in Indonesia. *Review of Indonesian and Malaysian Affairs* 48(1): 5–34.

Rosaldo, R. 2003. Introduction: The borders of belonging. In R. Rosaldo (ed.), *Cultural Citizenship in Island Southeast Asia: Nations and belonging in the hinterlands*. Berkeley, CA: University of California Press, pp. 1–15. doi.org/10.1525/california/9780520227477.003.0001.

Rosaldo, R. and W. Flores. 1997. Identity, conflict, and evolving Latino communities: Cultural citizenship in San Jose, California. In W. Flores and R. Benmayor (eds), *Latino Cultural Citizenship: Claiming identity, space and politics*. Boston: Beacon Press, pp. 57–96.

Sakti, V. 2013. 'Thinking too much': Tracing local patterns of emotional distress after mass violence in Timor-Leste. *The Asia Pacific Journal of Anthropology* 14(5): 438–54. doi.org/10.1080/14442213.2013.826733.

Satkorlak PBP NTT. 2006. *Upaya Penanganan Eks Pengungsi Timor Timur di NTT Tahun 2006 [Efforts to Handle the Ex East Timorese Refugees Problem in NTT 2006]*. Kupang: Satkorlak PBP NTT.

Schapper, A. 2011. Finding Bunaq: The homeland and expansion of the Bunaq in central Timor. In A. McWilliam and E. Traube (eds), *Land and Life in Timor-Leste: Ethnographic essays*. Canberra: ANU E Press, pp. 163–86. doi.org/10.22459/LLTL.12.2011.08.

Schurtz, H. 1902. *Age-Classes and Male Bands*. Berlin: G. Reimer.

Scott, J. 1998. *Seeing Like a State: How certain schemes to improve the human condition have failed*. New Haven, CT: Yale University Press.

Seran, H. 1996. Hakserak: The rites of sacrificial offerings among the Belunese on Timor Island. In S. Howell (ed.), *For the Sake of Our Future: Sacrificing in eastern Indonesia*. Leiden: CNWS Publications, pp. 245–61.

Seran, S. with M. Widyatmika, M. Bere, S. Nahak, R. Bau, Y. Nahak and D. Ishak. 2010. *Sistem Pemerintahan Tradisional di Belu [Traditional Government System in Belu]*. Kupang: Unit of Archaeology, History and Traditional Values, Department of Culture and Tourism, NTT Government.

Shacknove, A. 1985. Who is a refugee? *Ethics* 95(2): 278–84. doi.org/10.1086/292626.

Silva, K. 2010. Processes of regionalisation in East Timor social conflicts. *Anthropological Forum* 20(2): 105–23. doi.org/10.1080/00664677.2010.487295.

Smith, A. 2002. Timor Leste, Timor Timur, East Timor, Timor Lorosa'e: What's in a name? In D. Singh and A. Smith (eds), *Southeast Asian Affairs 2002*. Singapore: ISEAS, pp. 54–77.

Smith, D. 1997. The international history of grassroots associations. *International Journal of Comparative Sociology* 38(3): 189–216.

Solvang, I. 2005. Land rights: A gift for refugees in West Timor. *Forced Migration Review* 23(May): 60.

Stead, V. 2015. Homeland, territory, property: Contesting land, state, and nation in urban Timor-Leste. *Political Geography* 45: 79–89. doi.org/10.1016/j.polgeo.2014.05.002.

Stepputat, F. 1994. Repatriation and the politics of space: The case of the Mayan diaspora and return movement. *Journal of Refugee Studies* 7(2–3): 175–85. doi.org/10.1093/jrs/7.2-3.175.

Sudo, K. 2006 [1996]. Rank, hierarchy and routes of migration: Chieftainship in the central Caroline Islands of Micronesia. In J. Fox and C. Sather (eds), *Origins, Ancestry and Alliance: Explorations in Austronesian ethnography*. Canberra: ANU E Press, pp. 55–69.

Sunarto, K. with M. Nathan and S. Hadi. 2005. *Overcoming Violent Conflict. Volume 2: Peace and development analysis in Nusa Tenggara Timur*. Jakarta: UNDP–CPRU.

Sylvan, F. 1988. *The Legends of the Mauberes*. Lisbon: Fundação Austronésia Borja da Costa.

Tarrow, S. 1996. States and opportunities. In D. McAdam, J. McCarthy and M. Zald (eds), *Comparative Perspectives on Social Movements*. Cambridge: Cambridge University Press, pp. 41–61. doi.org/10.1017/CBO9780511803987.004.

Taylor, J. 1995. The emergence of nationalist movement in East Timor. In R. Barnes, A Gray and B. Kingsbury (eds), *Indigenous Peoples of Asia*. Ann Arbor, MI: The Association for Asian Studies, pp. 323–43.

Therik, T. 2004. *Wehali the Female Land: Traditions of a Timorese ritual centre*. Canberra: Pandanus Books.

Thu, P. 2012. Negotiating displacement: A study of land and livelihoods in rural East Timor. PhD thesis, The Australian National University, Canberra.

Thu, P. 2015. Displacement and informal repatriation in a rural Timorese village. In S. Ingram, L. Kent and A. McWilliam (eds), *A New Era? Timor-Leste after the UN*. Canberra: ANU Press, pp. 251–63. doi.org/10.22459/NE.09.2015.17.

Traube, E. 1980. Mambai rituals of black and white. In J. Fox (ed.), *The Flow of Life: Essays on eastern Indonesia*. Cambridge, MA: Harvard University Press, pp. 290–314. doi.org/10.4159/harvard.9780674331907.c15.

Traube, E. 1986. *Cosmology and Social Life: Ritual exchange among the Mambai of East Timor*. Chicago: University of Chicago Press.

Traube, E. 1995. Mambai perspectives on colonialism and decolonization. In P. Carey and G. Carter Bentley (eds), *East Timor at the Crossroads: The forging of a nation*. London: Cassell, pp. 42–55.

Traube, E. 2007. Unpaid wages: Local narratives and the imagination of the nation. *The Asia Pacific Journal of Anthropology* 8(1): 9–25. doi.org/10.1080/14442210601161724.

Turner, V. 1974. *Drama, Fields, and Metaphors: Symbolic action in human society*. Ithaca, NY: Cornell University Press.

Turner, V. 1977. *The Ritual Process, Structure and Anti-Structure*. London: Routledge and Kegan Paul.

Turton, D. 2005. The meaning of place in a world of movement: Lessons from long-term field research in southern Ethiopia. *Journal of Refugee Studies* 18(3): 258–80. doi.org/10.1093/refuge/fei031.

Tylor, E. 1871. *Primitive Culture: Researches into the development of mythology, philosophy, religion, art, and custom*. London: John Murray.

UN-Habitat. 2014. *Access to land in Indonesia: Reflections on some cases*. Working Paper on European Union's Aid to Uprooted People. UN-Habitat, Jakarta.

United Nations High Commissioner for Refugees (UNHCR). 2002. *Declaration of Cessation—Timor Leste*. 22 December. Geneva: UNHCR. Available from: www.refworld.org/docid/41657a7e4.html.

United Nations High Commissioner for Refugees (UNHCR). 2010. *Convention and Protocol Relating to the Status of Refugees*. Geneva: UNHCR.

United Nations Security Council (UNSC). 1999. *Resolution 1264 (1999) on the situation in East Timor*. Security Council Resolutions. New York: UNSC. Available from: www.un.org/docs/scres/1999/sc99.htm.

Van Gennep, A. 1960 [1906]. *The Rites of Passage*. M. Vizedom and G. Caffee (trans.). Chicago: University of Chicago Press.

van Klinken, G. with D. Bourchier and D. Kammen. 2002. The key suspects: An introduction. In H. McDonald, D. Ball, J. Dunn, G. van Klinken, D. Bourchier, D. Kammen and R. Tanter (eds), *Masters of terror: Indonesia's military and violence in East Timor in 1999*. Papers on Strategy and Defence No. 145. Strategic and Defence Studies Centre, The Australian National University, Canberra, pp. 67–81.

Waldron, S. 1988. Working in the dark: Why social anthropological research is essential in refugee administration. *Journal of Refugee Studies* 1(2): 153–65. doi.org/10.1093/jrs/1.2.153.

Wallis, J. 2013. Victors, villains and victims: Capitalizing on memory in Timor-Leste. *Ethnopolitics* 12(2): 133–60. doi.org/10.1080/17449057.2011.632958.

Warner, D. 1994. Voluntary repatriation and the meaning of return to home: A critique of liberal mathematics. *Journal of Refugee Studies* 7(2–3): 160–74. doi.org/10.1093/jrs/7.2-3.160.

Whitaker, B. 2002. Refugees in western Tanzania: The distribution of burdens and benefits among local hosts. *Journal of Refugee Studies* 15(2002): 339–58. doi.org/10.1093/jrs/15.4.339.

Wise, A. 2006. *Exile and Return among the East Timorese*. Philadelphia: University of Pennsylvania Press. doi.org/10.9783/9780812203929.

Wood, G. 1985. The politics of development policy labelling. *Development and Change* 16(3): 347–73. doi.org/10.1111/j.1467-7660.1985.tb00214.x.

Wurm, S. A. and S. Hattori (eds). 1981–83. *Language Atlas of the Pacific Area*. Canberra: Australian Academy of the Humanities.

Yudhoyono, S. 2005. *Transforming Indonesia: Selected international speeches with essays by international observers*. Jakarta: Office of Special Staff of the President for International Affairs and PT Buana Ilmu Populer.

Zetter, R. 1991. Labelling refugees: Forming and transforming a bureaucratic identity. *Journal of Refugee Studies* 4(1): 39–62. doi.org/10.1093/jrs/4.1.39.

Zetter, R. 2007. More labels, fewer refugees: Remaking the refugee label in an era of globalization. *Journal of Refugee Studies* 20(2): 172–92. doi.org/10.1093/jrs/fem011.

Index

www.ingramcontent.com/pod-product-compliance
Lightning Source LLC
Chambersburg PA
CBHW050808270326
41926CB00026B/4641